P9-DYY-522

WITHDRAWN

WITHDRAWN

The Once and Future School

AAW-1575
VC-LIBSTUDIES

The Once and Future School

Three Hundred and Fifty Years of American Secondary Education

Jurgen Herbst

ROUTLEDGE
New York   London

Published in 1996 by

Routledge
29 West 35th Street
New York, NY 10001

Published in Great Britain by

Routledge
11 New Fetter Lane
London EC4P 4EE

Copyright © 1996 by Routledge, Inc.

Printed in the United States of America on acid-free paper.

All rights reserved. No part of this book may be reprinted or reproduced or utilized in any form or by an electronic, mechanical or other means, now known or
hereafter invented, including photocopying and recording, or in any information storage or retrieval system, without permission in writing from the publisher.

Library of Congress Cataloging-in-Publication Data

Herbst, Jurgen.
    The once and future school: three hundred and fifty years of
American secondary education   /   Jurgen Herbst.
        p.   cm.
    Includes index.
    ISBN 0-415-91193-1 (cl). — ISBN 0-415-91194-X (pb)
    1. Education, Secondary—United States—History.   I. Title.
LA222.H386   1996
373.73—dc20   96-24908
                                                           CIP

To my Students and Colleagues

WITHDRAWN

Contents

List of Tables

Acknowledgments

For whatever merits my argument in this book may possess, I owe an abiding debt to my students and colleagues. They helped shape my thinking during the years of my teaching, first at Wesleyan University, Connecticut, and then at the University of Wisconsin–Madison. In discussion groups and seminars, in conferences and conversations, they proved, semester after semester, the complementary connection between teaching and research that arises out of the give-and-take of informed argument and results in the "joyful scholarship" of which Nietzsche wrote.

The specific occasion that prompted me to begin work on this book was a series of conferences arranged by Detlef K. Müller, Ruhr-University Bochum; Fritz Ringer, University of Pittsburgh; and Brian Simon, University of Leicester. This project resulted in the 1987 publication of *The Rise of the Modern Educational System*. As my three colleagues had set out to understand the history of European secondary education beyond the conventional national boundary lines and to interpret national developments in Germany, France, and England as parts of an evolving European system, so I began my inquiry into the development of secondary education in various American states in the hope of arriving at a better understanding of the historical development of an American system of secondary education. I am very conscious of my intellectual debt to the authors of *The Rise of the Modern Educational System*, and I will be gratified if they will accept this book as a token of my gratitude and as a worthy companion piece to theirs.

Every such academic enterprise involves more participants than the author alone. I have been fortunate over the years to have had the help of several highly talented graduate and undergraduate students as research assistants. All of them did more than unearth documents. They wrote research memoranda and papers, and I found their ideas and conclusions immensely helpful in criticizing and further developing mine. I express my sincerest thanks to (in alphabetical order) James Clark, Jack Dougherty, Nicholas Glass, David Levine, Christine Ogren, and Blair Williams, all students, at one time or another, in the Department of Educational Policy Studies at the University of Wisconsin–Madison.

A very special word of thanks should go to my colleagues at Madison and elsewhere who, over the years, have provided the atmosphere and support that alone sustain a scholar in that lonely quest of individual authorship. My deepest gratitude goes to Herbert Kliebard, who faithfully read every word of the manuscript as it evolved. I am grateful to Peter Lundgreen, who helped me with an earlier German version of parts of the manuscript. And how can I ever thank enough my luncheon companions Theodore Hamerow, Robert Koehl, Alfred McCoy, the late Felix Pollak, and Barry Teicher, who, week after week, listened patiently to my rambling about "the book"? They suffered more than they deserved, and they gave more than I could possibly have expected. It goes without saying that, however much this book owes to others, I alone am responsible for its mistakes of facts and errors of judgment.

I also gratefully acknowledge the support I received from the Wisconsin Center for Education Research and its director, Andrew Porter, from the University of Wisconsin Graduate School, from the Spencer Foundation, and from the archivists and librarians at the State Historical Society of Wisconsin, the University of Wisconsin–Madison Memorial Library, and the University of California–Berkeley library.

The last few months of work on this book were made especially delightful and productive for me through the hospitality I received at the Center for Studies in Higher Education at the University of California–Berkeley. My special thanks go to Sheldon Rothblatt, the director, who, together with his administrative aides, Barbara Briscoe and Diane Terry, made it all possible. I appreciated greatly the colleagueship of the center's fellows and associates, and benefited much from their stimulating conversations. My sincere thanks go to Geraldine Clifford, W. Norton Grubb, Torsten Husén, Clark Kerr, Hans Pechar, and Martin Trow. I also want to thank Akira Tachikawa at the International Christian University in Mitaka, Tokyo, and Edward Beauchamp and Jay Heffron at the University of Hawaii, who allowed me to try out my ideas in conversations and debates with students and colleagues in Japan and Hawaii.

Finally, there is one more indebtedness to acknowledge for which words fail me. That is to the part Sue has played in my life and scholarship. I only know that without her, this book would not exist.

Preface

In the decades following World War II, Americans have called for the reform of public secondary education. They have protested what they have held to be the excesses of progressive education and the "treason" of "life adjustment." Their demand for a return to academic rigor brought the curricular innovations of the "new math" and the "new social studies." When the Soviet Union's sputnik appeared in the skies, Congress responded with the National Defense Education Act of 1958. The 1960s crises of integration, poverty, and urban rebellions then shifted the spotlight from curricular to social and economic issues. This shift led to experimentation with alternative schools and concern with school-to-work relationships.[1] When, in the 1980s, the United States faced a deteriorating position in world markets and growing foreign, especially Japanese, competition at home, a renewed emphasis on curricular matters came to the fore.[2]

All the while, school administrators continued to portray the comprehensive senior high school as the embodiment of their and the nation's commitment to democracy in education. But dissatisfaction with the performance of public high schools, particularly in large urban areas, rose among parents and taxpayers until by the 1990s, the school-choice movement was seriously challenging the formerly only spasmodically contested dominance of the comprehensive high school.

Throughout these decades, Americans blamed public education, and especially the programs of our high schools, for the country's problems. Progressive education and life adjustment, many believed, had ill prepared Americans for the challenges of the post–World War II period.

Neglect of academic education at one time and of vocational training at another had made the nation vulnerable to the perils of the Cold War. The battles over integration and the general unrest of the 1960s found their flashpoints on college campuses and in urban high schools. When Japanese productivity, inventiveness, and quality workmanship were declared threats to the U.S. economy, the schools were again blamed for not having prepared their graduates for the challenge.

This study seeks to understand the nature of and reasons for this dissatisfaction with U.S. high schools, and the constant tendency to blame the schools for the nation's ills. I aim to do so through a historical inquiry into the curricular and institutional development of American secondary education from its beginning in 1635 to the closing decade of the twentieth century. "The Once and Future School" of its title refers to the nineteenth-century people's college, the extraordinarily effective urban high school of its days.[3] I will argue that although this school, as the product of a past era, cannot be resurrected, its spirit and mission, suitably adapted to conditions of the twenty-first century, hold the promise of a revitalized secondary education.

As a history of changing curricular and institutional goals and purposes, the book reconstructs the development of American public secondary education through an interpretation of the sometimes critical, sometimes promotional portrayals of individual authors, the reports of government-appointed or foundation-sponsored commissions and panels, and the accounts of the educators to whom I refer throughout as the schoolmen: the overwhelmingly male superintendents and employees of school-district, state, and federal education offices. Based on these writings, the account that emerges does not tell a story as it might have appeared in the reports and recollections of students and teachers, and it does not concern itself much with the quotidian events of school life—its logistics, its classes, its games, its participation in community life. It is instead a history that focuses on educational policy. Inevitably, a history based on such documents presents factual reports mixed with expressions of hope and intent or, when such was the case, with sentiments of disappointment and censure. It presents a potpourri of data, policy suggestions, and often generous portions of special pleadings. With all their obvious shortcomings, these testimonies have nonetheless shaped the American public's perceptions. They have been a central part of the debate on secondary education in the press and in various legislative bodies. They reflect how Americans have perceived the mission, accomplishments, and failures of their public high schools.

Tracing the curricular and institutional history of American secondary education, this study picks up its trail in the European past and follows it to its early days on the North American continent, through the colonial and early national periods, and through the nineteenth and twentieth centuries. It pays particular attention to the years between 1818 and 1893, which, framed by the Yale Report and by the Report of the Committee of Ten, witnessed the flourishing of the people's college. For the twentieth century, the study shifts its attention to the comprehensive high school as it emerged in response to the democratic challenge of providing secondary education for every young person. It traces this school's development to its ultimate floundering at the end of the century. Drawing on the record of 350 years of secondary education in this country, the study suggests for the twenty-first century that we replace the comprehensive senior high school's monopolistic hold on youth with up-to-date versions of the people's college. It proposes that there be a great variety of alternative institutions providing "careers in education" for individuals of senior high school age and older. In suggesting these innovations, the study assumes that knowledge of and respect for an institution's historical record is indispensable for the reformer or policy maker intent upon charting new paths into the future, and that the interplay of historical tendencies and contemporary circumstances will continue largely to shape the particular forms that institutions display at each stage of their history.

Finally, this study presents the history of American secondary education as part of the history of a North Atlantic civilization. Although international trade and industrial development today have alerted Americans to the transpacific as well as to the transatlantic world, and although Americans are bound by ethnic and religious ties to Africa, Latin America, and Asia as well as Europe, the historical roots of the American system of public education go back primarily to Europe. I therefore write of origins and of parallel developments in Europe and the United States; of medieval and Reformation Latin schools, *gymnasia,* and arts faculties; of the modernist-classicist debate in nineteenth-century Europe; and of American liberal arts and people's colleges. I call attention to the struggle over vocational education at the beginning of the twentieth century, and I point to the debt owed to European models. Conversely, I note the American influence on the development of comprehensive schools in Europe, and I suggest that as we approach the twenty-first century, the need for a restructuring of our educational systems and for providing lifelong "careers in education" is as great in Europe as it is in the United States.

Portions of this book have appeared in different form as "High School and Youth in America," in the *Journal of Contemporary History,* II (July 1967), 165–182, published also in *Education and Social Structure,* edited by Walter Laqueur and George Mosse (New York: Harper Torchbook, 1968); "Professionalization in Public Education, 1890–1920: The American High

School Teacher," in *Industrielle Welt: Bildungsbürgertum im 19. Jahrhundert*, part I, edited by Werner Conze and Jürgen Kocka (Stuttgart: Klett-Cotta, 1985), pp. 495–528; "The Regents of the University of the State of New York, 1784–1920: Secondary Education Emerges in the New Nation," in *The Colonial Experience in Education: Historical Issues and Perspectives, Paedagogica Historica*, Supplementary Series, vol. I (1995), pp. 317–333; "The American People's College: The Lost Promise of Democracy in Education," *American Journal of Education*, C (May 1992), 275–297; and "Von der Lateinschule zur Bewahranstalt: Die amerikanische Oberschule im Wandel 1635–1990," *Bildung und Erziehung*, XLVII (Juni 1994), 131–147. Material from the chapter "The Nineteenth Century Liberal Arts College" is to appear as "The Yale Report of 1828" in volume 3 of *The Classical Tradition and the Americas*, edited by Wolfgang Haase and Meyer Reinhold (Hawthorne, NY: Walter de Gruyter, forthcoming).

1

The Origins of Secondary Education

Medieval Cathedral Schools and Arts Faculties

Our traditions of secondary education have their origin in the *artes liberales* of the Middle Ages. These were the seven liberal arts of the trivium (grammar, logic or dialectic, and rhetoric) and of the quadrivium (arithmetic, geometry, astronomy, and music). Their study involved practice in the arts of communication: Latin, the common language of educated people in Europe, and mathematics, the universal language of numbers. The young students began their schooling with grammar, the lowliest of the seven arts, added the other two "trivial" branches, and finished their arts course with the quadrivium. Wherever schoolmasters and scholars were ambitious, they added a smattering of mental, natural, and moral philosophy.[1]

In Europe students pursued their Latin education in continental grammar schools, *gymnasia, lycées, collèges*, and university arts faculties and in English grammar schools and university colleges. In North America they did so in grammar schools, academies, and liberal arts colleges. Only toward the middle of the nineteenth century did we begin to recognize a curricular distinction between secondary and tertiary education. That is why in the early parts of this book I discuss Latin schools and colleges together. In Europe these institutions prepared their students for professional studies in the higher faculties of civil and canon law, medicine, or theology. In North America they sent students to professional school, apprenticeship, or practice.

Though Europe's universities opened first as professional schools—in Bologna, for example, lawyers were the first instructors; in Salerno, medical doctors congregated to learn from one another; and Paris gained fame as a theological faculty—the confusion of vernacular languages and the scarcity of cathedral and other Latin schools forced the universities to begin their own teaching of the liberal arts.[2] In this way the arts faculties came to supplement cathedral and Latin schools, and all of them taught the liberal arts.

The instruction youngsters and young men received served political and social purposes. The Church and governments sponsored and encouraged advanced education for reasons of state. They needed loyal and well-qualified diplomats and counselors, cardinals, administrators, priests, lawyers, physicians, and teachers to keep the ship of state safely afloat. To ensure a constant supply of such professionals, the Church and governments supported the institutions that produced them. Families sought education for their children beyond the elementary level to raise the esteem in which they were held by their neighbors and to improve their children's economic well-being. When a family heir achieved position and influence in the church, civil service or one of the professions, status and prestige were sure to accrue, even if his income remained meager by the standards of mercantile or industrial success.

Medieval Europe's Latin schools and universities thus served as indispensable pillars of empire and church. Because of the vital role the university *studia* played in ensuring the preservation of civil and ecclesiastical institutions, emperors and popes recognized them as privileged corporations. They authorized them to govern and organize themselves in their faculties.[3] As a result the medieval *studia* emerged as public powers equal to those of *imperium* and *ecclesia*.[4] In subsequent centuries their fortunes and influence would rise and decline, but they would never relinquish their claim to privilege and power. They would serve the modern princes of throne and altar as they had served the sovereigns of medieval empire and universal church.

The traditions of Western academic learning have always been considered a labor of the mind, not of the hand. The example that suggests itself is the medieval surgeon. Because he worked with his hands, contemporaries classified him with the tooth-pulling barber and the wound-dressing orderly. The book-learned physicians who dispensed their wisdom in oral and written instructions saw to it that the surgeon was not to be ranked as their equal.[5] From their beginnings in the medieval universities, the learned professions—the law, divinity, and medicine—all relied on the word as their one essential tool. Their novices received it first as students of the *artes liberales* and subsequently in the lectures and books of the learned *doctores* in the higher faculties. Education was book learning and mental labor.

Mental labor was held to be appropriate for men of leisure. It was not, in the main, considered suitable for women, serfs, or slaves. Though leisure and privilege were not required attributes of students who entered the medieval universities, they gradually became so until by the eighteenth century the sons of aristocrats dominated the student bodies of Europe's universities. On the Continent, advanced education included the Latin school as a preparatory step, the arts faculty as an apprenticeship, and one of the professional faculties as the final period. Because each of these stages involved a process of selection and elimination, it could truly be said that in advanced education few were called, and fewer yet were chosen to stay the entire course.

Schooling thus was an ordeal, if not by fire or water, then by words and their proper use. It brought the young man from his parochial home into the orbit of universal empire and nation state. Whether in the days of empire it was Latin as the universal language of educated men or, by the nineteenth century, a national language, it was always a language different from the vernacular he had spoken during his youth. This language became the scholar's mark of distinction. Language was his sign of achievement and it demanded respect. Ermine coat and golden tassel might indeed identify the scholar to the beholder's eye. But clothed in whatever garment and greeted with whatever honors, the scholar found it was his language that truly marked him as one of the elite.

After the Reformation

The Reformation shifted the fountain of academic power and influence away from universal church and empire to the secular sovereigns of territorial states and confessional churches. These continued to provide preparatory and professional education for the future civil and ecclesiastical servants of their respective realms. As before, academic training bestowed privilege and status, and brought the graduates wealth and influence. This naturally bound the latter to their benefactors who were also the founders and protectors of the universities. It also gave university graduates powerful incentives to preserve their own privileged status and to bequeath it to their sons and successors. Considerations of political influence and social status continued to weigh heavily when university affairs were discussed.[6]

As the influence of the Roman Catholic Church declined and the territorial-confessional churches gained power and became the instruments of their secular sovereigns, the emphasis on political concerns in university affairs became more pronounced. With growing secularization, the

3

social and economic background of the students also grew more varied.[7] To be sure, defenders of the medieval universities could and did proudly observe that their institutions had been open to new talent and that ecclesiastical princes had used them deliberately to bring fresh blood into the church.[8] Celibacy, after all, barred priests, bishops, and cardinals from supplying sons of their own. Yet by the sixteenth century a more worldly tone in the universities and a curriculum stressing civility as much as piety were undeniable. The gentrification of the universities had begun.

Because gentry and nobility valued the universities as proper training grounds for their sons and other young relatives, they came to regard the universities as means of insuring the survival of their families and houses. They welcomed the new emphasis on civility and gentlemanly virtue. They appreciated the worldly learning of the humanists, which, as *literae humaniores*, focused on grammar and rhetoric rather than on the logic of the scholastics before them. Mark Curtis put it well when he wrote of Oxford and Cambridge in the late sixteenth century: "The apostles of humanism were convincing the English gentry and nobility that the learning they preached not only instilled virtue and wisdom, but nourished the capacities and talents needed to manage affairs of state. . . . Learning fostered civility."[9] Sir Thomas Elyot's book, *The Governor*, became the model for the well-educated gentleman serving his king. Even future clergymen, educated in the colleges of Oxford and Cambridge, shared the new directions. "The parson in 1600," wrote Hugh Kearney, "was a gentleman among gentlemen."[10]

At the same time, the infusion of new vitality from below into the leading ranks of church and state slowed. The English colleges in particular were less concerned with training uneducated country youths from poor families in basic skills or with preparing them for professional careers. They concentrated on conveying good breeding, social graces, and the worldly skills of gentlemen and courtiers. Their students were the sons of the landed gentry, of merchants and professionals, and less so of artisans and yeomen. Everywhere in northern and western Europe the share of poor students began to decline.[11]

Secularization and gentrification accompanied other changes in the universities' curricula. The cumulative impact of the age of discoveries, of European expansion overseas, of the scientific revolution of the seventeenth century, and, eventually, of the industrial revolution, nationalism, and the spread of capitalism threatened the conventions of bookish learning and the reliance on the classical tradition of the word. For the settlement of disputed questions scholars relied less and less on the analysis of written texts and on disputations among learned men. Instead they collected artifacts and observed natural phenomena. They turned to the penetration of geographical and astronomical space, the experimentation with physical and biological objects, and the use of the products of these activities in commerce and manufacture. These activities together with the large-scale competitive struggle among the peoples of Europe for dominance, abetted and propelled by the energies of entrepreneurial capitalism, came to redraw the world of scholarship as they had reshaped the map and landscapes of the world. Johann Wolfgang Goethe put it succinctly when he had Faust change the biblical "in the beginning was the word" to the "in the beginning was the deed."

The institutional changes in education were unmistakable. Where once libraries had been the center and the only essential component of cathedral schools, monasteries, colleges, and universities, now botanical gardens; arboretums; physical, chemical, and geological cabinets and museums; and engineering laboratories and agricultural experiment stations appeared and altered the academic landscape. New types of schools were created to respond to the needs of sovereigns and industrialists. Colleges of mining and of engineering: higher schools of science and technology; and schools of medicine, dentistry, veterinary science, architecture and landscape gardening, economics and finance, and others were founded. They commenced their task of training specialists for the new world of industrial and commercial enterprise.

The Coming of Schooling

These changes ushered in an era in which the teaching of the liberal arts, particularly of grammar, its lowest branch, came to be more and more removed from the pursuit of investigations, research, discovery, invention, and professional training. As Philippe Ariés has pointed out for France, collegiate education turned into a program of schooling that aimed at instilling discipline and forming character. By the sixteenth century Parisian *collèges* no longer served as homes for students and masters but as day schools in which young grammarians learned their first lessons in Latin, logic, and rhetoric. These *collèges*, wrote Ariés, had by now taken on "the character of a modern educational establishment." Gone were the freewheeling days of instruction in the halls of the *rue du fouarre,* where students listened to lectures in the arts and philosophy under the guidance of masters who were themselves students in one of the higher faculties. Now, "the master giving instruction in the arts stopped being a scholar or thinker, a dialectician or logician famed for the originality of his thought, and became a pedagogue, a pedant, a mere laborer treated with scant respect." Schoolboys under discipline were his students. The modern secondary school had arrived.[12]

In the French *collèges* instructors taught grammar as well as the arts and philosophy and left only professional studies to the university faculties, but in the German-speaking countries only grammar moved into urban Latin schools while the arts, philosophy, and the sacred languages either remained in the arts faculties of the universities or were taught in the Continental *gymnasia illustria.* These municipal institutions functioned as nonuniversity arts faculties. Though they were not authorized to award academic degrees, they could educate future civil and church officials relatively inexpensively, and they provided prestigious employment for local doctors, ministers, lawyers, and teachers.[13] Everywhere, however, grammar was the prime subject in the rapidly developing urban Latin schools, the *gymnasia* and the *pedagogica.* Teachers used grammatical drill to instill discipline and to form habits of thought and attitudes in young pupils. In like manner, they relied on catechetical instruction to safeguard a proper moral education in the creed of the established confession.[14]

In many Calvinist cities and states the *gymnasia illustria* separated preparatory from university studies. Johann Sturm's *gymnasium* in Strassburg consisted of a lower school for Latin instruction and an upper division for the arts, philosophy, and theology. Calvin's Academy in Geneva was similarly divided into a *schola privata* for grammatical instruction and a *schola publica,* which offered Greek, Hebrew, philosophy, and theology. Many Dutch, German, and Scottish universities followed similar combinations.[15]

In England, just as in France, older fellows in the university colleges had originally taught students their Latin grammar. But after the separate establishment in 1382 of Winchester College as a Latin school, grammatical instruction moved from the university colleges into collegiate and noncollegiate Latin grammar schools. At St. Paul's and Merchant Taylor's in London, the government of such schools had been placed in the hands of trade guilds. Elsewhere, as in Harrow-on-the-Hill or at Charterhouse, private groups especially incorporated for the purpose directed these schools.[16] The curriculum corresponded to that of the *schola privata* in Geneva and to the *gymnasia* and *pedagogica* in Lutheran countries. As on the Continent, the collegiate and noncollegiate Latin grammar schools came to serve as preparatory institutions for the universities, which, in their arts faculties, continued to teach the arts and philosophy.

By the eighteenth century the separation of "schooling" from university studies was well advanced. Professional studies and the scholarly and scientific pursuits associated with them were carried out in the higher faculties and schools of the universities or they became the province of societies and academies specially created for this purpose.[17] By contrast, the Latin-based education in the English grammar schools, German *gymnasia*, and French *collèges*, in some of the Continental arts faculties, and in the English university colleges took on a more pronounced schoolmasterly, disciplinary tone. As Ariés put it, pedagogy had triumphed.[18]

The Modern School

The arrival of secondary schooling as distinguished from tertiary collegiate or university studies marked the beginning of modernity in education. Before the coming of the common school in the eighteenth century, schooling meant Latin instruction. By the mere fact of having embarked upon his studies, the Latin student had lifted himself above his fellow human beings into a realm of cultural elevation that did not require our modern distinction between secondary and tertiary education. This had been true in the European Middle Ages and also in the backwoods country of the American frontier. The differences between the curricula of European university arts faculties and of the *gymnasia illustria* of German cities were just as negligible as those between the Latin instruction in a nineteenth-century Ohio academy and a midwestern college. In both cases they were legal rather than curricular. Sovereign authorities had bestowed on European universities and American colleges the power to grant academic degrees. As municipal or private foundations, *gymnasia* and academies only rarely carried such authority.

This sameness of curricular purpose, however, was not to last. During the nineteenth century the distinction between secondary and tertiary education gradually hardened and became firmly drawn. In Europe this process had begun earlier but received its final form in the common school legislation of the major nation states. In the United States it gave rise to a great deal of uncertainty over the functions of the high schools. Should they be seen as "people's colleges" offering a college-like education for those who were never expected to attend a university? Should they perform as "connecting links" between the common schools and the universities and thus act as college-preparatory schools? Or should and could they serve both purposes at the same time? When after the turn of the twentieth century the third option prevailed, the high school was banished from tertiary and firmly assigned to secondary education.

This gradual crystallization of secondary schooling as a separate educational realm involved long and bitter disputes over the curricular contents of the schools. Although economic considerations had never been entirely absent in the educational planning of governments, families, and individuals, they had rarely played a major role until the onset of the industrial revolution. The increasingly dominant role of capitalist production and the commodity market with their attendant expansion of national and international finance brought demands for a corresponding shift in the curricula of established schools. An entirely new set of educational institutions was about to be opened. Until the closing decades of the nineteenth century, however, these demands remained remarkably ineffective. Little of what was taught in the most prestigious schools of the time—the German *gymnasia*, the French *lycée*, the English "public" schools, and the American academies and colleges—had a direct bearing on what we might call the "objective needs" of society. Training for manufacture, commerce, and finance was provided on the job, not given in schools. The prestige ranking of secondary schools and colleges corresponded closely to the degree their curricula offered the classics, "the dead languages," as they were called. Indeed, even when enrollment figures suggested that the schools' economic interests could be better served by studies in the vernacular, other modern languages, and the natural sciences, the classics, nonetheless, bore away the prizes and the renown.

The explanation for this apparent anomaly is to be found in the middle-class character of the modern secondary school's students.[19] It was no coincidence that toward the end of the eighteenth century the sons of the aristocracy increasingly moved into the universities, and the sons, and eventually also the daughters, of urban shopkeepers and artisans, of businessmen, manufacturers, and professionals attended the municipal Latin schools.[20] There came into existence in these schools a kind of urban middle-class social democracy with internal differentiating status lines all of its own. The European Latin school and the American academy served as common schools because they brought together the children of the lower and the upper middle class. But these schools also differentiated their students because usually, but not always, the sons of upper-middle-class parents stayed beyond the common years to receive advanced training. They concentrated on the classics or studied practical subjects like bookkeeping and surveying, a natural science like chemistry, or a modern language useful in commerce and business. Most students, however, left after the common school years to engage in a trade or apprenticeship.

Upper-middle-class parents and those who aspired to upper-middle-class status for their sons used the Latin schools and the academies as their means of social advance. For that purpose, the highest prestige accrued to the classicists with their linguistic and cultural training. The students of the practical or "real" subjects were left as the lesser players in the academic and social game. In this fashion secondary schooling acquired its characteristic function as a sorting mechanism.[21] Most usually, a family breadwinner's occupation exerted an initial directive influence over a child's choice or assignment of schooling. But in both Europe and the United States, the curricular opportunities available to a child as well as his or her academic performance could modify the initial path and point the child in a direction different from what might have been at first expected. This possibility of escape from a presumably predetermined vocational path and social position made secondary schooling the preeminent vehicle for social mobility within nineteenth-century bourgeois society.[22]

Middle-class education meant education for leadership in a capitalist society that was progressively becoming commercialized and industrialized. In Europe, Latin schools adjusted to this shift by including modern scientific and practical subjects. During the nineteenth century, new school types sprang up to offer curricula that stressed the natural sciences and modern languages and competed with the humanistic-classical schools. In the United States, academies accommodated growing demands for preparing students for commerce and industry. During the second half of the nineteenth century public high schools that pursued the same aim replaced these private academies. What was remarkable in this development, however, was that although modern scientific studies joined the classical linguistic subjects, no such change occurred in the schools' academic approach. Educators continued to interpret their task to be the preparation of leaders who, whether they worked as traditional professionals or supervised subordinates in industrial, commercial, or service occupations, would rely on their resources of mind rather than their practical experience. Despite its newly added concern with modern scientific studies, secondary education retained its emphasis on the word, on language, and on the labor of the mind. Theoretical understanding and book learning remained at a premium. Schools were not yet engaged in practical, applied, or vocational education. They did not yet seek to train their students to handle tools and materials. That was to come only with the rise of vocational education near the end of the century.

2

Grammar Schools, Colleges, and Academies in Early America

Grammar Schools Come to New England

When the English speaking white settlers first set foot on the shores of New England they did not waste much time before establishing Latin grammar schools and colleges. In 1635, five years after their landfall, the Puritan magistrates appointed a Latin schoolmaster for the city of Boston. Neither the threat of starvation nor the prospect of freezing to death in "a howling wilderness" deterred them from sending their future leaders to school. Their colleagues in Charlestown followed the next year, Dorchester acted in 1639, and Ipswich and Cambridge did likewise in 1642. The founders of the Massachusetts Bay Colony hired schoolmasters to prepare boys for college. In 1636 the members of the General Court, the colony's legislature, authorized the funding of what subsequently became Harvard College. They did this, so they informed their brethren in England, "to advance learning and perpetuate it to posterity, dreading to leave an illiterate ministry to the churches when our present ministers shall lie in the dust."[1]

In New England as in the other English-speaking colonies along the eastern seaboard, the Latin grammar school and the college were to play crucial political roles. An established colonial leadership of magistrates and ministers whose economic welfare and social position depended on the maintenance of their political hegemony, called on the scholars and schoolmasters in their realm to rally the resources of education to their support. New England's leaders saw schooling as the transmission of culture to future professionals that they might in time be capable of justifying the reformed way of life as it was practiced in the churches of the Bay

11

Colony. Given that context, schoolmasters and scholars were free to teach as they saw fit, provided they defended the reformed doctrine and familiarized their students with its foundation in Christian, classical, and humanist learning. For this, they were sure, nothing could serve better than instruction in the classical languages. No other institutions fulfilled that task more appropriately than the Latin grammar school and its more elevated cousin, the college.

The importance Boston's leaders assigned to the opening of the Latin school stands out when we recognize that it preceded by seven years official acknowledgment of the colony's responsibility for elementary education. In 1642 the Massachusetts General Court delegated that task to parents and to masters of indentured servants. It required them to teach their children and servants "to read and understand the principles of religion and the capital laws of the country." Parents who intended to send a son to the Boston Latin School had either to teach him to read or to find a neighborhood dame school or private writing school for the purpose. A year later the Boston Town Meeting agreed to support the Latin Grammar School for local boys. In 1647 the General Court then ordered that any town of one hundred families or more was to open a grammar school "to instruct youth so far as they may be fitted for the university." Fearing that Satan, that "old deluder," would attempt "to keep men from the knowledge of Scriptures," and resolving "that learning might not be buried in the graves of our fathers," the Puritans dedicated their grammar schools to the advancement of learning and the education of the ministry.[2]

Besides preparing New England's future professionals for their work, the Latin grammar schools were to instill in them a sense of a common culture. They were to accomplish this not so much through the reinforcement of the Puritan religious outlook—that was an obligation for all institutions, whether public or private, church, school, or family—as through the study of classical authors. The Latin grammar schools could concentrate on that function because their students were mainly the "moderately prosperous who planned and could afford to go to college."[3] Throughout the colonial period the boys who studied Latin read such authors as Aesop, Ovid, Tully, Cicero, and Virgil and, though to a minor extent, Greek writers such as Homer, Hesiod, and Isocrates. "It was to these authors," wrote Kenneth Murdock, ". . . that Bostonian writers of the time turned for classical allusions when they wished to adorn their pages with a tag of Latin or Greek and at the same time appeal to their readers with the effect that only a 'familiar quotation' can make."[4] The singular concentration on the classical authors supplied the sense of common culture that united New England's leadership.

Throughout the colonial period the pupils usually entered the seven-year course at age seven and were ready to enter college at age fourteen.

After 1789 the course took only four years, and some students entered Harvard at the ripe young age of ten. As in Europe's grammar schools, the boys' classical training was cherished more for the discipline it exacted on body and mind than for its curricular content. More often than not, the student would memorize the rules in Ezekiel Cheever's famous *Accidence*, the New England master's Latin grammar, then turn to the *Nomenclatura*, a Latin-English dictionary, and commit it to memory. There were other similar books that might have been used—Johann Comenius's *Orbis sensualium pictus* was one—until with a version of Corderius' *Colloquies* the student was ready for "construing" and "parsing," that is, the analysis of words and parts of speech. This memorizing of grammatical rules and vocabulary and its subsequent application in the analysis of texts trained the capacity for endurance, persistence, and patience of the student as much as of the teacher. Besides grammar, students studied Greek, rhetoric and logic, and simple arithmetic.[5]

Then as now, teachers varied in their skills, and during the seventeenth century New England schoolmasters began to introduce progressive methods of language teaching. They replaced the "ancient" or "vulgar" with the modern approach that shunned memorization. The advanced students, for whom the study of classical literature began usually during their third year, read and translated texts into English, orally one day, in writing the next, and, on the third day, back into the original Latin. Finally, the whole exercise was repeated with tenses altered as the master would require. Frequently, bilingual editions were used, where the Latin text was interspersed line by line with its English equivalent or where Latin and English appeared on facing pages. The master would ask students to read aloud or to repeat the Latin text as he read it to them. We may detect here the beginnings of what we moderns have come to know as the aural-oral method of language teaching. This use of bilingual texts made pointless the insistence on memorization. It encouraged the student to equate mastery of the language with understanding and speaking. For the students of these grammar schools, Latin may have been an "ancient tongue," but it was not a "dead language." Students used it as a tool of future professional reading and practice.[6]

The Collegiate Way

The requirements of the colonial colleges sustained this classical heritage in the grammar schools. They were similar throughout the colonies and changed little throughout the seventeenth and eighteenth centuries. At Harvard upon entrance, students had to prove their ability to read and speak Latin prose and to write Latin prose and verse. They had to read from the Greek New Testament and Isocrates. At Yale, common arithmetic was added in 1745; at the College of Rhode Island, in 1783. A boy from Massachusetts would most likely have entered Harvard College, but if his home was in Connecticut then, after 1701, he could also have gone to the Collegiate School, later known as Yale College. In either case he would have left behind him a municipal institution and enrolled in a college founded and supported by the provincial, that is, the colony's government. While he continued with grammatical studies throughout his freshman year, at both Harvard and Yale he would immerse himself in the medieval arts and philosophies; he would encounter the Renaissance study of the classical languages, including the Oriental ones, and the study of polite letters.[7] At Yale, as Frederick Rudolph wrote, he would be asked to translate the English Bible into Greek rather than into Latin, as at Harvard. "The first year," Rudolph continued,

> established language skills—tools; the second year provided depth in the study of logic—a method, another tool; during the third and fourth years, these skills and method were turned on the advanced subjects—natural philosophy, mathematics, and metaphysics—one at a time. And during all four years, every Friday and Saturday, all Yale students recited and disputed the key subjects—divinity and ethics. On Sunday the college worshipped together, and what may have appeared to be a day off for the curriculum was really the day when the curriculum fell into place, with the assistance of prayer, sermon, and Biblical explication from the president of Yale College.[8]

At William and Mary in Virginia, students were encouraged already in the grammar school to use Latin in "daily dialogues and familiar speaking together . . . [that they] may learn aptly to express their meaning to each other."[9]

As we have observed, language was the key subject in grammar school and college. Most of the textbooks were written in Latin. At Harvard the president gave his lectures in Latin. He spoke on logic, rhetoric, catechetical divinity, history, physics, the nature of plants, on Greek syntax and etymology, and on Hebrew grammar. He meant his words to inform the students and to demonstrate the use of language by example. The study of Greek and Hebrew continued throughout all four years at Harvard, and Aramaic or Chaldee and Syriac were added as well. When it pleased the president, he required instantaneous translations of the Bible from English or Hebrew into Greek. To be sure, the tongues were taught because they were the languages of the Bible. Yet one also gets the distinct

14

impression that in their very remoteness from the everyday concerns of colonial life, they served as a prized possession of a professional elite, identifying its members and distinguishing them from others. Morison quotes Samuel Johnson of King's College in New York as having said in 1759 that the knowledge of Hebrew was a "gentleman's accomplishment." And so indeed it was.[16]

Logic and rhetoric then introduced the student to the serious business of using the Latin language correctly and effectively. The student had to learn how to think and how to express his thoughts clearly and persuasively. Of the two subjects, logic was fundamental, indispensable for any professional hoping to make sense. It was, as one Harvard thesis held, "the most general of the arts and a standard for all other studies."[11] As such, students had to master its rules early in their careers. By their third and fourth years they no longer listened to lectures on logic but practiced the subject in the disputations they carried on in all of the languages taught. Morison relates that over the years Harvard remained open to the various systems of logic. Though Puritans generally preferred Peter Ramus as their guide in the subject, the logic of Aristotle and that of Descartes were taught at the college as well.

Rhetoric, to be sure, was no less indispensable than logic, for what would it profit the pulpit orator or the attorney if he could not inspire his hearers or persuade a jury by the elegance and fluency of his delivery? Rhetoric therefore was most extensively practiced at the college. In the Harvard curriculum of 1642, rhetoric and Latin declamations appear as the subject for all three classes on every Friday. The students listened to the president's introductory lecture, then were drilled by their tutors in written stylistic exercises, and topped off their work with oratorical declamations in both Latin and English. Occasionally there was a declamation presented in Greek, no doubt by the most proficient student of the class. If we look at the examples cited by Morison, we see that rhetoric and oratory were fun. They gave the students sufficient dramatic license and served as an appropriate counterweight to the more severely demanding drill of logic. Rhetoric at Harvard College, wrote Morison, was taught "as full-blooded and vital art, not as a flaccid and genteel introduction to Literature."[12]

The "trivial studies" of grammar, logic, and rhetoric found their practical applications in disputations in mental and moral philosophy. These also helped to counteract the dullness and dryness of study of which the students complained. For metaphysics and ethics, as the two philosophies were called, Aristotle served as the fountain of the principles. Harvard students encountered these in the textbooks of Gilbert Jack of Aberdeen, Caspar Bartholin of Copenhagen, and Bartholomäus Keckermann of

Danzig.[13] Metaphysics supplied the topics from which they derived theses like "space and time are mere logical abstractions," and "time does not really exist, but is a measure of existence."[14] These they then proposed and defended, and in doing so, they exercised and sharpened their logical and rhetorical skills.

Of the branches of Aristotelian moral philosophy, ethics far outshone politics and economics at early Harvard. President Dunster lectured on politics, but few graduation theses in this subject seem to have been offered. When students did propose such theses, they were primarily recipients of the master's degree who looked forward to political careers.[15] Undergraduates, however, preferred moral to mental philosophy, all the more so because Harvard kept ethics separate from theological study. Ethics was a practical matter of everyday concerns, and the graduating students felt no reluctance to argue their cases with humor and in high spirits: "Ethics is the corrosive plaster of vices," and "virtue comes with a good constitution, and vice-versa."[16] Moral philosophy, as everyone knew, was the finishing subject of a college education. It had its practical applications in everyday living, and there was no issue beyond its scope.

The crown of all efforts at practical application of the language arts was the recitations, declamations, and disputations. Walsh observed that "practically all of the American college statutes of the eighteenth century carry special injunctions on this subject of the disputation which was manifestly considered a cardinal factor in college education."[17] Students recited and declaimed to break the monotony of listening to lectures and of outlining systems. These oral exercises also served as examinations and as demonstrations of the students' acquired verbal skills. As Walsh related, referring to the College of William and Mary, "Students were expected to be ready in thought and speech, capable of responding to objections that might be urged against their opinions, but also thoroughly able to persuade hearers."[18] For future professionals, disputations brought practical education with a vengeance. Through their syllogistic training they increased the students' nimbleness of mind and taught them to think quickly on their feet, to express themselves accurately and with precision, and to speak effectively, compellingly, and elegantly—all skills of inestimable value to a future lawyer, minister, physician, statesman, or politician.

When during the late eighteenth century the syllogistic style of deductive argument went out of fashion and forensic debates became popular, the usefulness of debating became even more apparent. Induction, experience, and experiment having become essential parts of inquiry allowed debaters greater freedom to show off their argumentative skills and to choose topics of relevance to contemporary politics and society. But forensic debates also hastened the abandonment of the Latin language.

16

English was now more frequently used in the debates and as language of conversation.[19]

For the students, however, life at the college was not all study. To be away from home in the company of fellow students and tutors was a radically new experience. It introduced the freshman to the "collegiate way of living."[20] He quickly learned that there was more to education than listening to lectures and reciting in class. Eating, drinking, playing and praying in the daily and nightly company of his peers and under the scrutiny of tutors and president shaped character and molded behavior of the colony's future elite. Lifted out of their diverse domestic environments and forming a society of their own, the students of the college community ranged widely in age from ten to thirty, but less widely in social background. Although most came from professional and well-to-do business and farm families, scholarships and the opportunity to teach school during the winter permitted a few scions of the less fortunate to benefit from the college as well. Still, until by the middle of the eighteenth century the rising spirit of rebellion infected the colleges as much as society, the "collegiate way" prevailed and accustomed the students to find and accept their place in society within and outside the college.[21]

From Latin Grammar School to Academy

Until late in the eighteenth century public Latin school and college each enjoyed a monopoly: the school in the city that nurtured it, and the college in its province. The collegiate monopoly survived until 1766, when it was broken for the first time with the chartering of Queen's College as rival to the College of New Jersey at Princeton.[22] The Latin schools lost their privileged position much earlier; other schools, not all of which offered an advanced education, had sprung up. Because the line between elementary and secondary instruction was never clearly drawn, many of these schools taught whatever parents said their children needed, with little regard to any set level of instruction.

As was true in England and on the Continent, the public Latin schools did not restrict themselves to a purely classical curriculum. Not all boys intended to continue to college and into careers as ministers, lawyers, physicians, or schoolmasters. Morison estimated that in New England fewer than half did so.[23] Thus, the Latin schools functioned also as common schools. Already in the seventeenth century a town meeting might insist on the schoolmaster's teaching English as well as Latin and offering the latter only to those boys whose parents requested it.[24] In the eighteenth century, Shipton explained, in towns where only one or two Latin pupils signed up, the schoolmaster spent most of his time teaching reading, writing, spelling, and "cyphering" to older and younger students alike.[25] Only in larger schools with many Latin scholars could he devote most of his time to teaching the classical languages and leave to his assistant, the usher, the task of teaching the lower grades.

English scholars now went not only to the Latin schools but also to the newly appearing public and private writing and grammar schools. In Boston "instruction was available in a long list of non-classical subjects" already before the Revolution.[26] Private writing schools supplemented the elementary reading schools, and their language of instruction was English. One purpose they served was the formal education of girls, though the intellectual fare the schools offered was meager. "Even if a girl went off to boarding school," wrote Robert Middlekauff, "she came away with very little of intellectual value." She learned how to read, received a good dose of religious training, and was instructed in needlework. Girls who were sent to finishing schools could add dancing, music, and polite literature, and, if the school showed academic inclination, painting, geography, and history as well. Then there were such special skills as "genteel cookery" and "ornamental handwriting."[27] Girls, unlike boys, were not to be prepared for work in the professions. They were to help men in the home as wives and mothers, and their education was directed toward that purpose alone.

In the private grammar schools the master taught both English and Latin to boys and girls alike. Much like their public counterparts, these schools too clung to the traditional academic curriculum, but they also offered everything "useful," from bookkeeping to sailing and from accounting to shorthand. Shipton tells us that one such school in Boston at the end of the seventeenth century charged tuition slightly higher than that required of an out-of-town student at the public Latin schools, though it was lower than what was usual at Harvard College. Some schools, like New London's Union School in Connecticut, were incorporated and the schoolmaster hired by the proprietors. One, like James Manning's Grammar School in Rhode Island, was connected with a college. Most were the personal private businesses of their masters. Add to this that local parsons often boarded boys and taught them Latin privately, and the variety of situations and opportunities becomes apparent.[28]

As time went on, the diversity of opportunities for schooling increased. A rising demand for instruction in the trades, in business, surveying, bookkeeping, mensuration, and navigation ushered in academies with modern curricula in mathematics, geography, astronomy, the sciences, and modern languages. Private initiatives responded to the needs of an expanding business and trade, and began to rival the public thrust for the classical training of the commonwealth's future leadership. By the end of the eighteenth century's first decade, Shipton tells us, there were 210 scholars attending Boston's grammar schools, 220 the writing schools, and 100 one private school. During the next ten years, enrollment decreased by 20 percent in the grammar schools and doubled in the writing schools.[29] Toward the end of the eighteenth century, academies outranked the Latin grammar schools in popularity and numbers. The tide had begun to turn. The demands of working people in the New England towns now challenged the monopoly of state-sponsored classical education, traditionally promoted through society's leadership in the colonial legislatures.

The change was noticeable in small towns in the remote hinterland and also in "long-settled and relatively wealthy towns close to the cultural centers of New England," wrote Jon Teaford. Communities failed to maintain their grammar schools. In Worcester, for example, the townspeople instructed their representatives in the General Court:

> Use your endeavours to relieve the people of the Province from the great burden of supporting so many Latin grammar schools, whereby they are prevented from attaining such a degree of English learning as is necessary to retain the freedom of any state.[30]

This growing lack of popular support for the grammar schools disturbed New England's colonial leadership and contributed to its sense of doom and decline. People no longer saw schooling as appropriate only for future professionals but as desirable also for tradesmen and farmers, businessmen and merchants. The academies now could effectively compete for students with the Latin schools. Worse, after the middle of the century, court enforcement of the grammar school law lapsed, and, Teaford concluded, "during the Revolution, the grammar school tradition collapsed entirely."[31]

Why this reversal of priorities? Why, as Teaford put it, were "both the courts and the legislature . . . content to allow the grammar school tradition to die a slow and gradual death?"[32] The answers are many. It was no longer plausible to justify a classical education as necessary for the defense of the commonwealth. Colonists now believed that trade and industry better served the commonwealth than the commitment to the reformed way of life. The interests of the ecclesiastical establishment no longer prevailed over those of a rising bourgeoisie more interested in profits than in culture. With independence, a chiefly theological justification of a classical education had become meaningless for all but ministerial students. Arguments for classical training lacked conviction in a trade- and business-minded environment.

What was involved, however, was less a matter of exchanging one type of education for another than one of finding ways to accommodate society's various educational interests. As the continuance of Latin in many academies showed, a decline in classical education did not mean its disappearance. A case in point was the story of the beginnings of Benjamin Franklin's academy in Philadelphia. In the founder's own words, the school was to teach the sons of the city's artisans and small merchants "those things that are likely to be most useful and most ornamental." The students were to learn writing and arithmetic useful for their business and to become acquainted with literature and history. The aim was to enable them to hold their own in the give and take of everyday life and politics. Those who wanted to move on to college were to attend the academy's Latin school. The fact that Franklin's dream of equal status for English and Latin masters remained unfulfilled—the prestige of the classical studies and the power of the city's social leadership backing the classical curriculum were too great to allow the English master equal pay with the Latin master—showed only too well how academic tradition won out over practical purpose. If further proof was needed, it came in 1755 with the reorganization of the academy as the College, Academy, and Charitable School of Philadelphia. Its Latin school and a newly formed philosophical school made up the college, whereas the English school remained in the academy.[33]

The history of the Phillips Exeter Academy, incorporated in 1781 in New Hampshire, also shows that Franklin's case was not unique. According to the school's charter, the academy existed

> for the purpose of promoting Piety and Vertue, and for the education of Youth in the English, Latin, and Greek Languages, in Writing, Arithmetic, Musick, and the Art of Speaking, Practical Geometry, Logick and Geography, and such other of the Liberal Arts and Sciences or Languages, as opportunity may hereafter permit.

An examination certificate of 1795 testified that a graduate had studied not only Latin, Greek, rhetoric, logic, arithmetic, geometry, astronomy, natural and moral philosophy but also English, French, geography, history, and natural law.[34] These listings of subjects bespoke an impressive curricular catholicity, and proponents for a classical and an English curriculum both should have been well satisfied.

Although the founders of the Phillips academies in Andover and Exeter had announced their aim to teach their students above all "the great end and real business of living," they favored the college-preparatory

Latin school.[35] Not before 1808 did the Exeter trustees officially recognize the existence of an English department for non-college bound students. But then they let it be known that they tolerated but not especially desired the presence of these students. By contrast, the Latin students were exempt from certain examinations given to "mere English scholars."

The English scholars continued to be scorned, even though the English school attracted students and expanded its offering. By 1818 its three-year curriculum comprised instruction in grammar, composition, forensics, declamation, logic and rhetoric; geography; ancient, modern, and especially United States history; arithmetic, algebra, geometry, plane trigonometry, mensuration, surveying, navigation; chemistry; astronomy; and natural, moral, and political philosophy. In 1832 it included French and Spanish as electives.[36] The trustees, however, charged the English students with "bad habits" and "want of capacity." A committee reported that

> the English Room is liable to be filled with the idle and stupid. Under these circumstances, we believe that the benevolent purpose of the Founder would be more effectually carried out by appropriating the funds of the Institution to the instruction of young men of talents and promise, in a thorough Classical Course of study, including, as heretofore, all those Mathematical & other English branches belonging to such a course.[37]

In 1848 the trustees abolished the English department and kept only an extended English course for college-bound students. But even this course was not to last, and it disappeared after 1853. The Exeter trustees intended Phillips Exeter Academy to remain a college-preparatory school in the classical way. As late as 1923 the school's historian remarked that the academy "has remained a cultural school, where the humanities, Latin and Greek, still hold the most prominent place," and where of the natural sciences only elementary physics and chemistry are taught, "and of those only the amount prescribed for entrance to college."[38] The trustees never made their peace with the advocates of modern instruction. At Exeter, preparation for college remained "the great end and real business of living."

Private Control and Public Purpose

In the state of New York, private academies and colleges had come under the general supervision of the Regents of the University, a public body that, in turn, was subject to the supervisory and directive power of the state legislature. The academies had developed out of unincorporated elementary writing and private English grammar schools. They had added their Latin departments only when they applied for incorporation. Some were located in cities, usually as day schools, but the majority were boarding schools in rural areas. Only a few could count on income from an endowment. Most depended on tuition payments and sought to attract as large and diverse a clientele as they could. Thus they continued to offer elementary and practical instruction and both a classical and a modern curriculum. In their classical departments they prepared male students for entrance to a college. Through their teaching of the sciences and modern languages, they equipped others for life in the world of business and manufacturing.

Initially, the Regents had regarded as their chief objective to prevent an indiscriminate proliferation of financially and intellectually weak institutions. They had valued the academies chiefly for the classical education offered in the liberal arts. To this end, they used their power of incorporation and, after 1813, their authority to distribute the revenues of the State Literature Fund. Taking the number of students enrolled in an academy's classical course as the prime indicator of the school's quality, the Regents made the amount of support depend on that number. By that means they provided an incentive to the academies to favor the classics and mathematics over all other subjects. They in effect penalized the academies' English schools and discouraged those academies that included utilitarian subjects like surveying, navigation, and bookkeeping.[39]

With this policy the Regents quickly lost touch with the state's residents. Both urban and rural families had come to rely on the academies for the elementary and advanced English education of their sons and daughters. They feared the Regents' policy of favoring the support of a classical education as a threat to the continuing existence of the often less well endowed schools. They expressed their unease to the State Assembly, which accused the Regents of championing the male offspring of the well-born and the rich. In 1817 the legislators intruded on the until then exclusive prerogative of the Regents and began to charter most of the new academies. By 1841 they had chartered all of the female, and during the next decade also all of the coeducational academies.[40] In 1821 the Assembly's Committee on Colleges, Academies, and Common Schools had also urged the Regents to support studies "which fit the student for the useful occupations of ordinary life," specifically for "that most important employment, the business of the school master."[41] The academies, the legislators said, were "people's colleges." They continued the work of the common schools on a higher level and served the common schools by educating their teachers, both male and female.[42]

The Assembly's pressure showed results. In 1822 a Regents committee suggested to the entire board that it might consider increasing the number of academies that prepared "men for the active duties of life." New Yorkers were not likely, this committee said, to demand university preparatory schools on the model of the German *gymnasia* or French *lycées*: "The habits and condition of the Community preclude the separation of a portion of its members into a distinct class, devoted solely to the cultivation of polite literature and the sciences." The committee would rather see advanced training in modern subjects for non-college-bound students.[43] Four years later the Regents themselves asked that science be taught as a useful branch of knowledge "rather [than] as an accomplishment."[44] They argued that in their preoccupation with the classics, too many academies and colleges had ignored the needs of the state's middle classes for education in "mechanic pursuits and manufacturing establishments."[45] The Regents urged that colleges and professional schools offer courses of popular lectures in agriculture, chemistry, and mechanics, and that academies add more instruction in chemistry, trigonometry, geometry, surveying, algebra, bookkeeping, French, and Spanish.[46] In 1829 they incorporated the Oneida Institute of Science and Industry, "a public school [that] intended to combine horticulture, husbandry, and the mechanic arts with literature" and appealed to "the indigent classes" because it integrated remunerative labor into its curriculum.[47]

As the 1830s approached, the Regents appeared to have made their peace with the ascendancy of practical scientific studies over the classics. They acknowledged that the curricular division between modern and classical subjects tended to separate students who attended the academies from those who went to a college. To students in the academies, they wrote, the mathematical and physical sciences were central, whereas for college students literary pursuits and moral philosophy were "almost always the companions of leisure and wealth." Social class thus played a role in the students' choice of institutions and assigned more of them to the academies than to the colleges. This, the Regents said, was "the natural result of our social condition."[48]

The Regents accepted this division and the accompanying move from literary to scientific studies for two reasons. One was the role of science in the economic development of the state, particularly in the construction of the Erie Canal. According to Frank C. Abbott, the Regents' most recent historian, a minority of politicians, businessmen, scientists, and entrepreneurs on the board, men deeply involved in the development of the canal, had taken the initiative. Stephen Van Rensselaer, canal commissioner and founder and benefactor of the Scientific Institute that bears his name; De-Witt Clinton, New York's governor and chief promoter of the canal;

Simeon DeWitt, the state's surveyor general; and several others had championed the cause of scientific education as essential for the welfare of the state. The second reason was the Regents' awareness that if they were to ignore the economic pressures, their academies would soon be obsolete. This had become apparent when in 1831 the New York legislature incorporated the University of the City of New York as a public institution. It was to happen again when sixteen years later the New York City Board of Education created another public institution, the New York Free Academy. Although the academy was to prepare students for the city's colleges in its five-year classical course, its main function was, through a modern scientific curriculum, to prepare the children of the city's middle classes for careers in the trades and in business and manufacturing. Aware of these competing initiatives from the state's largest urban center, the Regents responded by accepting the Free Academy in their distribution of the Literature Fund. They no longer hesitated to embrace a scientific institution catering to lower-middle-class students.[49]

Further pressure for the academies to open themselves more widely to lower-middle-class and to female students came through the Assembly's push, already referred to, to train teachers for the common schools. The legislature and the state superintendent felt that because of their wide distribution in the hinterland and their low expense, the academies were a more cost-efficient form for the education of teachers than a proposed state normal school.[50] The Regents, reluctant at first to consider that proposal, fended it off with the help of friends of a public normal school. In 1832, however, they gave in and authorized the use of the Literature Fund for the training of teachers in the academies. By now the legislature had become suspicious and, to make sure that the moneys from the fund were distributed proportionally to the students in the English as well as in the classical course, asked the state superintendent to supervise the teacher-preparation departments in the eight academies that had established them. Thus, writes Abbott, by 1837 "the Regents were removed for a time from direct responsibility for teacher-education programs in academies over which they had general surveillance."[51]

Reactions to the new program were mixed. Teachers and trustees of the academies generally welcomed it because teacher-education departments brought added revenues, broadened the academies' base among the voters, and raised the general level of the common schools in the neighborhood. Other observers noted that in the academies teacher education was a stepchild at best. In a report to the state superintendent, Professor Alonzo Potter of Union College stated that the students rarely completed the three-year course. Many felt that the study of the classics, mathematics, or a modern language "will enhance the estimation in which they are held, not only as teachers, but in any other pursuit." Hence, they were "extremely anxious to embrace such opportunity."[52] Matters were even more discouraging in the female academies. The establishment of teacher-education departments there was superfluous because, as the state superintendent said, the ordinary course of instruction was "in itself sufficiently adapted to prepare female teachers of schools."[53]

The legislature concluded in 1844 that academies, having traditionally been centers for the education of teachers for academies and colleges, were not well qualified to prepare teachers for the common schools. It therefore opened a state normal school in Albany and withdrew its annual contribution to the academies' teacher-education departments. To add insult to injury, the executive committee of the State Normal School charged that the academies' teacher-education departments had allowed students to follow their own "whims," had not subjected them "to a rigor of daily examinations," had not exposed them long enough to recitations, and had not instructed them in vocal music, drawing, and the theory and practice of teaching.[54] Matters were adjudicated a few years later in a compromise. Teacher education in the academies and the State Normal School came under the supervision of an executive committee jointly established by the Regents and the superintendent. The academies' wide distribution across the state worked to their advantage, and by 1849 the legislature reauthorized the funding of teacher education in the academies.[55] Slowly, ever so slowly, did the academies find their place as schools for the advanced education of the children of the state's working middle classes.

3

The Nineteenth-Century
Liberal Arts College

The Colleges and the Modern Curriculum

As chapter 2 showed, neither the impatient urging of the legislature nor the encouragement of some more enterprising Regents had succeeded in making the New York academies enthusiastic champions of practical or useful studies. Viewing themselves as defenders of a century-old tradition of the *artes liberales*, conservative trustees continued to look upon arithmetic and geometry as practical sciences not suited to enhance the prestige of their institutions. But the growth of industry and modern communications had moved the more-open-minded trustees to accept the quadrivial subjects and natural philosophy as studies worthy of a gentleman's attention.[1] This was even more true of the trustees of liberal arts colleges. At Yale College, for example, the books of Isaac Newton and of other members of the Royal Society had been purchased for the library in 1714.[2] The presidency of Thomas Clap then brought a surge of interest in mathematics and natural philosophy, and the *theses physicae* defended at commencement during Clap's years from 1740 to 1766 included propositions on mechanics, physics, astronomy, chemistry, and biology.

Another index of the growing importance assigned to the natural sciences was the appointments to professorships in mathematics and natural philosophy, chairs second in importance and rapidity of establishment only to those of divinity. At the College of William and Mary, the first professor of mathematics was appointed in 1717, and Harvard followed with Isaac Greenwood in 1727 and John Winthrop in 1738.[3] In the College of Philadelphia and King's College in New York, the active commercial and business life of the cities encouraged a more practical orientation with greater stress on such applied skills as surveying, measuring, navigation, commerce, husbandry, law, and government. In 1750 Theophilus Grew was appointed the College of Philadelphia's professor of mathematics, and King's College followed in 1761 with Robert Harpus in the chair of mathematics and natural philosophy. Their teaching brought greater specialization in mathematics, chemistry, botany, and mineralogy.[4]

College presidents never doubted that the study of the classical languages was fundamental and necessary for any other scholarly pursuit. They also never questioned that a collegiate education included the study of nature as well as of tongues. But for many Americans outside the colleges, such liberal views did not go nearly far enough. Caught up in the pervasive and impatient boosterism of the era of westward expansion, they were ready to ignore the liberal arts colleges altogether, and they clamored for more easily accessible institutions of advanced education. As settlements sprang up beyond the Alleghenies and, as one commentator put it, a "money-making mania" began to grip the new nation, advanced education, too, took on the aspects of business enterprise.[5] Ministers offered Latin instruction in their homes to aspiring preachers. Lawyers and physicians banded together and opened proprietary law and medical schools. Businessmen and entrepreneurs promoted grammar schools and academies as attractions for "the better kind of settlers." Thus, as Daniel Boorstin remarked, the American "booster college" made its appearance, and, in Richard Hofstadter's view, "the great retrogression"—a precipitous drop in academic standards—came to characterize American education beyond the common-school level.[6]

Although in the frontier areas of the West academies and proprietary schools may indeed have suffered from lack of academic respectability, the established colleges in the East were hardly affected by such "retrogression." Their study of the *artes liberales* continued to exclude the practical and useful subjects. When, like King's College and the College of Philadelphia, they introduced the teaching of medicine, they did so through the establishment of professorial chairs or faculties in separate medical schools associated with, but not part of, the college. Similar developments occurred in the other professional fields of law and divinity.[7] Such conservatism brought upon the colleges a series of vociferous condemnations. Teaching the "dead languages" was nothing but drudgery, rote learning, and uninspired pedantry, the critics thundered. It was of no help to a generation that was to subdue mountains, dig canals, construct turnpikes and railroads, throw bridges across rivers, and turn woods and plains into granaries and pastures. The colleges were hostile to agriculture and engineering and unwilling to open their gates to the sons and daughters of farmers and workingmen. All they did, asserted the detractors, was to foster an aloof snobbishness of a ruling class.

Such accusations came not only from unknown laymen and ill-tempered and rabble-rousing journalists but from reputable alumni as well. In 1827, Judge Noyes Darling, a Connecticut state senator, Yale College alumnus, and member of the college corporation, asked his fellow Yale trustees to substitute other academic fields for the study of the classical languages. As politician, Darling shared his constituents' enthusiasm for steamboats, canals, and Connecticut's beginning industrialization. Having listened many times to the adventure stories of trading and whaling, he queried whether Yale had anything to contribute to this new world of technology, trade, and geographical expansion. Looking at the college's traditional offerings, Judge Darling thought the answer was obvious. His challenge roused the Yale faculty to a spirited defense of their pedagogical practice.

The Yale Report: Defense of the Classics

According to one of Yale's historians, that defense, the Yale Report of 1827, was "the most influential educational statement ever to emanate from Yale."[8] On one level it presented a spirited *apologia* for the classical curriculum. On another, and more important one, it became the definitive statement of the philosophy of the *artes liberales* as they were taught in nineteenth-century American liberal arts and "people's colleges," in academies and high schools.

Professor James L. Kingsley, renowned classicist, sought to defeat Judge Darling's proposal to remove the classical languages from the college curriculum with traditional arguments; none of his points were new. The classics were useful, he wrote, because on them were founded the literatures of every European country. Their study helped form taste and disciplined the mind in thought and diction. It provided a standard for determining merit in literature, architecture, and sculpture. "Classical discipline, likewise, forms the best preparation for professional study."[9] To depart from past practice and abandon the study of the languages would endanger everything the college had represented in the past. Worse yet, it would compromise the meaning and quality of the college degree, and thus the college would devalue its own currency and "put at hazard the very means of its support and existence."[10]

The committee of the corporation endorsed Professor Kingsley's statements. "The learned world," it wrote, "long ago settled this matter, and subsequent events and experience have confirmed their decision."[11] Patriotic Americans, concerned for "civil and religious liberty," demanded that the country's future lawyers, physicians, statesmen, ministers, or businessmen be steeped in the intellectual discipline and skills that the classics strengthened in students.[12] The committee went even further and recommended, provided the faculty agreed, that "the terms of admission . . . be gradually raised . . . , especially in the classics."[13] This would prevent the college from declining to the status of "a mere academy," keep its degrees from becoming valueless, and save the college itself from becoming "directly accessary to the depression of the present literary character of our country."[14]

The Yale Report: Faculty Psychology

As a definitive statement of the philosophy of the *artes liberales,* the report gave classic expression to what was known as nineteenth-century faculty psychology, the scientific bedrock on which rested the Yale scholars' philosophy of mental discipline. In the 1820s faculty psychology was not a new theory. Its history can be traced back to classical antiquity. Its curricular requirements included the classical languages and literatures as they had been modernized by the results of the revival of literary learning in the Renaissance and were permeated by a commitment to reformed Christianity. It supplemented this intellectual fare with an at least cursory overview of modern scientific and social ideas and theories that had emerged during and after the scientific revolution of the seventeenth and the political upheavals of the eighteenth centuries.

For the students, faculty psychology manifested itself primarily in the emphasis on mental discipline. "The two great points to be gained in intellectual culture," Yale's President Jeremiah Day had written,

> are the *discipline* and the *furniture* of the mind; expanding its powers, and storing it with knowledge. The former of these is, perhaps, the more important of the two. A commanding object, therefore, in a collegiate course, should be, to call into daily and vigorous exercise the faculties of the student. Those branches of study should be prescribed, and those modes of instruction adopted, which are best calculated to teach the art of fixing the attention, directing the train of thought, analyzing a subject proposed for investigation; following, with accurate discrimination, the course of argument; balancing nicely the evidence presented to the judgement; awakening, elevating, and controlling the imagination; arranging, with skill, the treasures which memory gathers; rousing and guiding the powers of genius.[15]

The Yale scholars viewed the curriculum as a finely tuned and evenly proportioned assembly of "branches of study" or "modes of instruction," each chosen for its disciplinary value to train a particular faculty. Was it just a fortuitous coincidence that those subjects thought to be most valuable for the purpose of mental discipline—the classical languages, mathematics, and natural science—were also those of longest use in the schools, familiar to every schoolmaster and university scholar?

However that may have been, faculty psychology, wrote Sheldon Rothblatt, had always been a teacher's philosophy *par excellence*. It placed the teacher in control of his pupil's education by making him the expert who knew which of his pupils' faculties needed special training and who could adjust his tutorial labors to the greatest advantage of the pupil. It was the teacher's task, Rothblatt reminded us, "to see that the faculties of mind were properly cultivated, that the will was strengthened, the judgment improved, the imagination warmed or excited, the reason developed, the understanding enlarged, or the moral powers exercised. . . . [But the] most important of all his teaching responsibilities was stimulating the memory."[16]

As the Yale scholars made clear in their report, they appreciated that an emphasis on the training of faculties permitted, even demanded, that subjects be chosen for their disciplinary rather than their informative or vocationally useful value. This allowed them to separate those academic disciplines that were basic to all intellectual endeavor from those that were taught primarily for vocational or professional purposes without necessarily tying the curriculum to the "cultivation of literature," or keeping it forever estranged from "the acquisition of science." Theoretical approaches and mental discipline were available to the college student of any field, provided he avoided a preoccupation with their merely factual and applied aspects.[17]

Another key demand of faculty psychology was, according to President Day, to bring into play "*all* the important mental faculties," and to do so in a balanced fashion. If literature and science were taught in unequal proportions, wrote Day, "there is a distortion in the intellectual character."[18] Their insistence on balance allowed the Yale scholars to keep open avenues for future curricular developments without having to capitulate to the anarchy of a proliferating curriculum that would destroy the coherence of a collegiate education.

Finally, the report reminded its readers that the Yale students were immature and untested boys who had barely emerged from the protective custody of the parental home. Unlike so many of their contemporaries in the English colleges, they had neither been socialized in residential grammar or public schools nor nurtured in clerical families. Unlike also their fellow students in the German universities, they had not undertaken a prolonged course of secondary studies at the successful completion of which they would have received a "certificate of maturity." In continental terminology, they were "pupils" rather than "students," adolescents rather than adults. The college they now attended corresponded to the German *gymnasium* or the French *lycée*, not to the Continental university. Thus, the Yale scholars wrote, it was "necessary that some faithful and affectionate guardian" take these boys by the hand and guide their steps. The college, they asserted, should be a family, an *alma mater*, in which students lived together in common residences and the faculty could act *in loco parentis*.[19]

The English Precedent

For the Yale scholars, the closest model of their pedagogical practice had been the colleges of the English universities. Some twenty years before they published their report, Edward Copleston, then fellow and later provost of Oriel College, Oxford University, had presented a similar apologetic argument for tradition and mental as well as physical discipline for collegiate education. In 1810 Copleston had sought to refute accusations published in the *Edinburgh Review* that his university had "been doing useless things for a long time." In *Reply to the Calumnies of the Edinburgh Review Against Oxford*, he argued, just as the Yale faculty would do, that the classical languages were as necessary to a well-rounded college education as the modern sciences. But in marked contrast to the Yale Report, Copleston's *Reply* was purely defensive and without the benefit of philosophical grounding. As a result, it lacked the Yale Report's psychological and pedagogical pertinence.

Critics, Copleston stated, should properly distinguish between the "cultivation of literature" and "the acquisition of science." The former had ever been the chief object of a college education, and the models provided therein by the ancients had never lost their value. Tutorial instruction in literature to small groups of three to twelve students was superior to public lectures that aimed at the "acquisition of science."[20] Lectures, Copleston conceded, held advantages for the self-disciplined and inspired student, but they could not be "the most effectual means by which instruction is to be conveyed to the minds of the great majority of students."[21] At Oxford, professorial lectures on science were not part of the required work for the college course anyway. Their contents were not included in the degree examinations. Literature clearly outranked science in the Oxford curriculum.

Lectures on science, Copleston pointed out, had been available—though not required—at Oxford in experimental philosophy, in astronomy, chemistry, mineralogy, and botany. In these studies, he wrote, "the ancients are not made our guides." Modern authors and experimenters were freely drawn upon. For more than a century, Copleston reminded his readers, Aristotle's physics had been replaced by Newton's natural philosophy, and mathematics had advanced beyond geometry to conic sections and calculus. In chemistry, students could find out about neutral salts and the decomposition of alkalis. There was, then, no justification in declaring that Oxford checked the progress of science and kept its students "back to the measure of the ancients."[22] But because the study of science could neither detract from nor add to the power of eloquence, the charm of poetry, the force of historical examples, or the instructiveness of moral and political reflection, it remained of distinctly secondary importance.

Copleston also took great pains to differentiate the work of the colleges from that of the university. As private institutions, the colleges offered a liberal education that cultivated literature; the university inquired into science and publicly presented the factual results of its work. A liberal education, whether offered in colleges or grammar schools, preceded university studies and, as one of its benefits, prepared students for them. This was the wisdom of the ages, grounded in tradition and the nature of things.[23] Subsequently "individuals may engage in the task of discovery," wrote Copleston, "and they are better fitted for that task, if they be well informed in what is already known." A liberal education, therefore, was basic and as such more important than university studies. The latter, Copleston emphasized, were "the subordinate, and not the leading, business of education."[24]

By comparison with the Yale Report, Copleston's essay suffered from its disregard of faculty psychology. Copleston saw it as no more than a suitable argument for linking the traditional curricular fields with the pedagogical objectives of a collegiate education in the liberal arts. Thus it supplied a respectable *ex post facto* rationale for the teaching of the ancient languages and mathematics. That was all. As Peter Slee has pointed out, Oxford defended the choice of the subjects it taught not because they provided the best match for the demands of faculty psychology but because their difficulty made them tools *par excellence* for the disciplining of unruly boys. Their mastery required of the students unremitting, tiresome, and often boring application and persistence; qualities that college dons prized as means of character training. "By requiring the student to adopt skills appropriate to another—alien—mode of experience the curriculum required more effort on his part than could reasonably be elicited from any subject read in English alone."[25] The English universities at the beginning of the nineteenth century certainly believed in mental discipline, but for them it meant little more than hard work in difficult subjects.

Yale College and the New Republic

The vibrant spirit of early republicanism and continental expansion gave the Yale Report much of its driving power. Its authors, foremost among them Professor Benjamin Silliman, Yale's professor of chemistry and mineralogy and the editor of the *American Journal of Science and Arts*, were keenly aware of the entrepreneurial spirit that pervaded the developing country. Unlike their fellow scholars in England, they accepted the new industrialism. They wanted their students to assume responsibility for its guidance, not to become its most bitter critics. They also viewed themselves as generalists in the classical sense. When they insisted on language as the key subject of instruction, they did so not, like their Oxford colleagues, solely for its disciplinary use but for the humanistic values it embodied. They said repeatedly that they were interested in educating men, not in training technicians, specialists, or narrow professionals. Leaders in a democracy like the United States had to be able to respond to and represent everybody. Referring to the lawyers and Lords in the houses of Parliament, the Yale scholars asked: "Ought the speaking in our deliberative assemblies to be confined to a single profession?"[26] Their answer was a decided "No." They let it be known that in their college they were not educating gentlemen leaders for a class-based society. That, they implied, may have been the self-assigned task of the Oxford dons, but it was not theirs.

The theme of the college's awareness of its place in the world and its acceptance of its obligations to society came through again and again. In a democratic country, wrote President Day, where a college was the one place where education could be thorough, theoretical, and basic, it had to be available to everyone who qualified.

> Our republican form of government renders it highly important, that great numbers should enjoy the advantage of a thorough education. . . . [I]n this country, where offices are accessible to all who are qualified for them, superior intellectual attainments ought not to be confined to any description of persons. *Merchants, manufacturers*, and *farmers*, as well as professional gentlemen, take their places in our public councils. A thorough education ought therefore to be extended to all these classes.[27]

Yale was a liberal arts college in a republic. It therefore required a republican theory of education in the *artes liberales*. This the Yale Report was meant to supply.

Yale's Curriculum

Reading the Yale Report, one has to remember that members of the faculty and of the corporation wrote it as an *apologia* for past and then-current practice. One has to assume that not all of Yale's students, and particularly the undergraduates, shared the glowing assessment. However effectively advanced and professional students were persuaded by the lectures and sermons of the professors to remain at the college after graduation, this was not always true of Yale's undergraduates.[28] Not all professors lectured, and of those who did, not all did it well. President Day, for example, restricted his demonstrations to mathematical proofs, and, if we are to judge by students' comments, Professor Kingsley's lectures on the classical languages were less than inspiring.[29] On the whole, Yale's faculty members, believing in enforcing physical and mental discipline, supervised recitations more than they lectured and did little to arouse intellectual curiosity and enthusiasm or to stimulate experimentation and inquiry. George W. Pierson summarized it well: Yale College "operated on the assumption . . . that the better part of a college education was a training in good habits: habits of worship and devotion; habits of industry and exact study; good moral and physical habits; habits of square and manly dealing."[30]

But in their report the faculty gave matters a different twist. They set out to document that Yale College students were offered far more than the recitations of the classical course. And then they listed their lectures: Kingsley lectured to all four classes on Latin, Greek, and Hebrew; Denison Olmstead spoke before the juniors on natural philosophy, and Silliman gave his presentations on chemistry, mineralogy, and geology to the senior class and the postgraduate students of Yale's Medical Institution. Silliman employed laboratory equipment to demonstrate the professional applications of his subject, and he relied on the collections of Yale's mineral cabinet.[31] Professor Chauncey Allen Goodrich lectured on rhetoric and oratory, and drilled his students in English and Latin composition, in forensic disputations, and in declamations. Nathaniel Taylor, Yale's Dwight Professor of Didactic Theology, served the community as the minister of New Haven's Center Church. He and Eleazar Fitch, the college professor of divinity, persuaded a group of graduates to continue divinity studies under their guidance.

President Day's committee took special pains to stress the innovative aspects of Yale's curriculum. It reported to the trustees that "whole sciences have, for the first time been introduced; chemistry, mineralogy, geology, political economy, &c."[32] Others might have pointed out that many of these changes involved nothing more than the introduction of different texts in familiar subjects and thus scarcely proved any fundamental alteration. Kingsley, for example, had expanded instruction in Greek by adding Homer and the anthologies *Graeca Minora* and *Graeca Majora* to the ever-present New Testament, and in mathematics he got his students to read Euclid.[33] For the professors, however, the changes were meaningful and real. Yale moved with the times.

The professors' case was strongest in the natural sciences. There the introduction of new subjects, especially in natural history and philosophy, was more radical. So were the reasons given by the professors. Silliman pointed to chemistry's usefulness to medicine. "No physician can hope to keep pace with his profession who does not attend to this science," he said. Balloonists would benefit from knowing the properties of hydrogen gas, and every practitioner in agriculture and industry could expect new discoveries and inventions that would contribute to the future prosperity of society.[34] Silliman underlined chemistry's novelty as well as its promise as a tool for assuming leadership in the expanding economy of state and country.[35] The same motivation lay behind his introduction of mineralogy and geology.[36] To add the three sciences meant that his students would be prepared to cope with the demands of a changing world while maintaining their customary positions of a ruling elite.[37]

What mattered to Silliman was that science was taught for theoretical understanding rather than for practical application. The scientific curriculum was not designed to acquaint students with the minutiae of the natural and industrial worlds but with their basic principles. The liberal arts and sciences were the college's province, not vocational or professional studies. By shaping character, forming habits, cultivating taste, and providing opportunities through scientific lectures for students to become acquainted with the latest studies and discoveries, a Yale education was designed for leadership in all fields.

College and University

The introduction of new sciences with laboratory equipment and mineral cabinets inevitably raised the question whether the college would or should develop into a university and add research instruction to its duties. The Yale scholars were aware of earlier suggestions that American colleges, like those of England, might be associated with one another in a university.[38] The dispersal of American colleges across the country, however, made this pattern inadvisable. They also knew of the German model of elective subjects, which Harvard had introduced in 1825 and of the opening of the University of Virginia in the same year as an association of eight professional schools.[39] Speaking of European, especially German, universities they said: "We hope at least, that this college may be spared the mortification of a ludicrous attempt to imitate them, while it is unprovided with the resources necessary to execute the purpose."[40] As to professional schools, Day and his colleagues did not give it any thought at all. Yale was a college, devoted to the *artes liberales*, no more and no less. The Yale faculty wanted neither to abandon tutorial recitations nor to exchange the cohesion of an integrated uniform curriculum for elective offerings of a variety of new disciplines. Yale students, they thought, being two to three years younger than their European counterparts, were far too young and unprepared for university work; they required strict, disciplinary supervision. "Would parents in this country," Day asked, "consent to send their sons, at the age of sixteen, to an institution in which there should not be even an attempt at discipline, farther than to preserve order in the lecture room?"[41] For the American college, serving the needs of a democratic nation, there really was no model to copy anywhere on the globe. If a kindred institution could be found at all on the Continent, the Yale scholars wrote, it would have to be the German *gymnasium*. But the *gymnasium* was a day school without common meals and family-style living, and thus it, too, could not really provide a model for the college.

The Yale Report in Retrospect

In speaking about their college, the Yale professors and trustees wrote what one may well call the *magna charta* for liberal arts institutions of secondary education in the United States. Their blueprint applied to the curriculum of institutions of general education that took up their work where the common schools left off. These institutions were of two kinds, the liberal arts colleges like Yale and the "people's colleges" usually found in larger urban centers or, as academies, in rural areas. The liberal arts colleges expected their graduates to enter upon professional careers, but both types of colleges prepared their graduates for any future work they might consider.

As the Yale scholars saw it, this curriculum embodied enough flexibility to guarantee that students would be exposed to all "those branches of knowledge, of which no one destined to the higher walks of life ought to be ignorant."[42] In addition to the curriculum, "the collegiate way" of the liberal arts colleges, their common extracurricular and social experience, provided the unifying bond that held together the country's future leading elite. Had these scholars still been alive 140 years later, they would have agreed with Pierre Bourdieu that "the sharing of a common culture . . . is probably one of the surest foundations of the deep underlying fellow-feeling that unites the members of the governing classes, despite differences of occupation and economic circumstances." Should a nation replace "the collegiate way" with "a system of teaching geared more and more exclusively to preparation for an increasing variety of occupational activities," it would endanger "the cultural integration of the educated class."[43] The Yale scholars knew that in their developing nation, the college experience and the resulting cohesion of the nation's elite were the most potent antidotes to the threat of cultural dissolution.

The problem the Yale scholars wrestled with was the problem of culture in a business civilization. Was it true, as Judge Darling and his supporters contended, that the colleges were "not adapted to the spirit and the want of the age; that they will soon be deserted, unless they are better accommodated to the business character of the nation"?[44] Did or would or could the liberal arts colleges, the embodiment of academic culture, prepare their graduates for the entrepreneurial capitalism of an emerging business society? The Yale faculty left no doubt about their commitment to play their role in shaping the country's future leaders in every area of life from politics and the traditional professions to business, industry, and science. But they were going to do it in "the collegiate way" best suited to their traditions and capabilities. Other educational institutions might pursue aims of their own and provide information and technical skills. Academies taught "a little of everything," and professional schools and practical settings gave mercantile, mechanical, or agricultural training.[45] The college's work was more basic. It prepared students to benefit from subsequent professional instruction by teaching them to rely on their native ingenuity, skill, and intellectual abilities to continue learning on their own.

But there was more to the Yale faculty's reaction than a stubborn belief in the superiority of their practices and beliefs. They were convinced also that beyond a certain point, the siren songs of the outside world were dangerous and traitorous to the inherited faith and customs of the American people. The new entrepreneurial spirit, necessary and promising as it was for a developing nation, also held dangers and temptations. By its individualistic bent it could prove fatal to the sense of commonwealth and national destiny. It encouraged individuals "of a very limited stock of knowledge" but endowed with "a driving, bustling spirit" to show off "the tinsel of . . . literary ornaments" acquired through a superficial education and tempted them to push themselves "forward into notice and employment."[46] An education such as the college provided, the faculty believed, would inoculate their graduates against the insidious influences of a creeping commercialism, a reckless individualism, and a rampant desire for self-promotion and aggrandizement. With its balance of factual knowledge and moral instruction, Yale would safeguard the republic against such treason.[47]

4

The People's College

The Coming of the Urban High School

In the country's large urban centers, the people's college became the successor to the academy, which was most usually found in rural areas.[1] In both institutions students opted, with few exceptions, for the modern curricula rather than for the classical course. What established the people's college as an institution parallel to the liberal arts college was its adoption of the educational philosophy of the Yale Report. The report's emphasis on mental discipline and on the academic study of the liberal arts and sciences defined "the college course" as the proper curriculum for all of the country's post-common-school institutions of general education. The only curricular difference between the liberal arts college and the people's college was that the former concentrated on the classical languages, the arts, and the sciences, the latter emphasized primarily mathematics, the natural sciences, and the modern languages. Both stressed a predominantly academic approach and had no room for the applied sciences and practical studies.

The people's college as an urban high school owes its existence to the rise of the common schools, which helped popularize the principle of free schooling supported by the local property tax. It had been only a question of time for the idea of free schooling to be extended to the secondary level. In the cities, a population of artisans, shopkeepers, and other small businessmen wanted an education for their sons that could serve their vocational aims; an education that could be offered close to home; and an education that children could enter and leave as the fam-

41

ily budget and other considerations required or suggested. Though the proposals for and descriptions of secondary school curricula during the first half of the nineteenth century contained few, if any, direct references to the Yale Report, the emphasis on mental discipline recommended it as the appropriate model. Speaking of a period as late as the 1890s, Edward Krug could still write that "most of the school men . . . agreed that the purpose of the schools was to furnish mental training or training of the will. Mere information was disparaged, although concessions were made at times to something called the furniture of the mind."[2] The furniture of the mind, of course, was a phrase made memorable in the Yale Report.

In the decades after 1820 free public high schools opened their doors in the urban centers of the United States. As an upward extension of and part of a city's public school system, these schools were meant not only to provide opportunities for the upward mobility of the children of small business and artisan families but also to serve the public interest of urban economic development. Trade and manufacturing demanded workers skilled in reading, writing, and computational skills beyond those taught in the common schools. A national and international market required businessmen and entrepreneurs familiar with conditions of life outside the boundaries of their own community, acquainted with foreign customs, and able to communicate in foreign languages.

The high school as people's college was to combine the academic study of practical skills familiar to most Americans from the academies with the teaching of modern natural sciences like chemistry and geology as carried out in the liberal arts colleges. In addition, it was to foster among the working classes of the cities a consciousness of common economic and social-class interests that was to parallel the "collegiate way" of the liberal arts colleges. In the nineteenth century, Benjamin Franklin's "rising people" of the eighteenth were to find their "way to wealth" in the urban high school.

The Urban High School: Boston

The first public high school opened in Boston in 1821. Other Massachusetts towns followed, until by 1839 twenty-six such schools existed in the state. By that time high schools had also spread to other states and had begun their work in Philadelphia, Baltimore, and Charleston. By 1851 eighty cities had public high schools.[3] The curriculum of the Boston school included the usual academy subjects: English, geography, history, arithmetic, algebra, geometry, trigonometry, navigation, surveying, and natural and moral philosophy. Mr. Gould, principal of the venerable

42

Boston Latin School, no doubt piqued by the appearance of a competitor, commented two years later that

> public opinion and the wants of a large class of citizens of this town have long been calling for a school in which those, who have either not the desire or the means of obtaining a classical education, might receive instruction in many branches of great practical importance which have usually been taught only at the Colleges.

Noticing that the classical languages were neither required for entry nor taught, Gould was especially irritated by the school's name, English Classical School for Boys. He expressed hope that eventually a change of name would express more adequately the school's real function. In 1824 his wish was granted, and the school came to be known as the Boston English High School.[4]

Despite his displeasure over the school's original presumption, Gould readily agreed with the town's school committee that it offered a curriculum that—except for the absence of classical studies—was in all respects equal to that of a liberal arts college. The Boston English High School served the people of Boston as an alternative not only to a private academy but also to a liberal arts college. A subcommittee of the Boston School Committee described the school's purpose:

> A parent who wishes to give a child an education that shall fit him for active life, and shall serve as foundation for eminence in his profession, whether Mercantile or Mechanical, is under the necessity of giving him a different education from any which our public schools can now furnish. Hence, many children are separated from their parents and sent to private academies in this vicinity, to acquire that instruction which cannot be obtained at the public seminaries. Thus, many parents, who contribute largely to the support of those institutions, are subjected to heavy expense for the same object in other towns.[5]

Relative inexpensiveness and the opportunity of receiving appropriate advanced training while staying at home were the school's salient advantages.

The English High School for Boys became an unqualified success. To be known in Boston as a student of Boys High was a recommendation that assured easy employment in countinghouses and trade and mercantile establishments. It aided a young man to set up his own business as shopkeeper, tradesman, or entrepreneur, in most cases without ever having completed the full three-year course. As Michael Katz has pointed out, although schools like this evidently aided the propertied small bourgeoisie of the cities, they did not draw many students from families of workingmen and women who could ill afford the loss of their children's wages.[6] Mayor Josiah Quincy cherished the Boston school for its payoff to the city's business life. He saw no reason to object to the taxpayer-financed largesse for middle-class boys.

The story was different, however, for Boston's middleclass girls. School reformers and the parents of girls set out to convince the taxpayers that a high school for girls was ultimately as cost-efficient and beneficial as one for boys. Certainly, they argued, the city would benefit when girls received further education for their expected roles as wives and mothers. In addition, before marriage and motherhood or as widows and spinsters, women, young and old, could aid the city as teachers in the common schools. The arguments were persuasive, and in 1826 the city opened a high school for girls.

Yet the school did not last long. Within two years the mayor, the aldermen, and members of the school committee found that the school had become too successful. "From the known circumstances of females, between the age of eleven and sixteen," complained Mayor Quincy, "there is no reason for believing that any one, once admitted to the school, would voluntarily quit it for the whole three years; unless, indeed, in the case of marriage."[7] As Quincy saw it, sending girls to high school was not cost-efficient. Girls were neither trade- nor profession-minded and, unlike boys, rarely obtained employment or other opportunities before they graduated from school. Thus their stay in school, argued the mayor, was but a waste of the taxpayers' money.[8]

Mayor Quincy's views prevailed for nearly a quarter of a century, until the advocates of a girls high school found a winning argument in the lack of common-school teachers. Just as in New York State the academies had taken up teacher education, so now the city of Boston, finding that parents hesitated to send their daughters out of the city to the state normal schools, decided that a municipal secondary school for girls could best respond to the desire of many of the city's parents for the further education of their daughters, and, at the same time, alleviate the shortage of teachers in the city's common schools. A city normal school opened its doors in 1852.

For middle-class Bostonians, however, a normal school was not enough. What they really wanted was a high school that could open the doors to occupations other than common school teaching. Besides, the city fathers and schoolmen soon discovered the malaise that beset most other normal schools in the country: few of its graduates went into teaching; those who did, did so for only a few years.[9] As the school's headmaster would later remark: the school's "normal features were soon quite overshadowed by the high school work."[10] Bostonians thus decided within two years to rename the school the Boston Girls' High and Normal School. Its curriculum offered a two-year high school program with a third-year normal course added on. Teacher training thus provided the argument that girls were being given the same opportunities their brothers had enjoyed since 1821.

The Urban High School: Philadelphia

When in October of 1838 Philadelphia opened its Central High School, another people's college was born. As did its Boston counterpart, this school for boys appealed to the city's lower middle class of shopkeepers and artisans. Alexander Dallas Bache, its first principal, from 1839 to 1842, defined the school's purpose as providing "a liberal education for those intended for business life."[11] Its curriculum, although academic and collegiate, was to be directed toward practical purposes. At the outset, it offered a two-year English sequence that went beyond the ordinary elementary preparation and was meant for boys who could not afford or did not desire to attend one of the full, four-year courses. Of the latter, the modern-language course was the principal one. It was intended for the majority of students who were expected to enter careers in commerce, manufacturing, and the useful arts. Finally, there was a four-year classical program for those boys who intended subsequently to attend a liberal arts college.[12]

With its concentration on a single, common curriculum of academic scientific instruction for all students and on business preparation as its central purpose, the four-year modern language course highlighted the school's nature as a people's college. This intent was brought home vividly in 1849 when the school was authorized to grant academic degrees and, two years later, when the masters organized themselves as the faculty that was to govern the school. Calling themselves professors, the teachers constituted the well-paid elite of the city's grammar-school masters. The school's nature as a people's college was emphasized again in 1854 when the faculty dropped the classical course and in 1856 when it eliminated the two-year English curriculum. As the school's historian, David Labaree, observed: "Central's curricular uniformity makes it similar to mid-nineteenth century colleges and quite different from other early high schools," many of which offered both an English and a classical course.[13]

The four-year common English and modern-language curriculum underscored the school's intent to serve the local business community. Students were obliged to spend 34 percent of their class time on science and mathematics, 21 on modern languages, 14 on history, 12 on vocational instruction, 11 on English, and 8 on other studies.[14] Even though the curriculum was designed with practical purposes in mind, the professors, for the most part, took a scientific rather than a vocational approach. Just like their colleagues in the liberal arts colleges, they carried out laboratory demonstrations with the school's "philosophical apparatus" to illustrate scientific theory. Only secondarily did they acquaint their students with practical tasks.

In his history of Philadelphia Central, Labaree points out that it was precisely this academic atmosphere in which the school presented its training for business that constituted its greatest strength and value. Except for the absence of the classics, of dormitories and commons, Philadelphia Central *was* a college. The ideology of common schooling for all its students represented its version of the "collegiate way." To be sure, Central's students, unlike Yale's, were not educated to become "gentlemen." But they were groomed for positions in the city as men of affairs, if not men of letters. As John Hart, the school's second principal, said in 1843, Central did not aspire "to educate boys above their business, but for it."[15] The conduct of students mattered at Central, and until 1859, the students' grades reflected behavior as well as academic performance. In these ways the school combined cultural aspirations with business mentality and confirmed for or bestowed on its graduates the "cultural property" of the middle class.[16]

The Urban High School: New York

In New York City, as in Boston, agitation for a public free high school had begun in the 1820s. A high school was to provide an alternative to the preparatory Latin Grammar School of Columbia College and other private, fee-charging grammar schools. By 1825 the High-School Society, a group of private citizens incorporated by the legislature, succeeded in opening a high school for boys and, in the following year, added a high school for girls. The society intended to offer low-cost instruction that would prepare the boys for "the active business of life" and the girls for their duties as wives and mothers.[17] Because the society's schools employed student-monitors as instructional staff and thus could undercut the private schoolmasters' fees, the masters vigorously combated the schools and by 1831 succeeded in shutting them down.[18]

New York's Public School Society, responsible for the city's common schools, also expressed interest in sponsoring a high school. but before its efforts could bear fruit, it was replaced in 1842 by the City Board of Education. The board petitioned the state legislature for a high school charter and in 1847 obtained the incorporation of the Free Academy for the City of New York. Board members had complained that the city's private colleges—Columbia and New York University—were too expensive and interested only in students who looked toward careers in the professions. Because the colleges failed to attract the graduates of the city's common schools, a public high school could serve as a collegiate school for the children of nonprofessional families who desired advanced training for careers in business and industry. In such a school, board members said,

> the courses of studies to be pursued will have more especial reference to the active duties of operative life, rather than those more particularly regarded as necessary for the Pulpit, Bar, or the Medical Profession. . . . [Thus] the laboring class of our fellow citizens may have the opportunity of giving to their children an education that will more effectually fit them for the various departments of labor and toil by which they will earn their bread.

Boys, they said, would study chemistry, mechanics, architecture, agriculture, navigation, and physical as well as moral and mental science. The city would have a people's college of its own.[19]

Four years later the board's Executive Committee repeated once more that it did not view the academy as a connecting link between the common schools and the private liberal arts colleges, but as a public "substitute" for both the private colleges and academies. Board members argued that the Academy's students neither came from nor intended to enter the professional class. But neither, as Carl Kaestle later observed, did they come from families of unskilled laborers and servants. The bottom quarter of the work force was almost entirely absent and blacks were excluded altogether.[20] The academy's students were the sons of lower-level white-collar fathers, of artisans, and of skilled laborers. Their aim was social and economic advance in their business.

During the 1850s and 1860s, however, the school's preparatory program became more important. It consisted of two five-year courses: one stressed the ancient languages; the other, the modern subjects. A third, called the "partial" course, accommodated those boys who wanted to leave before graduation and enter directly into business. When in 1854 the legislature authorized the academy to award academic degrees to the graduates of its five-year courses, the school was on its way to becoming a college in law as well as in fact.[21] Two years later, making full use of its newly received authority, the academy bestowed eight M.A. degrees on its resident graduates. Finally, in 1866, the Free Academy was reincorporated by the legislature as the College of the City of New York.[22] New York City's people's college had become a liberal arts college.

The Urban High School: Somerville

The public high schools in Boston, Philadelphia, and New York were schools for boys. The prior existence of the Boston Latin School may have predisposed Bostonians to think of secondary education as a male preserve; yet, as pointed out above, strong sentiment existed already in 1821 to accommodate the wishes of middle-class parents for the advanced education of their daughters. In Philadelphia and New York the stories were similar. The University of Pennsylvania and its predecessor, the College of Philadelphia, had catered to boys, as had Columbia College and New York University. Central High and the Free Academy had followed that pattern, but, just as in Boston, the coming of schools for girls could not be delayed indefinitely. In 1848 Philadelphia opened its Girls' High School and New York followed in 1870 with its City Normal School.

Where, however, such preexisting local institutions for the advanced education of boys were absent, the common-school tradition of coeducational instruction prevailed, and high schools opened for boys and girls together.[23] Somerville, Massachusetts, a suburb of Boston, was an example. Here, girls attended the high school from its beginning in 1852. Their number was roughly twice that of the boys. When, beginning in 1862, students began to graduate, for ten years two-thirds of the school's graduates were girls.[24]

There were several reasons for the school's attractiveness for girls. Other than for positions as teachers in the common schools, employment opportunities for teenage girls were rare. Those that existed provided wages half those boys received and did not materially improve the girls' family incomes. Thus, just as in Boston, few girls left the school before graduation, and then mainly for reasons of health. Given the prevailing views on gender roles at midcentury, the parents of girls were less concerned with their daughters' vocational training or academic preparation for business than they were with their readiness for marriage and motherhood. Because they believed a cultural "finish" would add luster to a girl's reputation, prepare her for a few years of school-teaching, and, at the same time, increase her chances for marital happiness, parents encouraged their daughters to remain in school throughout all four years

48

and not to miss the last two, which were devoted to academic-cultural studies.[25] It was only during the 1880s, when girls began to enroll for commercial courses or looked forward to transfer to normal school or college, that this pattern of a finishing school for girls became less obvious.

Despite the preponderance of girls, schoolmen had defined the school's purpose and curriculum largely with boys in mind. The sequence of courses suggests this. As Reed Ueda tells us in his history of the school, the subjects of "most immediate practical value" were offered in the first two years; languages and philosophy were taught during the last two. Thus, Ueda wrote,

> students could take immediately the courses that provided communication skills and knowledge useful for white-collar work, and then leave. As a result, from the time of its founding in 1852 until the end of its first decade, the school did not produce a single graduate.[24]

This did not bother the school committee, whose members had argued, even before the school had opened its doors, that instruction should prepare graduates of the common schools directly for practical life. Committee members had not wanted a Latin grammar school that stressed the "recitative dexterity" favored by the classical studies. They wanted a school specializing "in studies more accurate and practical." Its best students, the committee members stated, were not going to be "prodigies capable of working incomprehensibly and mysteriously," but young people with "strong, progressive, well-balanced faculties which it would be an honor to our town . . . to train to distinction and usefulness, without calling for foreign aid."[27] It is obvious from this that at least the Somerville school committee had not counted on female students and the kind of finishing school their presence appeared to call for. The committee had wanted a people's college that, utilizing the faculty psychology of the Yale Report, prepared boys for the world of work.

Although the presence of female students thus introduced a somewhat discordant note in Somerville's conception of its people's college, the demographics of the student body did not. At the beginning of the school's first decade, 55 percent of the school's students came from white-collar families, 31 percent from homes of skilled laborers, and 8 percent from those of semiskilled laborers. The fathers of only 4 percent were listed as unskilled, and those of 2 percent as unemployed. At the same time, the city's male labor force consisted of 30 percent white-collar workers, 32 percent skilled laborers, 5 percent semiskilled laborers, and 33 percent unskilled laborers. Thus in Somerville as in New York, the children of white-collar families were overrepresented, and those of unskilled laborers were few indeed. At the end of the decade, the proportional share of youngsters from white collar and unskilled labor families was roughly the same; that of skilled labor and artisan families had gone up; and that of semiskilled labor families had decreased.[28] During the 1860s, then, the share of small property-owning families as well as of foreign-born parents, chiefly from Great Britain, increased again, and demonstrated once more that the school benefited most directly the children of white-collar and artisan families.[29]

The Urban High School as People's College

The urban people's college was the distinctive educational institution of the pre– and early post–Civil War era. As a tax-supported public secondary school, it was intended for young people desiring an education beyond the elementary curriculum of the common schools. It was open to all who, in the language of the 1893 Committee of Ten, showed "themselves able to profit by an education prolonged to the eighteenth year, and whose parents [were] able to support them while they remain[ed] so long at school."[30] The people's college had come into its own when the public high school appeared and replaced the private academy. It was meant to serve its supporting community as the prime supplier of academically trained leaders for the world of business and industry, and, in the case of girls, of well-prepared matrons in schoolroom and home.

For its guiding philosophy, the urban people's college had adopted the faculty psychology of the Yale Report. It instructed its students, both male and female, in traditional and modern academic disciplines. Its educational ideals combined a vigorous and well-trained intellect, an ethical integrity that acknowledged the obligations educated individuals held toward their communities, and an individual independence that rested on the awareness of the power that flowed from knowledge. It bestowed on its graduates what David Labaree called the "cultural property" of the middle class, that is, "all those cultural traits . . . that are considered valuable to possess as a result of their association with the dominant culture."[31] The people's college represented an admirable, though not entirely successful, attempt to join the desire for equality of opportunity with the determination to provide a quality education.

Because any educational institution reflects the prejudices and social practices of its time, barriers of race, class, and religious faith prevented many young people from being admitted. Prevailing views of gender roles prescribed that the school's primary aim was to serve male students. Its program benefited female students only incidentally by creating parallel

50

high schools for girls or, where a high school served both genders, by assigning girls to separate classes in normal training and, later, commercial work and domestic economy. Nonetheless, within the limitations of its time, the people's college embodied the American dream of enabling young people to raise themselves above the worldly attainments of their parents.

With its academic and cultural program, the people's college was a finishing, not a preparatory, school. It sent its graduates immediately into the world of work, marriage, and home. It did not expect them to continue their education in other schools of higher rank. People's college graduates, whether male or female, were thought to be as ready and well educated for their respective future tasks as were the graduates of the liberal arts colleges and professional schools for theirs.

The people's college derived its unique place in American educational history from its having merged the common-school idea with the academic curriculum of the private academies. Its ability to provide its students with both practical advantages and cultural endowments made it the defining educational institution for the American middle class of the nineteenth century. As such it was the American counterpart to the German *gymnasium,* the French *lycée,* and the English endowed grammar school, all of which Detlef Müller and his colleagues described as their societies' "defining institutions." The difference, of course, was that the European societies had developed their defining institutions as schools for the children of the educated bourgeoisie, and charged them with preparing boys for careers as future professionals and higher civil servants. The American people's college, however, was meant to prepare the children of the nineteenth-century successors to Benjamin Franklin's "rising people" for careers as small businessmen and entrepreneurs and as their wives and helpmates. The people's college thus was the defining educational institution of the urban lower-middle class. Whether in Europe or in the United States, these defining educational institutions succeeded, as Hilary Steedman put it, in converting "social hierarchies into academic hierarchies in such a way that academic hierarchies became the obligatory mediators for social groups maintaining or improving status between one generation and the succeeding one."[32]

The era of the people's college drew to a close toward the end of the nineteenth century. As more students, both male and female, wanted to be prepared for continuing schooling in colleges and universities, the people's college changed its character. It added college preparation to finishing for business, housework, teaching, or employment. For its female students, it introduced classes in office work and domestic economy. As we shall learn in subsequent chapters, manual education and eventu-

ally vocational instruction turned the people's colleges into the multipur-
pose high school of the twentieth century. A chapter in the history of
American education drew to a close. "For a brief and shining moment"
the American people's college had defined secondary education as sufficient in its own right and on its own terms for all its students regardless
of their future destinations. It had been democracy's college, a concept
Americans lost sight of throughout most of the twentieth century. It is,
however, a concept that we need not have lost forever and that, as I shall
point out in a later chapter, with suitable modifications, we may recover
for the twenty-first century.

5

State Systems of Secondary Education

The Systematization of Secondary Education

The preceding chapter introduced the people's college as the defining institution of American mid-nineteenth-century urban middle-class democracy. The urban high school, however, had not been the only public institution devoted to the post-common-school education of American youths. Latin grammar schools, as we know, antedated the common schools. Other public high schools had grown out of local common schools or had once been private academies. These schools, however, had been or had become parts of state systems and had come under state supervision and direction. Though reflecting local needs and aspirations, they had also been intended to prepare their graduates for continuing collegiate study, and their programs and curricula had been designed with the requirements of statewide university systems and private colleges in mind. To use the terminology of the nineteenth century, these high schools were meant to prepare their graduates for college, and the people's colleges were to prepare their students for "the active life."

Such sharp differentiation of purpose, however, never corresponded to reality. As the number of students attending the college-preparatory schools increased, so also grew the discrepancy between the schools' announced purpose and their actual function. Families desiring further preparation for business and domestic life for their sons and daughters were more numerous than those seeking college admission for their sons. Politicians and schoolmen exploited the always latent and often open antagonisms of class and gender and deplored the "aristocratic"—today we would say "elitist"—implications and connotations of preparation for college. By the 1870s the country was ripe for a searching debate over the high school question: What was the public high school's primary mission: to prepare for college or to prepare for life?

However imperfectly the systems of preparatory education were accomplishing their task, the existence of secondary schools prior to and after the opening of urban high schools kept alive the idea of state responsibility for secondary education. To be sure, these systems were not all alike in their details. In Massachusetts the Latin grammar schools had served as preparatory public feeder schools for Harvard College, the state's public university until after the Civil War. After the incorporation of Williams College in 1793, they fulfilled the same function for the private colleges. In Georgia, New York, and in Michigan, private academies received public subsidies. Until the opening of Oglethorpe College in 1835, the Georgia academies sent their graduates to the university; thereafter, they also prepared them for the private colleges. In New York, the academies and private colleges both came under the administrative supervision of the Regents of the University of the State of New York. In Michigan, the state system had included private academies as branches of the university. However much they differed in detail, all of these states, in one form or another, had in their early history experimented with the idea of an integrated secondary-collegiate system and made it a part of the American experience in secondary education.

As I have pointed out in prior chapters, this process began in 1635 in Massachusetts even before Harvard College had opened its doors. The Boston Latin School was the first of its kind, and it was founded by the city upon the urgent request of the General Court. Soon it became evident that local communities resisted the legislature's pressure for more such schools, and that wherever Latin schools had been opened, only a minority of their students stayed for the Latin course and intended to attend college. But it was this minority that attracted the interest of colonial and later state authorities and prompted them to concern themselves with the founding and maintenance of secondary schools. If local authorities favored the academies with their practical training, colonial and state legislatures focused their attention on preparatory and collegiate institutions. In what follows I shall review the development of the state-sponsored college-preparatory secondary schools in Georgia and then discuss their history in New York and Michigan.

The Georgia State System

From New England this state concern with secondary education as college-preparatory education was transplanted to Georgia. There a number of graduates of Middlebury and Yale colleges were instrumental in designing the university system of that state.[1] At its beginning, the University of Georgia consisted of a few preparatory academies and Franklin College at Athens. Similar to what later would develop in New York, the University was responsible for preparatory education in the private academies in the counties and for the collegiate studies at Franklin College in Athens. The Senatus Academicus, consisting of the university's board of trustees and a board of visitors made up of high state officials, had been created to determine the academies' curricula and to recommend their instructors. It also supervised the state's common schools.[2] Josiah Meigs, president of the Senatus and of the university, asked the trustees on November 11, 1803, that the academies be "furnished with teachers able to qualify the Youth of the State (by teaching particularly the learned languages) for admission into the Collegiate family at Athens."[3]

Meigs's prayer was not answered and, absent a steady supply of well-prepared students for Franklin College, the trustees saw to it that in 1804 a grammar school was opened at Athens to supply students for the college and to furnish "a means of acquiring a good English education."[4] Beyond that the trustees agreed with the desire of many Georgians to open grammar schools and academies for their daughters as well as their sons. "Nothing should be withheld," the Senatus Academicus resolved in 1805, "which would tend to the encouragement of science in both sexes."[5] Just as New Englanders had expressed opposition to the classical curriculum of the academies, so now Georgians wanted their academies to serve as English schools for everyone and as finishing schools for their daughters.

Class-based antagonisms divided the proponents of the modern academy curriculum and the supporters of the classical university-preparatory studies. The latter complained in 1827 in a statement issued by a committee of the university's Senatus Academicus that the "county academies intended by the System to be ramifications to the Mother Stock of learning, has [*sic*] as yet ministered but little to the advantage of their common parent." The academic learning there, they continued, was "so scantily diffused, or so imperfectly communicated, that there is sometimes almost wholly a deficiency of the necessary information resulting from those sources, when the candidates apply for admission to the College."[6] What they tried to say was that the applicants to Franklin College were insufficiently trained in the classical languages and that the champions of classical learning found scant support in the state.

On the whole, the Georgia university system with its private academies in the counties under the supervision of the Senatus Academicus was not a glowing success. As Merton Coulter reported, the senators rarely responded with reports "in sufficient numbers and of information exact enough to meet the purpose in view." Though there was no lack of academies across the state, they did not cooperate with Franklin College in an effective statewide system.[7] They rather served a local clientele that appreciated them as social equalizers and took great pride in the acquisition of learning. Those few students who intended to move on to Franklin College studied the classics. The majority, however, were content with an English education.[8] Local concerns and hard economic times never allowed the state system to flourish. For all practical purposes it came to an end in 1837, when the state ceased to fund the county academies.[9]

The Regents of the University of the State of New York

As described in chapter 2, the New York Regents, not unlike the Senatus Academicus of Georgia, had initially thrown their authority behind the classical college preparatory curriculum of the academies and, by the 1830s, had only reluctantly made their peace with the modern scientific curricula and with normal instruction for future teachers. As in Georgia, this policy had not met with the approval of many state residents and, in New York, had also aroused the opposition of the legislature. Thus when in 1847 the New York City Board of Education sought to obtain the incorporation of a free, that is, public, academy, the board turned to the legislature for action rather than, as one might have expected, to the Regents.

The Regents experienced further setbacks when in 1853 the legislature reduced their original jurisdiction over the state's secondary institutions and passed the Union Free School Act. The act permitted local school districts to consolidate and grade their common schools and to inaugurate academic or high school departments.[10] To be sure, the legislature placed these departments under the supervision of the Regents and their requirements for distributions of the Literature Fund. But even that safeguard was compromised when, with the establishment in the next year of the Department of Public Instruction, the state superintendent was authorized to extend his supervisory powers to both the academies and the academic departments of union free schools. Given the Regents' heightened sensitivity to threats to the academic quality of the schools under their supposed supervision and given the superintendent's commitment to broaden the scope of secondary studies within the common school system, their joint supervision was bound to become troublesome.

Matters looked worse for the Regents when it became apparent in subsequent years that the academic departments of the union free schools began to outnumber the academies. The growth of the academic departments led to the transformation or closing down of many of the smaller academies until around 1878 the two types of secondary schools were equal in number.[11] When, in their desire to maintain standards, the Regents began to scrutinize these departments closely as they applied for acceptance under the Literature Fund, the local school boards were infuriated.

Committed to uphold the high standards of the academies while, in a general way, approving the wider opportunities provided by the academic departments of the union schools and the state's public high schools, the Regents were pulled in different directions. In that quandary, they gave priority to their conviction that the academic departments and high schools did not prepare their students adequately for college. "Young people," they reported, "have not infrequently received diplomas of graduation in the so-called higher studies, when they could not sustain an examination in the lower."[12] By 1865 the Regents therefore introduced academy entrance examinations in the preliminary studies of arithmetic, English grammar, geography, and spelling. They limited state support to those students only who could pass these examinations.

Immediately members of the Assembly demanded to abolish the Board of Regents and "to place our Academies, Colleges, and Free Schools under a more efficient management."[13] Faced with this threat, the Regents withdrew the proposal and in March 1870 divided the academic departments into preparatory and academic classes. They apportioned the Literature Fund to students in the academic classes who had attended a minimum of four months or had been studying the first book of Virgil, Caesar, Sallust, or Cicero.[14] Because this move lowered the number of academic students and withdrew state support from those in the increasing preparatory ranks, it further enraged school boards, whose local tax base was not always sufficient to support the students in the advanced classes, especially when the boards ignored the entrance qualifications set by the Regents. The Regents, on their part, complained that the academic departments had become "only one of the grades of the school," and were not "elevated into a position of such distinctive prominence as to excite ambition in scholars to secure the qualifications prescribed by the law for admission to it."[15] The old conflict between local interest and central authority, first experienced in colonial Massachusetts, appeared once more.

These difficulties led to a compromise of sorts when the legislature agreed to a new system of examinations. Advanced graduation examinations were added to the preliminary examinations and the system became effective on January 1, 1881. The graduation examinations had been designed with the classical college entrance course in mind but affected primarily the two English courses that prepared students for careers in business. The Regents had come around to seeing the academies and the new academic departments for what they were for most of their students: people's colleges serving the state's industrial and business expansion. At the same time, they had persevered in their insistence on maintaining the schools' academic quality which they judged by the rigor of the college preparatory program. The examinations were to accomplish this, and the Regents could proudly point out that the state now administered statewide examinations, a practice that had been known until then only in Prussia and France.[16]

Even so, the Regents remained dissatisfied. They had not made their peace with the normal departments that they had introduced in 1832. They continued to distrust them as "merely a pretense," and they regarded the payments from the Literature Fund to them as "only a species of gratuity."[17] They also did not cease to lament the increase in the number of academic departments in the public schools, and looked back longingly to the academy of yesteryear, which, they said,

> stood higher, comparatively, in the educational scale, than the academical department of today. The studies were more distinctively classical and more in the line of a liberal culture. . . . For such a school, there will be always a place and a career of great honor and usefulness.[18]

The Regents' ambivalence over the rise of the public high schools illustrates the country's general uncertainty over the place of secondary schooling in the educational system. Was its primary task to prepare students for college or was it to speed them on their way into careers in business and industry?

The Michigan System of Public Education

The idea of a university as a statewide administrative system of education had first been developed in the United States in New York and Georgia. In Europe, it was embodied in the Napoleonic University of France. It was to find yet another incorporation in what was to become the state of Michigan. There the fancifully named "Catholepistemiad" was created in 1817 as a system that, on paper at least, included common schools, academies, colleges, and a university proper.[19] Its first Classical Academy, located in Detroit, offered instruction in Latin, Greek, and English, as well as in writing, composition, rhetoric, geography, arithmetic, surveying, bookkeeping, and navigation. It differed in no significant ways from the usual private academies of its time and, wrote a trustee of the school in

1820, if provided with a "competent teacher," a number of boys "might be prepared to enter collegiate studies."[20] A college or university, however, was not going to be available in Michigan until 1841, when the first students entered the state's university at Ann Arbor.

For the opening of the university, the people of Michigan had to wait for the state to be accepted into the union in 1837. At that time, the Michigan Regents were authorized also to accept nine private academies as branches that were to act as feeders to the university. Receiving state funding, the branches each were to have a classical, a normal, and an English department to prepare students for the university, teaching, or business. Plans were entertained also for an agricultural department in one of the branches. The superintendent emphasized the pivotal role these academies were to play in the system as indispensable support of both the university and the common schools. Without the branches, he wrote, "the University itself cannot be expected to prosper; and equally important are they, to the success of the primary schools, being as they are, the sole means of obtaining a full supply of competent teachers." In an accompanying report, the Regents stated that of the 161 pupils to attend the five then-existing academies, 10 intended to become teachers in the common schools and 111 to enter the university. The remaining 50 had not at that time declared their plans but, the Regents felt sure, many of them would enroll at Ann Arbor. When one notes that the Regents also stated that though female departments had been authorized, all the existing academies functioned as university branches for boys, the primarily college-preparatory nature of these schools stands out.[21]

During the following years the stringent financial conditions of the state led to several branch closings. By 1841 only five were in operation. Pressures increased that questioned the emphasis placed on the collegiate-preparatory course. The superintendent, obviously worried about unfavorable publicity, stressed the teacher-training function of the academies: "*Merely* as preparatory seminaries for an admission to the main university," he wrote, "branches could hardly claim an expensive support out of the public fund; but, as the means of giving to the state qualified teachers for the common schools, every consideration unites to have them sustained." He similarly desired to stress the importance of "a theoretical knowledge of agriculture," though he was constrained to admit that he could not tell "how far this branch of the required studies has been taught."[22] Perhaps he could derive some comfort from the fact that by August of 1842, a little over a quarter (54) of the 210 students attending the branches were women. On the other hand, another list showed that 110 out of 174 students were enrolled in the department of classical languages.[23]

When the ax fell in 1846 and the legislature abolished state appropriations to the branches of the university, State Superintendent Ira Mayhew seized the opportunity and vigorously argued that the common-school system stood ready to take over the functions performed in the past by the branches. He pointed to the growth of union school districts, which with the economies achieved through the consolidation of small districts promised to provide an attractive alternative. Union schools, Mayhew argued, "combine all the advantages of the ordinary common school and the academy." They should be established, he continued, "in all the principal villages, in which students may qualify themselves to enter the University." And then he coined a phrase that was to describe public college-preparatory institutions as the term *people's college* had defined the schools preparing their students for the world of work. "Union schools constitute the only reliable *connecting link* between our primary schools and the State University" (italics added). According to Mayhew, the union schools were first of all democratic institutions, free of tuition charges and open to everyone. Second, they were excellent substitutes for normal schools with built-in model schools supplied by their primary departments, and third, they were preferable to the private academies, which often required their students to leave home and indulged them with lax discipline in order not to lose them as fee-paying clients.[24]

As one might expect, Mayhew's proposal offended the champions of the private academies, who had found supporters in the university's board of visitors. The visitors were much dismayed over the lack of academic preparation found among the entering students at the university. For this, they blamed the inadequate training of the state's common-school teachers. As remedy, they proposed to revitalize the university branches through increased funding of private grammar schools, academies, and seminaries, as well as through the establishment of public high schools and a state normal school. In the following years the superintendent gave lip service to these suggestions but maintained that the eventual final answer to the problem was going to be the continued spread of the union schools.[25]

From Union School to High School

By the middle of the century, Mayhew's view of the union school as "the only reliable connecting link between our primary schools and the State University" had won the day. The university Regents wrote in 1853 that "the union schools will become the elementary, classical and scientific schools preparatory to the collegiate or Gymnastic department of the

University." Enamored of Prussian educational institutions and reluctant to concede too much to the state superintendent, the Regents accepted the union schools as institutions somewhat lower in academic standing than the Prussian *gymnasia*. In that belittling attitude the Regents were joined by the Detroit Board of Education, whose members were similarly critical of their own union schools. The city's union schools, they reported, were middle schools at best and therefore could not offer the classics. Their curriculum did not extend into the higher or high school grades. In Battle Creek, however, the union school was reported to offer a full college-preparatory program with Latin, Greek, English, mathematics, physiology, philosophy, and history. Apparently, then, conditions varied in different cities, and the state's union schools, while not everywhere including the high school grades, were on their way to function as college-preparatory schools.[26]

The superintendent, however, dissented from this view. Despite his reiterated demand that "between the Primary School and the University there is a chasm, deep and impassable, which requires to be thoroughly bridged," and despite his declaration of the Michigan union school as the "connecting link" between common school and college, he was keenly aware that he faced a far larger constituency than those concerned with preparation for college. To reassure these taxpayers, he wrote in his 1858 Report that union schools

> are not, what they are sometimes supposed to be,—a distinct order of schools, like academies, and constituting an intermediate link in our chain of schools, their chief office being to connect the Primary School with the University, by being converted into what are known as Preparatory Schools. This I say is *not* their chief office.

Union schools, he stated, were "rather an outgrowth from, and an improved condition of our Primary Schools," and were therefore more properly understood as graded schools.[27]

In what sounded like an argument for the urban people's college, the superintendent went on to say that in remote rural areas as well as in densely populated communities the union schools' "first and the prominent object in arranging a course of study, must be the fitting of youth who frequent these schools for the discharge of the duties of life, and not for admission to a higher grade of schools."[28] But because in Michigan the branch academies had lost state support, union school districts, he added in 1859, had been authorized by the legislature to establish high schools. These had taken the place of academies just as "the substantial homes of our industrious citizens" had replaced "the Indians' wigwams." They now also served as preparatory schools to the university, but this was their subordinate rather than their main office.[29]

Changing his tune once more, the superintendent added that the time would come when increased populations would demand more precisely graded schools. This would then lead to the establishment of intermediate and advanced grades, as had happened in New York City, where the Free Academy as high school had become the crown jewel of the public school system.[30] By the late 1860s the superintendent reported that high school grades had indeed become familiar in Michigan union schools and furnished "the means for acquiring the elements of a more liberal education" and "all needed *facilities* to such pupils as desire to prepare for our State University."[31] The road that had led from the establishment of the primary schools to the introduction of graded and union schools and from there to the high schools had been straight and unbroken. Now the high schools served a double purpose: they continued the union schools' mission of fitting youth "for the discharge of the duties of life" and they had taken on the branch academies' task of preparing students for the university.

The Kalamazoo Decision

The appearance of the high school in Michigan, whether in the form of advanced classes in a union school or as a separate institution, and the attending uncertainties over the two distinct missions it was to perform led to vigorous debates all across the state. When the late 1860s witnessed a marked increase in the rate of high school openings, opposing voices came to be heard.[32] Skeptics questioned not only the wisdom of the superintendent's enthusiasm but also the authority of local school boards to burden all taxpayers with the expense of high school instruction when only a very small segment of the state's youths were involved. They argued that as the history of the branch academies had shown, institutions of secondary education had always been parts of higher education to be financed by the state's university fund rather than by the common-school fund. The state constitution, the critics asserted, had prescribed English, not Latin, as the language of instruction in the common schools and had not authorized a state superintendent to be paid from tax funds.[33]

The opponents of the high school saw its college-preparatory curriculum as the most objectionable part. "Instruction in the classics and in living modern languages," they stated, was "in the nature not of practical and therefore necessary instruction for the benefit of the people at large, but rather as accomplishment for the few, to be sought after in the main by those best able to pay for them." When in January of 1873 the charges were brought before the Ninth Judicial Circuit Court of Michigan, however, the three complainants did not distinguish between the high school's college preparatory and practical purposes but asked that the court restrain the school board of Kalamazoo from levying taxes for the support of the local high school. If high schools were to continue, they suggested, they should "be paid for by those who seek them, and not by general tax."[34]

Superintendent Oramel Hosford had previously warned that "to make the high school departments self-sustaining by charging tuition would be to abolish them," would condemn the graded schools "to return to the conditions of the district schools," and would rob the school system "of its unity and glory."[35] Judge Charles R. Brown agreed with him and ruled that the history of public schooling in Michigan amply demonstrated that the legislature had full powers to provide the schools it deemed necessary for the welfare of the state and that the English-language clause in the state constitution referred only to its mandatory use in general subjects, not to instruction in other languages.

The decision was appealed but reaffirmed in July of 1874 by the Michigan Supreme Court, Associate Justice Thomas Cooley writing the opinion. Justice Cooley held that when voters of a school district had agreed to support a high school, school boards could freely decide what the purposes and the curricula of such schools were to be. Referring specifically to Superintendent Mayhew's 1849 report, which had described intermediate schools as *connecting links* between common school and university, Cooley stated that historical precedence in Michigan left no doubt that schools intermediate between the common school and the university had from early on in the century prepared young men for the university. The Kalamazoo decision, sometimes called the "magna charta" of the American high school, thus provided the legal base for the high school's college preparatory function.[36]

Even before the Michigan Supreme Court had issued its opinion, the University of Michigan had taken the initiative in recognizing the state's public high schools as potential feeder schools. It set up an accreditation system under which university faculty members visited high schools and inspected their curricula and instruction. If these met the university's admission standards for its literary or scientific course and were endorsed by a vote of the university faculty, the graduates of such a school were admitted to the university's scientific department without entrance examination. The state superintendent declared himself satisfied with this arrangement and reported that "such a policy cannot fail to prove a stimulus to the high schools throughout the State, and lead to the adoption of better devised courses of study, to more profitable instruction and thorough collegiate preparation." He endorsed raised entrance requirements for the university's classical and civil-engineering course and added that even though few high schools in the state met these requirements, there was every reason to assume that they could do so in the future. Michigan's public high schools were now taking on the role played by the state's early private branch academies.[27]

Three years later the university expressed its willingness to admit students without examination to any one of its courses if the high school could pass muster with its offerings in that field. Working through the State Association of City Superintendents, the state's high schools, on their part, prepared a recommended syllabus that in its combination of idealistic goals and realistic considerations reflected the then-current expectations of what the state's high schools might accomplish.[38] Most significant in that context was the omission of the classical languages. Although high schools in some of the larger cities did offer Latin and Greek, this could not be expected as a general rule.[39] The state superintendent himself admitted that few of the state's high schools were able to prepare their students for all of the university's courses. The state's recommended high school syllabus was intended only "to meet the requirements of a general course for those whose studies end with the high school and a preparatory course to the scientific department of the University."[40] The classical high school course emerged as the weakest of the "connecting links."

The realities of high school attendance in Michigan indicated that despite the extended discussions in the superintendent's reports over the preparatory function, most of the school's graduates prepared for "practical life" rather than for the college classroom. Statistics of fifty-one Michigan high schools showed that in the five years from 1876 to 1881, only 3.71 percent (68) of the 1,831 graduates had planned college attendance.[41] The figure corroborates the angry remarks of a speaker at the 1883 meeting of the State Teachers Association who complained that the state's high schools prepared 5 percent of their students in Latin and 3 percent in Greek but "shamefully" neglected the 90 percent who intended to go into business. This neglect was particularly acute in the smaller high schools, which did not have the means to pursue both a college-preparatory and a business course and which, for the sake of prestige and under pressure from parents, opted for the former.[42] Though the paths followed by secondary education in Michigan were different from those in New York, they led to the same question: What was the high school's primary purpose? Was it to prepare its students for practical life or for college?

6

Midwestern Democracy

The Democratic Imperative

By the second half of the nineteenth century the high school's purpose had everywhere become a subject of vigorous dispute. As we saw in chapter 5, in western New York and Michigan academies had been replaced by high school departments of union schools and were eventually transformed into public high schools. In the trans-Appalachian areas of the country, schoolmen and parents fought hard to gain public tax support for the high school as connecting link to the colleges and universities, even though the great majority of the schools' students did not go to college. In the eastern cities where most high schools functioned as people's colleges it was the influx of female students that brought to the fore a concern with the college-preparatory function of the school. Though more and more high schools had come into being through a gradual extension upward of the common schools, throughout the decades from 1850 to 1880 they still remained "uncommon" schools for the nations' select youngsters. By 1890 they enrolled only 6.7 percent of the country's fourteen- to seventeen-year-olds.

During the 1880s, however, the number of public high schools had increased more than tenfold. A trend became apparent, and Americans, particularly the nation's schoolmen, began to interpret the rising demand for the high school as what I shall call "the democratic imperative."[1] The strength of this imperative initially derived from the desire of economically favored middle-class parent-taxpayers to provide opportunities for their children's social advancement. It was not to take long until parental desires were pushed aside by the schoolmen, whose professional self-interest demanded greater institutional proliferation and administrative specialization.

In midwestern and western states, where the lines of social class demarcation were less visible than they were in the older, eastern sections of the country, an alliance of schoolmen and middle-class parents in cities, towns, and villages readily coalesced around the district high school that had grown up in the union school districts. Here the distinctions between people's college and connecting-link high school, between preparing for life and preparing for college, were unimportant. Having grown up, as it were, grade by grade out of the local district school, the high school began to be seen as an advanced common school, serving the upwardly mobile segments of the district's population. This growth from below contrasted sharply with the older traditions of Europe and colonial America, where secondary schools had provided the initiation into advanced education rather than the capstone of elementary education.

Despite its relatively small and select student body, the high school in its local development, especially in the tendency to house its grades in the existing district school building, facilitated the near-universal adoption of the democratic rhetoric. Theodore Sizer tells us that in Illinois, as also in Connecticut, no more than 15 percent of all high schools were conducted in buildings of their own. This fact alone, Sizer wrote, demonstrated "that high schools were the natural outgrowth of common schools." If, then, one considers that "teachers of secondary subjects were drawn from the lower grades and often continued along a course more suitable for eight-year-olds than teen-agers," the absence of a clear distinction between elementary and secondary schooling becomes ever more apparent.[2]

As high schools grew out of district schools, the multiplicity of purposes often blurred the differences between normal, elementary, and secondary instruction. This was particularly true when the added grade or grades served primarily as normal or teacher-training classes that usually included a review of the elementary curriculum. Because few of these schools had a four-year program, they were well described by the Franklinian phrase that they served *any* student for *any* purpose, provided that we understand that "any student" meant a white middle-class youngster and that "any purpose," when applied to boys, in most cases meant preparation for life and occasionally for college.[3] Whether or not girls eventually went to college, the high school prepared them to become teachers or homemakers.

The founding of the National Education Association in 1870 and the accompanying growth of the schoolmen's professional bureaucracy shifted the democratic imperative away from its reliance on parental desires. In Illinois, this became apparent when in the early 1870s the state superintendent began his crusade for the township high school. Taxpayers and popularly elected rural school district officials viewed township high schools as threats to district democracy. They were loath to see their authority and opinions ignored and their decisions overturned by an emerging state and township bureaucracy. In other states, the schoolmen, eager to "professionalize" their activities and make schools efficient and businesslike, picked up on Horace Mann's pet project of the 1840s in Massachusetts and declared war on the district schools and their "unprofessional" directors. As in Illinois, "the educators in overalls who managed the country schools" resisted, and they did so in the name of democracy. Local district school officials, representatives of grassroots democracy, and state and township schoolmen all claimed to speak for democracy in education.[4]

Public and Private in Illinois

District, township, and state school officials agreed in viewing the public high school as their finest example of democracy in education. In the high school, they said, "the child of the cottage and of the palace shall meet on terms of perfect equality, except as one excels the other in scholarship," and "even the poorest may pass on to the realization of cherished hopes."[5] As in New York and in Michigan, so also in Illinois the high school had slowly emerged as the top department of the common schools in union school districts. This development had begun in the mid-1840s and leveled out during the 1870s to resume again after 1880.[6] Legislation recognizing high schools and providing a legal basis for their existence was passed in 1855, 1857, and 1872, and the State Supreme Court endorsed this legislation as constitutional in 1872 and 1874.[7]

The democratic imperative propelling the statewide crusade for public common and high schools targeted the private academies or "select schools," as the greatest enemy. A committee at the State School Convention in October of 1844 referred to the academies as "nurseries of pomposity and contemptible vanity" that, though they might be "of occasional advantage to individuals," were "a positive curse to the public in such a population as exists generally in Illinois."[8] Fifteen years later the state superintendent used similar language in expressing his displeasure. Admitting that private academies and seminaries had "for more than two centuries . . . been considered indispensable links in our American system of education," he now concluded that they had "done more to retard the progress and sap the life blood of the Common Schools . . . than all other causes put together." They were aristocratic rather than democratic because "only those able to pay the stipulated entrance fee can ever gain admittance to its sacred walls."

The superintendent's resentment did not derive solely from the "aristocratic" nature of the select schools but, rather, more from their popular appeal. The academies were "rivals" of the common schools, he said, "from first to last in their claims for support," and in drawing to themselves "the older and more advanced pupils." Thus the common school was "robbed of one of the prime elements of success" and dragged "out a miserable existence beneath the shadow of its more fortunate rival."[9] As long as the common school was unable to offer advanced work for older students, it could not compete with the select private schools and was condemned to an inferior position.

The schoolmen's fear of the academies was not without foundation. Academies had spread across the country with amazing speed and frequency. They followed the first wave of settlers and, by boosting a settlement's reputation, became a favorite instrument of promoters and land speculators to attract families of "the better sort."[10] As Paul Belting pointed out in his study of secondary education in Illinois, the academies thrived under the educational laissez-faire policies of the state's early legislatures. *Individualism* and *democracy* were nearly synonymous terms, and the academy promoters and teachers ranged from conscientious religious ministers and political leaders to "parasitic, itinerant individuals [who] thought that teaching was the easiest means of existence."[11] For the public schoolmen many of these schools represented educational anarchy, professional incompetence, and unrestrained greed.

As in the older parts of the country, in the Midwest, too, the academies were popular institutions that offered whatever their clients demanded: an elementary education of basic skills; a modern business-directed curriculum of bookkeeping, science, and modern languages; the classical languages for their "cultural" value or as preparation for college. In Illinois between 1818 and 1848 the legislature chartered no fewer than 125 academies, and there is reason to think that the number of unchartered academies was even larger.[12] By promising, although not always delivering, free education to the children of the poor and of Indians and by offering normal instruction and refraining from religious discrimination, the academies claimed to offer public services and frequently received public subsidies. Even though incorporated as private institutions, they were very much a part of the state's educational establishment.

Although the schoolmen resented the private academies, they generally held a far more favorable opinion of the private colleges. The colleges supplied the common schools, and particularly their higher grades, with teachers. The Illinois superintendents had been forced to rely on them as sources of teachers and as early as 1849 had asked the governor to apply the state's college and seminary fund "to such of the colleges and seminaries as shall provide for educating a required number of teachers of common schools."[13] Twenty years later, Superintendent Newton Bateman set aside the public schoolmen's dislike of "aristocratic" private institutions and repeated his predecessor's request that colleges take on the task of preparing common school teachers. He argued that elementary and high school work should be carried out by the state with help from the "higher and broader culture which belongs to the colleges and universities." Public and private institutions, he asserted, were "indissolubly linked together." They were "parts of one great system," and "their relations should be close, confidential, and sympathetic."[14] He did not appear to think that private colleges were aristocratic, pompous, and vain.

But this reliance on private colleges was more a marriage of convenience than of mutual recognition. Bateman, whom Abraham Lincoln had once called "my little friend, the big schoolmaster of Illinois," regretted that the state did not have a public university like Michigan. He looked forward to the day when such a university would be established in Illinois and when, presumably, the public schools would no longer have to depend on the private colleges.[15] The University of Michigan, he wrote in 1865,

> is in many aspects the first of its class on the continent; and the reason is, it is in sympathy with, and a part of, the free school system of Michigan; it is borne upward and onward by the same resistless popular power that underlies and moves forward her public schools. It is the grandest demonstration in the United States of the perfect symmetry and strength of a state system of popular education.[16]

What Illinois needed, wrote Bateman, was a state university as the crown of its public school system. He was confident that it would eventually be created. Three years later his faith was rewarded when the Illinois Industrial University opened its doors in Champaign-Urbana.

When Bateman wrote the above lines in 1865, Illinois already had one institution of public higher education: the State Normal University near Bloomington. Opened in 1857, this school owed its existence to a coalition of public schoolmen and proponents of industrial and agricultural education. The schooolmen, seeking to free themselves from their dependence on the private colleges and taking their cue from New York and Michigan, had always wanted a state normal school. They hoped that in collaboration with their allies they could do better and create a genuine state university on the Michigan model. They were to be disappointed in that hope. Despite the deliberate use of the term *university*, the institution near Bloomington remained a normal school throughout the century and became a university only in 1908 when it granted its first bachelor degree.[17]

Like most Illinois public schoolmen, Bateman was torn in opposite directions. He and his colleagues were crusaders for the public schools, yet their success depended on their cooperation with the private colleges. They had to acknowledge that by 1860 Illinois's one public state institution—the Normal University—had to compete with twenty-one private colleges or universities, while Michigan's three public universities faced only six private colleges.[18] The overwhelming presence of private institutions in Illinois forced the state's schoolmen simultaneously to endorse the colleges and to condemn the academies and seminaries. The colleges accepted their graduating students and educated the common-school teachers; the academies competed with the common schools for funds and students and, by undercutting the establishment of high school grades, blocked and threatened to halt the advance of the public school system. In Illinois, the frequency and stridency of calls for public institutions of advanced education corresponded to the ubiquitousness of private colleges and academies.

Illinois Union Schools

As in Michigan, the call for union schools had set in motion the development of the high school in Illinois. In 1852 a common-school supporter in Peoria asked the state superintendent to create school districts large enough to support schools with both elementary and high school departments and to require that counties and townships have a union high school for the graduates of the district schools.[19] The superintendent accepted the proposal and, in the following years, asked for township high schools that would qualify their graduates "for any profession or pursuit of life" and "would encourage and sustain our colleges and academies" by furnishing "greater facilities to those aspiring to a collegiate education."[20] He had accepted the popular view of high schools preparing their students for both life and college. In 1859 he announced that union graded district schools had proved their superiority over the private academies. "Nearly two-thirds" of the academies, he wrote, had "thrown up their organization and reorganized under the Common School law." They now were open free of charge to all the children of the district. "All castes are thus done away with," and "the poor man's children enter the school room on an exact equality . . . with the rich man's child."[21]

As public graded union schools appeared in larger numbers, they de-creased the need for colleges to offer preparatory classes. When in 1867 Illinois considered the creation of a state industrial university as the cap-stone of its public school system, Bateman charged that those colleges whose preparatory departments taught more students than were enrolled in any of their collegiate courses were colleges in name only. Statistics gathered at the time illustrate his complaint: in Illinois's private colleges and seminaries 2,441 students pursued a full course of study and 1,618 a partial course, and 3,299 pupils attended the preparatory departments.[22] Bateman argued that for every five legitimate college students on Illinois campuses there were four pupils who might have been better served in a public high school. Colleges unable to compete with legitimate high schools, Bateman declared, should "perish by the competition. . . . Such so-called colleges are pretentious cheats," and should be pushed from the field by the public high school.[23]

As gratifying as the spread of public high schools was to the superin-tendent—he reported 108 for 1870, "an average of about one to each county in the State"—the overwhelming majority of these "schools" were high school *departments* rather than separately housed high schools. Most of them were located in rural areas. The superintendent of Clay County in the southeastern quadrant of the state reminded Bateman that over 60 percent of the state's children were taught in ungraded country schools. "The school of the town cannot educate the child of the country," he wrote, and asked that more attention be paid to the rural areas. In Car-rollton, Greene County, thirty-five miles north of St. Louis, for example, the seventh grade of the district school served as a two-year high school department offering a combination of grammar and high school work, in-cluding drawing and bookkeeping, and Latin as an elective.[24]

The full-fledged high school, however, appeared to thrive only in or near the state's larger cities. In Chicago, such a school had begun its oper-ation in October of 1856 with 125 students, both boys and girls. It offered four courses of instruction. The three-year Classical Course was "recom-mended to all who intend to give their children a collegiate education, or who design them for teachers, or for any other occupation or profession, in which an acquaintance with the ancient languages is deemed desirable." The English Course, likewise of three years, was intended for students who looked toward careers in "trade, commerce, manufacture and the me-chanic arts." "Young ladies desiring to become teachers" could choose the Normal Course of two years. And students who wanted to remain a full four years in the school could sign up for the Classical and English Course, which included the full range of the school's offerings.[25] The Chicago High School was a school for any purpose.

In his 1870 census of the state's high schools, Bateman included the high school departments of district schools. The simultaneous decline of graded schools from 722 in 1869 to 641 in 1870, makes it apparent that he had now classified graded schools as high schools. But in the state's rural areas, full-fledged high schools were still rarities. In the cities, their advocates stressed the college preparatory opportunity of these schools, but in numerical terms that was the high schools' least important function. As a contributor to the *Illinois Teacher* pointed out, not even the Boston Latin School had sent more than an average of thirteen of its graduates annually to college, and the high schools in Chicago and Cincinnati had each sent no more than "a squad of from five to seven young men" annually. The author concluded from that: "The high school must do its own work without reference to the college, in a few favorably-situated places attaching the preparatory work to itself as an addendum."[26] By 1870 the urban high school was still primarily a people's college.

The Township High School

Bateman's enthusiasm for the township high school prompted him to encourage passage of legislation that would authorize erection of such schools upon petition of fifty voters and an affirmative vote of the township. Such a school, he rhapsodized,

> plants in the midst of every township adopting the plan, a school, the influence of which will, in time, favorably affect the tone of society, and nearly every interest of the community, not excepting the value of real estate and other property; for it will invite those who seek homes where they can educate their children without being parted from them—families of means, intelligence and refinement—whose coming is a blessing to any community. It will powerfully tend to equalize the educational facilities of the State, which are now overwhelmingly in favor of cities and villages.[27]

Bateman now promoted the rural township high school much as land speculators and business entrepreneurs in the areas west of the Appalachians before the Civil War had advertised academies and seminaries as "booster colleges."[28] Again and again he returned to the theme of democracy: The public high schools made it possible "for the whole body of our youth to know *something* of the beginnings of *higher knowledge*, . . . they help to break down the barriers that have too long kept the youth of the country schools at a disadvantage."[29]

Table 6.1 Illinois Township High Schools, 1880–1900

Year	All High Schools (N)	Township High Schools (N)	Township High Schools %
1880	110	6	5.5
1882	144	5	3.5
1885	161	7	4.3
1886	169	8	4.7
1887	179	7	3.9
1888	191	8	4.2
1889	204	9	4.4
1890	208	10	4.8
1891	223	9	4.0
1892	233	9	3.9
1893	246	8	3.3
1894	239	9	3.8
1895	258	11	4.3
1896	272	13	4.8
1897	284	12	4.2
1898	299	13	4.3
1899	311	15	4.8
1900	321	17	5.3

Source. Various issues of the reports of the superintendents of the state of Illinois.

Township high schools, however, did not live up to Bateman's expectations. Rural Illinois voters were hesitant to support schools beyond the boundaries of their district (Table 6.1). By 1890 only 10 of the state's 208 high schools were township schools, and their relative percentage did not increase before the end of the century. The schoolmen's democratic imperative again met its match in district democracy.

The state's first township high school at Princeton, Bureau County, was opened in 1867. At that time it was the only school offering high school work in the county, and thus, from the beginning, it drew students from outside the township. In its first year 17 of its 174 students and by the mid-1870s, one-quarter of its students came from other townships, demonstrating that however hesitant voters were to fund such a school, there was demand for its services. The school offered a five-year program, though its principal, Henry S. Boltwood, frankly admitted that the first two years were "really grammar school work." More important, as the township high school sent several of its graduates to college, it demonstrated that it was responding to the demand of some of the parents for college-preparatory work. He showed that in the third year Latin or German, rhetoric, algebra, English history, physiology, botany, and zoology were added, and that students in the classical course could select Greek instead of the natural sciences. English students could drop Latin after one year and exchange it for French or German. Of the 113 students who had graduated by 1876, 24 men and 9 women, nearly 30 percent, had gone on to further study in colleges or professional schools.[30]

Cook County and Champaign County, each home of large cities, also boasted early township high schools. From 1869 to 1883 Jefferson High School in Cook County operated in the town hall. It presented a four-year program and, like Princeton High School, did not reach advanced subjects until the third year. Then, algebra, rhetoric, botany, and bookkeeping were added, and natural philosophy, physiology, natural history, chemistry, and astronomy followed in the fourth year. Caesar and Cicero were offered on demand, but the principal did not state how frequently that happened.[31]

Bateman's college enthusiasm was equaled, perhaps even surpassed, by that of A. F. Nightingale, the principal of Lakeview Township High School in Cook County. Demonstrating a particularly vigorous form of the democratic imperative, Nightingale denounced the carelessness of well-off parents who sent their children to private academies and deplored the tendency of the common school to generate among its students greater love for business and business college than for the "infinitely more practical discipline of university study." He regretted that the Illinois State Supreme Court had indicated that high school attendance could not be made compulsory, because he saw the high school as a "wedding-clasp uniting the common school and the college." The township high school was "the *sine qua non* of the perfection of our public school system." At Lakeview, he rejoiced, "the college spirit is uppermost in the school," and even though nearly two-thirds of his pupils were girls, they were actuated by "the same ambition for university discipline" as the boys.[32]

Benefiting from the closeness of Chicago, the school admitted thirty-eight girls and thirty-five boys to its preparatory classes in May of 1874. Two years later the school offered a college-preparatory as well as a scientific or civil engineering curriculum, the majority of its students enrolling in one of the college preparatory classes. A classical course offered four years of Latin with German or French and additional sciences added in the third year, and Greek as optional during the last two years. A German course allowed the student to substitute German for Latin throughout, with Latin or French as a second language during the last two years.[33]

Like the Princeton and Jefferson township high schools, Champaign County's township high school, located in Tolono, roughly ten miles south of the cities of Urbana and Champaign, offered a two-year review of grammar school studies of arithmetic, reading, spelling, penmanship, arithmetic, grammar, and geography. For three more years a student had the option of Latin or German, Greek, and classes in history, English literature, and natural science. The trustees intended, so the annual report stated, "to give a scholar his choice between a good practical education or a thorough preparatory for any college."[34]

Democracy's Schools

The township high schools like the district high schools served a variety of purposes. Schools in rural areas covered the entire spectrum from a catch-up grammar school program to college-preparatory work. Urban schools concentrated on a classical college preparatory course. If in the eyes of their proponents their primary purpose had been to offer more extensive opportunities for advanced education to young people who lived in small districts with relatively meager resources, the small enrollments indicated that rural folks were not so easily convinced. If others had envisaged them as "connecting links" to the colleges, Superintendent Bateman's successor, S. M. Etter, in marked contrast to his predecessor, reminded them that perhaps they misunderstood the democratic imperative. He declared in his report for 1875–1876 that a school board's first duty was to provide for a strong common-school education before its members thought of introducing the curricula of seminaries, academies, colleges, or universities. "No board," he said, "has a right to adopt a policy that will sacrifice the best interests of a large majority of the pupils to the individual advantage of a small minority."[35] The high school was first of all a people's college and only secondarily a college-preparatory school.

Five years later, Etter's successor, James P. Slade, returned to Bateman's position, endorsing the connecting-link function when he referred to *Richards v. Raymond*. In that case the Illinois Supreme Court held that the laws establishing township high schools were constitutional, and a school board could levy taxes for their maintenance, even though "the course of study prescribed was different from that contemplated by law."[36] This decision was confirmed in *H. W. Powell et al. v. The Board of Education, etc.*— Illinois's Kalamazoo decision—in which the Supreme Court upheld the teaching of German in the Belleville high school as permissible under the state school law.[37] There was now no longer any question that the high school had become an integral part of the state's common-school system and that its directors were empowered to shape its curriculum in any direction the voters approved.

By the early 1880s Illinois schoolmen had reason to be gratified. The spread of the high school had been steady though less than spectacular.

The state's schools had been recognized at the Philadelphia Centennial Exhibition in 1876 and had been awarded a Gold Medal Diploma at the Paris Universal Exposition two years later. Superintendent Slade could proudly relate reactions from France that singled out the American high school as "essentially national . . . original . . . [and] removed from European ideas." These high schools were, a French commission had reported,

> of one body with the common schools, . . . administered by the same authorities, supported by the same funds, and intended for the same population. . . . They are in the fullest sense popular schools— schools intended to give the people the best, purest, loftiest results of liberal education. . . . One graduate will enter the university, another will go into business: there will be differences of occupation among them, but there will be no inequality of education. So far as social equality can possibly be reached on this earth, it is attained by the American high school. . . . If it be true that the prosperity of a republic is in the direct ratio of the replenishment of its middle classes . . . then the high school of the United States, whatever it may cost, is the best investment of national capital that can possibly be made.[38]

When foreign commentators endorsed the American high school as an instrument of democracy, Americans could well be satisfied.

Democracy and equality did not extend only, as the foreign commentators never failed to point out, to rich and poor, but also to male and female. The superintendent's statistics showed that although there were more boys than girls in the lower grades of the district school, numerical parity between the sexes was reached by the fourth grade. Thereafter the percentage of girls climbed continually, and once the high school grades were reached, it moved from 63 percent in the ninth grade to 73 percent in the twelfth.[39] In the eyes of the schoolmen, at any rate, the midwestern high school extended democracy and equality to gender as well as to class.

Still, there were questions. Racial segregation in the schools remained a subject rarely faced and discussed, but the numerical dominance of girls in the upper grades led to some anxious soul-searching among the schoolmen. Why did boys leave school and seek early employment while girls apparently remained satisfied with what the curriculum had to offer? Why was there a difference between rural and urban areas in the percentage of female and male students found in the state's twelfth grades? In small towns of from 5,000 to 10,000 inhabitants a little over two-thirds (67.5 percent) of twelfth graders were girls, but in cities of more than 5,000 inhabitants nearly three-quarters (73.6 percent) were girls.[40] Why were country girls less likely to stay in school than those in cities? Did they marry earlier? Were they needed at home more often, or could they find work more easily than their sisters in the cities? And, conversely, why did a larger percentage of boys stay in school longer in the country than in the cities? Were the attractions offered them in the cities more potent than those found in the country? How could or should the schools react to these figures?

If the French commentators were right in saying that the American high schools were representative of a middle-class culture, did this mean that this culture as it was nurtured in the schools was essentially urban and female? Did it embody what the Spanish-American philosopher George Santayana had called the "genteel tradition," the culture of the mansion rather than that of the skyscraper, the world of literature and the arts rather than that of business and aggressive entrepreneurship?[41] What cultural as well as economic function was the high school to perform in and for American democracy? As the 1890s approached and the high schools continued their slow but steady expansion, these questions remained unanswered.

7

Between Town and Gown: The High School in Wisconsin

Private Schools and Public Systems

In the midwestern sections of the country parents spearheaded the drive for public tax-supported high schools to take over the private academies' role as college-preparatory institutions. Public school administrators welcomed the parental "democratic imperative" and used it to push for the inclusion of secondary education in their states' public school systems. Their purpose, however, was better served if they could promote the high school program as a suitable preparation of every youngster for all the various opportunities of adult life, not just as a preparation for college or university. By emphasizing English, science, and the modern languages the schoolmen believed they could appeal to male students and thus serve two purposes: to counteract both the high school's reputation as "aristocratic"—a reputation gained through its offerings in the classics—and its preponderance of female students. Thus, while arguing strongly that the high school prepared its students for life *and* college, their self-interest inclined the schoolmen to favor preparation for life over preparation for college. As developments in Wisconsin show, for various reasons the schoolmen's relationship to the university remained strained until in the late 1880s they reached a compromise with the faculty over the university's entrance requirements.

From the beginning, Wisconsin schoolmen had thought of a state system that allowed young people uninterrupted ascent from common school to university. They followed the Michigan example and relied on the academies and other private secondary schools to fill the gap between the two. From New York they adopted the idea that the academies were to provide teachers for the common schools.[1] In the constitutional convention of 1847 the delegates not only granted tax exemptions to the colleges but also assigned the "residue" of the state's school fund that had not been expended for the common schools to the private academies and the projected public normal schools.

Expectations for the speedy completion of a comprehensive system of public education were not unreasonable. When Wisconsin achieved statehood in 1848, there existed four private colleges and sixteen incorporated academies in the state, far fewer than in neighboring Illinois.[2] Few as they were, these private institutions served as platforms on which a public system could be erected. They also provided a foundation for the education of the state's teachers. It is understandable, therefore, that many of the state's early educators spent their careers in both private and public institutions and easily shifted between them as the occasion suggested.

Eleazer Root, who participated in the 1847 constitutional convention and was to become the state's first superintendent of public schools as well as the first president of the University Board of Regents, is a good example. He had gained his familiarity with education as headmaster of female seminaries in Virginia and Missouri. In Wisconsin, he served as the president of the Prairieville Academy, which in 1846 had become Carroll College. Yet despite his involvement in private institutions, he became one of the most outspoken advocates of public education. He foresaw a system of public schools that would bring "the advantages of a chartered academy" to every town and would be crowned with "the university acting in harmony with the entire system."[3]

Root was not alone in his faith in the compatibility of private academies and public education systems. John McMynn, who began his career as the first principal of public high schools in 1849 in Kenosha and in 1853 in Racine, after 1856 served for more than twenty years as university regent. After service in the U.S. Army during the Civil War, he became agent for the state normal schools, and in 1864 was elected state superintendent of public instruction. He remained in that office until 1868. Eight years later he evidently did not find it difficult to switch from public to private employment; from 1876 to 1882 he served as principal of the Racine Academy, a school whose primary aim was the preparation of students for university entrance.[4] In Milwaukee, Peter Engelmann, a graduate of the University of Berlin, presided over "Engelmann's School," a German-English academy, from its beginning in 1851 until his death in 1874. Like so many other refugees of the failed revolution of 1848, Engelmann was a strong promoter of public education and founded his private academy only because he felt the lack of public support for adequate advanced schooling. At the academy's fiftieth anniversary in 1901, City Superintendent Henry O. R. Siefert, himself born in Germany, highlighted the school's contributions to the city's public life. He pointed to the "rational methods of teaching" practiced in the academy, to the beneficent influence of academy-trained teachers in the city's public schools, to the academy's "early introduction . . . of the Kindergarten system," and the establishment of "our magnificent museum." Although in both Milwaukee and Racine the relationships between private and public educators were cordial, they were especially so in Milwaukee, where, unlike in Racine, the private academy emphasized its commitment to the city by teaching its graduates the modern natural sciences as preparation for entry into the city's business life.[5]

Similar accounts can be given of other localities. In Washington County, where private academies were opened in Barton in 1853 and West Bend in 1865, the first superintendent of public schools was Frederick Regenfuss, a German immigrant trained at a teacher seminary in Altdorf, Bavaria. Regenfuss had opened the Milwaukee German-English academy together with Peter Engelmann in 1851, and then served as county superintendent of public schools from 1861 to 1875. When he left that office, Washington County had four public schools with high school departments. Regenfuss, however, returned to head a private bilingual school and ended his educational career as principal of a German-English select school in West Bend.[6] Although the special situation of a German-English educator certainly influenced Regenfuss's decision to head private bilingual academies, it nonetheless shows again that there was no impassable gulf separating public schoolmen from their colleagues in private schools and that educators, whether teaching in public or in private schools, were heavily influenced by local issues.

Local Interests and State Concerns

Given the virtual interchangeabilty of Wisconsin's early private and public educators, the state's pioneers of public secondary education pursued a double-track policy. On one track, they followed the lead of Horace Mann and Henry Barnard and advocated the creation of union school districts that they expected would eventually form their own high school departments. On another track they encouraged reliance on private academies and their eventual conversion to public high schools. In either case they knew such conversions were dependent on local initiatives. As in Illinois, the democracy of local and district school administrations presented the greatest obstacle to centralized direction and severely restricted the state superintendents in the exercise of their duties. In dealing with Wisconsin's school districts, independent city school systems, and township or, after 1861, county systems, the state superintendents could influence only through persuasion. Their favorite means were their annual or biennial reports.[7]

Thus it should not come as a surprise that Wisconsin's high schools differed widely in their academic offerings, their location in commercial buildings, common schools, or edifices of their own, and in the number of their students, teachers, grades, and classrooms. They were to be found primarily in villages and cities and to a far lesser extent in the rural townships.[8] As in other states, they had first appeared as union schools and high school departments in the more heavily settled southeastern sections of the state. They were augmented by the steady conversions of academies into high schools. Their diversity and concentration in urban areas and their neglect in the rural countryside reflected the wishes of different localities and ignored the common educational needs of the commonwealth, which, as in all developing societies, were to be addressed primarily through the university. Thus while much of the rhetoric of the state superintendent stressed system building and the high schools' connecting-link function, the schools themselves and their local advocates responded to local concerns. They resembled the people's colleges of other urban centers, served the commercial needs of their communities, and supplied teachers for the common schools.

Aspects of the history of schooling in Racine may serve as illustration. In that city, the high school had been opened in 1853 and produced the state's first graduating class in 1857. It consisted of two boys and eight girls.[9] By 1879 the social composition of the student body of Racine High School and the intended professional destination of the majority of its graduates demonstrate to what extent even a midwestern urban high school resembled an eastern people's college more closely than the "connecting link" envisaged by Eleazer Root. In 1879 nearly two-thirds of the school's students came from blue-collar homes, nearly one-third from white-collar homes, and a mere 3.7 percent from professional families,[10] (Table 7.1). Twelve years later State Superintendent Oliver Wells found that in 119 of the state's 177 free high schools, 2,732, or 51 percent, of the 5,377 parents paid less than $1,000 in poll or property taxes annually; 1,304, or 24 percent, paid between $1,000 and $2,500; 1,125, or 21 percent, paid between $2,500 and $10,000; and only 216, or 4 percent, paid more than $10,000. Wells pointed out that farmers, unclassified day laborers, and widows constituted "more than two-fifths of all the patrons," and he concluded that "the high schools are pre-eminently the schools of the common people."[11]

Table 7.1 Social Origins of Racine High School Students, 1879		
	Number	Percent
Professional	5	3.7
Bankers	2	1.5
Doctors	2	1.5
Clergymen	1	0.7
White Collar	43	32.1
Merchants	25	18.7
Manufacturers	8	6
Salesmen	5	3.7
Barbers	2	1.5
Clerks	1	0.7
Hotel keepers	1	0.7
Teachers	1	0.7
Blue Collar	86	64.2
Mechanics	45	33.6
Day laborers	15	11.1
Farmers	15	11.1
Sailors	11	8.2

Source: Wisconsin Journal of Education, new series, IX (1879), 137.

If by "the common people" Wells meant the broad ranks of the American middle class including blue- and white-collar workers in city and country, then he was undoubtedly right. In Wisconsin as elsewhere, the nineteenth-century high school was a middle-class institution. Absent from its ranks were the scions of wealthy elite families, and absent likewise were those at the very bottom of the social pecking order in city, village, and country. But whether we refer to the "common people" or to the "middle class," within each category gradations of influence and status surely existed. Stories abounded of mutual distrust among high school students from village and country and of social discrimination against the latter by the former, particularly when such distrust and discrimination were fueled by ethnic differences.[12]

High School and University

The children of well-off professional families did not, as a rule, prepare themselves for admission to the university in the state's high schools. They were more likely to rely on private tutoring and on the continuing, though often intermittent, presence of private academies. University sources verify that however effective the state's high schools were in preparing their graduates for work in their communities, they did not send them to the university. In 1878 half of the students who attended the university's regular courses had received their secondary education in the university's preparatory department.[13]

In its relationship with the public schools, the university was constantly embarrassed by its preparatory department. Its very presence discouraged the already feeble efforts of the city of Madison to begin a high school of its own. Secondary schooling in Madison had begun as a private business run exclusively for and by women. When the university opened its doors to students in February of 1849, it invited the Madison Female Academy to play host to its preparatory department of twenty boys. The curriculum covered the spectrum from elementary subjects like reading, writing, and arithmetic to the requirements of an English school with grammar, geography, algebra, and bookkeeping, to the traditional collegiate fields of Latin and Greek. The university faculty was not happy with its assignment of preparatory work in a female academy but agreed with the chancellor, who wrote in 1851 that it

> must be continued until the academic or union schools, one in each township, embraced in the plan of public instruction for the State, shall be put into successful operation, and relieve the University from an office, which does not properly belong to it, and which will be better performed by the township schools.[14]

The university did not regard its host, the Madison Female Academy, as a proper training ground for future university students but said that it expected the public schools to provide the remedy.

The newly established Madison school district sought to oblige when in 1854 the Female Academy closed its doors. But it found that, for financial reasons, it could not provide a district-owned schoolhouse and was forced to arrange for instruction in a church. The measure persuaded the university that this was not an opportune time to drop its preparatory instruction and shift it to the district. Five years later Madison High School had moved into the building once owned by the Madison Female Academy, and Henry Barnard, who had become chancellor of the university, suggested that the high school take over the university's preparatory department. Opposition, however, came from the university faculty and students who argued that the high school did not have enough room and that it was demeaning for the students to be sent away from the campus. Thus by 1860 the preparatory school was still on campus and Madison High School, for its part, soon closed again for lack of funding. School-university relations in Madison were not at their best, and for the next two years only a private, tuition-charging high school for girls provided post-common-school instruction in the city.[15]

It is not surprising that given this history of repeated moves and indecision, the preparatory department was to become a burr under the saddle of the state's public school establishment. From the start the preparatory department had competed actively for students with Madison's efforts to establish a district high school. It allowed its pupils to select "branches usually taught in English High Schools, without reference to the regular collegiate course . . . although [it had been] designed mainly for the instruction of Classical Students."[16] Even though the faculty was reluctant to engage in preparatory work, the university remained highly dependent on such work and was not in a position to give it up early or easily. As late as 1865 the preparatory department furnished the university's single-largest student contingent, and during the 1870s its enrollment ranged between 15 and 30 percent of the whole.[17]

The faculty was torn between its desire to be rid of high school work and its intent, were the work to continue, to raise its academic level. When the Regents sought to placate the schoolmen in 1858 by proposing to drop the English subjects and to concentrate on the teaching of the classical languages and algebra, faculty members heartily agreed. Ten years later they accommodated their conflicting impulses by demanding that the preparatory sequence generally be reduced to one year except for candidates for the College of Letters. The candidates would have to take an additional two-year course in Latin and Greek. That two-year sequence remained as a subfreshman requirement even after 1880, when the preparatory school was finally officially closed.[18]

Madison High School, in the meanwhile, bore the brunt of the preparatory department's adverse effects. It had reopened in 1863 but did not receive a building of its own until 1874. According to Joseph Schafer, it never became very successful in its work until the university preparatory department was abolished in 1880.[19] In its first three years of separate existence, from 1875 to 1877, it graduated a total of fifty-eight students, thirty-one boys and twenty-seven girls. Of these, forty-one had taken the college preparatory work of the modern courses, both classical and scientific, and more than half of these were girls. Only seventeen had opted for the ancient classical course, requiring both Greek and Latin, and more than 80 percent of these were boys.[20] The schoolmen would have liked to have seen an even larger total enrollment and larger percentage of boys preparing themselves for university entrance, which would have hastened the disappearance of the preparatory department. They had nurtured that hope particularly after the legislature in 1876 had granted free tuition to all state residents, and the university, on its part, had begun to accredit high schools whose graduates it would admit without entrance examination. Madison's high school then became the first in the state to be granted that privilege.[21]

By the end of the 1870s neither Madison's district high school nor the university preparatory department were resounding successes. Focusing on the university's side of the story and the relationship between that institution and high schools in the state, the university's historians, Merle Curti and Vernon Carstensen, highlight

> the difficulty that was faced in bringing the high schools into a satisfactory relationship with the University while at the same time maintaining and, when possible, raising University entrance requirements. Some representatives of the high schools objected that the University was competing with the high schools, and others protested that to make the high schools serve as preparatory departments of the University was to divert them from their primary purpose. And when representatives of the University insisted too vigorously that the University was the head of the public school system and as such should receive all high school graduates, representatives of the sectarian colleges protested.[22]

What nobody wanted to acknowledge was that even with a university, however small, in its midst, Madison could hardly afford two competing high schools.

When, then, in 1880 the preparatory department closed except for its classes in Greek, the response was not unanimous either. John Bascom, president of the university, conceded that it had been a prudent step, though, as he said, "taken not without some solicitude" and only after some urging from the high schools. But there remained doubts as to its wisdom. "The High Schools of the State," wrote Bascom, "are not yet in a condition to do all the work required of them." He and others pointed to public normal schools and private academies and seminaries as suitable alternatives.[23] As for the schoolmen, they knew that only large high schools could afford to give due attention to college preparation for the small percentage of students who desired it. Small schools, if they attempted it, inevitably had to shortchange the large body of general students.

But in 1890 the *Wisconsin Journal of Education* editorialized that high schools and the university had worked out their problems. This was due in large part to the university's openness, quite unusual for American universities at that time, to popular and progressive currents of thought. By 1886 students could choose among four curricular tracks. A general scientific course would lead them to a bachelor of science degree, an English course and the modern classical course each concluded with a bachelor of letters degree; and only the ancient classical course offered the traditional bachelor of arts degree.[24] In this way the university had become more hospitable to a greater diversity of students and thus permitted the high schools to design curricula that at one and the same time prepared students for university study, took into account "the wants of the local community," and were "well adapted to pupils who do not look beyond the high school."[25] The *Journal* rejoiced that high school and university had come to a mutually acceptable solution.

The Free High School Law of 1875

The Wisconsin schoolmen's fight to eliminate the university preparatory school as a competitor was soon overshadowed by their struggle to open up the state's vast agricultural areas for public secondary schooling. Just like their brethren in Michigan and Illinois, Wisconsin's superintendents faced a population reluctant to vote increased taxes for this purpose. Only in the larger villages and cities had it been possible to inaugurate high schools.[26] Even there this was possible only after considerable efforts by the proponents of public schooling, who appealed to the economic interests of a growing mercantile middleclass. Most citizens still thought of private academies as appropriate feeder schools for colleges and the university. They saw no great urgency to provide for tax-supported high schools that would offer an advanced education in English or commercial subjects. If the superintendent was to be successful in popularizing the high school as a fitting school for business and trade in agricultural lands, he had to persuade taxpayers that the school could do both equally well: prepare the few students for the university and enable the many to become efficient contributors to their community's wealth. There was no longer any point in speaking of either people's colleges or connecting links. The high school had to be both.

In that crusade, the successive incumbents in the state superintendent's office served as cheerleaders. In their annual reports they pleaded for a more efficient and centralized school system. Superintendent Josiah Pickard won his first victory when in 1861 the legislature replaced the township organization of district schools with the county superintendency. In his report of 1862 Pickard urged cities and villages to grade their schools and encouraged townships to promote the creation of union districts for high school purposes. He appealed to parents who desired advanced academic instruction as business training for their sons and a finishing or normal school education for their daughters, and he also addressed those who thought of sending their children to college or university and preferred a free high school to a fee-charging academy as preparatory institution. Knowing how ill-prepared the state's public education system was to take on these tasks, Pickard continued to assure the friends of private schools that their academies and colleges were still very much needed to help satisfy the state's educational needs.[27]

Pickard's successor, John McMynn, adopted Illinois superintendent Bateman's crusade for the town high school. Quoting at length from Bateman's sixth biennial report, he argued that with district boundaries abolished and a township organization in place, the rural high school would no longer lag in quality and efficiency of instruction behind its city and village cousin.[28] But it was Superintendent Edward Searing who during his time in office from 1874 to 1878 urged the cause of the public high school with unprecedented vigor. Searing was particularly disturbed about the high number of boys who, he said, even in the best high schools left for work and contributed to the nearly all-girl composition of graduating classes.[29] He pointed once more to the lamentable lack of opportunities for advanced instruction in the rural areas and to the overextension of the elementary schools that resulted when their teachers tried to supply that lack. He gratefully acknowledged the support he had received from "the friends of university or collegiate culture," but added that this was not where "the great popular need" was located. What was missing were not

> a *few long ladders* by which to climb to the solitary peak whence all the wisdom of the earth is under view, but rather many short and convenient and inexpensive ones by which to climb to the broad and fair and wholesome table-land of secondary or academic culture. What is everywhere needed is not so much the *preparatory* school as the *supplementary* school. Therefore, without special and immediate reference to the interests of the University and of those comparatively few pupils who in any event will seek therein that superior culture to which peculiar ambition or peculiar wealth may lead them . . . it is my conviction that the system we need to inaugurate is a system of township rather than of county schools.[30]

A system of township rather than county high schools as supplementary rather than preparatory institutions—that was the aim of Searing's crusade for a free high school law to benefit the state's rural areas.

Searing took as his model the free high schools of Maine. These schools gave instruction in "the ordinary academic studies, and especially the natural sciences in their application to mechanics, manufactures and agriculture." They were "peoples' high schools for a superior English and scientific education . . . and affording the general culture demanded by the increasing business, manufacturing and mercantile wants of the times." To that general curriculum, the prospectus stated, "may be added the higher mathematics, modern and ancient languages, and belles lettres."[31] Maine's high schools continued the tradition of the people's colleges of the eastern cities. Because their chief business was supplementary to the common schools and because their classical collegiate training was incidental, they had little in common with the "connecting links" of Michigan.

But Searing undercut his own campaign for the supplementary township high school when he also insisted that thought be given to the additional creation of preparatory high schools and to curricula that were to be used in both kinds of schools. Searing obviously wanted to please both constituencies, the supporters of the supplementary and the fans of the preparatory high school. As it turned out, each of his three recommended high school courses enabled its graduates to enter the university; that had become possible because the university no longer required Latin training of all applicants.

The original supplemental character of Searing's high school curriculum remained apparent only in the inclusion of German as an elective in the two nonclassical courses. In one of them, a student could select German in place of bookkeeping, rhetoric, mental science, or political science; in the other, German could take the place of bookkeeping and rhetoric only. For Searing German was a "practical" subject like bookkeeping and rhetoric and not a field of collegiate study. German highlighted his "supplementary" nature of a high school education that went beyond the common-school subjects while still responding to local needs or wants. The Germans, Searing noted, "were among the most appreciative and ardent supporters of the high school plan." Two German-born legislators, Speaker Frederick Horn and Assemblyman Herman Naber, were instrumental in guiding the high school bill to victory.[32] But it may well be doubted that they did so, as Searing somewhat disingenuously suggested, because Germany was "universally acknowledged to be the world's educational center."[33] Wisconsin Germans, it seems safe to say, were, by and large, more interested in preserving their culture and language than in basking in the reflected educational glory of their former homeland.

Still, the slowness of the spread of high schools in the state's agricultural areas continued to disappoint the superintendent. Matters were made more precarious and urgent in 1877 through the legislative statutory revision of the 1875 law. The revision required that in order to receive state aid, high schools had to be conducted for a minimum period of three months each year in a building not devoted to any other school purpose. This hit particularly hard the high school departments of graded schools in rural areas, just those that the law had originally been intended to help. Beacuse the revised law also limited aid to $500 a year to any one district for a period of three years and required that districts be established by the voters in a special election and not be created simply by the conversion of an ordinary common school district, it again handicapped the rural township schools above all others.

Searing's successor, William C. Whitford, regretted these "pernicious restraints," which deprived "a large majority of the free high schools . . . of the opportunity to receive State aid," and asked that they be reconsidered.[34] Under the 1877 amendment, only two or three of the eighty-five high schools aided under the 1875 law could have continued to receive such aid in 1878. Whitford's plea fell on fertile ground, and in February of 1879 new legislation restored the aid to rural schools.[35] But the increase in the number of high schools aided—three—was minimal, and the termination of grants after the initial statutory five-year period in 1881 decreased the number of aided schools to seventy-eight. Superintendent Whitford was justified in announcing in December of 1879 that "the primary object in the establishment of these schools has not been realized to any great extent—viz.: the creation of town high schools. Only three of this kind have been organized in the past four and a half years."[36]

Conflicting Purposes

In subsequent years Wisconsin educators, like those in other states, continued to debate the various missions of the high school: to prepare its students for college; to upgrade the quality of the common schools by encouraging and training its students as future teachers; to qualify its graduates for business; and to inspire them to good citizenship. The pages of the *Wisconsin Journal of Education* bear witness to this debate. Unanimity was nowhere to be found. Proponents of all these purposes, singly and in various combinations, had their say. As Superintendent Robert Graham wrote in 1886, they spoke "always in hopeless disagreement, owing to the absence of all conception of the high school as adjusted to schools below, as well as to the schools above."[37]

Most contributors acknowledged that the high school, willy-nilly, had to contend with varied demands, most prominent among them the double mission of preparing for life and preparing for college. For some, that translated itself into each high school's having to offer an English and a classical course, courses that instructed students in varied proportions in the academic fields of mathematics, science, language, and literature.[38] Others still clung to the view originally proposed by Edward Searing, that the high school supplement the common school and pay primary attention to the skills needed in practical life in the students' home communities. Thus they pointed to such "practical" skills as bookkeeping and sentential analysis and argued that if the high school were organized as preparatory school it would only "render ease of access to secondary work for the common school pupil a myth."[39]

Statistics reported for 1882 tended to underline the proposition advanced by Superintendent Graham that the high schools were "largely attended by such as seek for a better equipment for immediate and active business than the common schools can afford, and not in any great numbers by those seeking fit preparation for collegiate courses of study." Only 367 students, or 5.62 percent, of the 6,528 students enrolled in high schools aided under the 1875 law graduated and thus had embarked on a course that *might* take them to college or university. But after the university's decision in 1886 no longer to require of all applicants for entry a high school preparation in a foreign language, that percentage was to climb steadily. By 1892 it had nearly doubled.[40] Nonetheless, in 1890 Superintendent Jesse B. Thayer emphasized once more that the high school was "chiefly valuable . . . in its relation to the work of associated lower grades of the same school, and to the work in surrounding country district schools."[41] The resolution of this issue, if there was to be one, would obviously not be found in Wisconsin alone. But in the meantime, the merging of preparation for life and for college had fatally undercut the high school's ability to serve as a people's college. Regardless of the number of students who intended to go on to college, the high school had given up the last vestige of its character as a people's college and had become a school whose programs reflected college entrance requirements.

8

Growing Pains

Expansion and Its Effects

During the last two decades of the century the growth of industry in the bourgeois societies on both sides of the Atlantic brought rising pressures to bear on the systems of secondary education. In the United States the high school had become the favorite instrument of the middle classes for their children's social and economic advance. This was true as much for artisans and small entrepreneurs in the cities, who relied on the people's colleges, as for businessmen and professionals in rural areas, who looked toward the connecting-link high schools.

In Europe, the authors of *The Rise of the Modern Educational System* tell us, the situation was similar. There, Heinz-Elmar Tenorth wrote, "The school as an institution can be traced primarily to middle-class consciousness." He endorsed Fritz Ringer's point that social role and prestige and transmitted ways of thought, not economic or technological change, constituted the driving force of educational development.[1] It was not the modern scientific curricula of the late-nineteenth-century secondary schools but their revitalized classical curriculum that commanded the highest prestige. As Brian Simon wrote for England:

> The ethos, mores and indeed institutions of traditional education became the models increasingly accepted by the middle class and the new social forces now bidding for hegemony. The culture of the gentry and aristocracy was in fact accepted by leading sections of

the bourgeoisie. . . . The educational objectives of the new middle class now became ambivalent.[2]

The preference of parents for and the support given to the classical course in the college-preparatory curricula of American high schools at a time of increasing demand for graduates trained in the sciences and modern languages pointed to the same ambivalence.

Trying to explain this phenomenon in Europe, Detlef Müller and his colleagues suggested that a rising bourgeoisie realized that once larger numbers of their own ranks had access to secondary education, the value of such educational currency was bound to decrease. Because most of the middle-class children attending secondary schools were attracted to the practical curricula of the modern scientific-technical schools, the prestige ranking of the older, traditional classical schools could only go up. Thus even members of the middle classes, fully supportive of the newer schools, nonetheless regarded the traditional English "public" schools as models and pacesetters. Many of them wanted their children prepared for Oxbridge and thus ultimately for careers in the professions and public service. Their ambivalence made them waver between admiration for the modern schools and allegiance to the traditional institutions.

In the United States the prestige of the classics was linked to the growth in high school enrollments that initially was propelled by female students. In the early years of this trend, career motivations played a minor role for women.[3] When in the cities it became less necessary for teenagers to seek work or, because of child labor legislation and popular concern with vagrancy and delinquency, less possible to find employment, continuing attendance at school became an attractive and viable option for male youngsters as well. What David Labaree has called "the acquisition of cultural property"—speech patterns, tastes, manners, style, academic credentials—rather than opportunities for work-related schooling served as enticement.[4] When we add to this the democratic imperative—parental desire to see their children advance socially and economically combined with the schoolmen's ambition to expand their sphere of influence—we understand better why the schoolmen not only were uncertain about the high school's purpose but also had to cope with slowly but steadily increasing numbers of students. During the years between 1890 and 1920 the percentage of fourteen- to seventeen-year-olds in school increased nearly fivefold, from 6.7 to 32.3. In absolute numbers the increase was even more astounding: enrollment in grades 9 through 12 rose nearly elevenfold, from 202,693 to 2,200,389.[5] Over time, institutional momentum and societal pressures saw to it that what at the beginning was viewed and appreciated as an opportunity for the motivated few gradually became compulsion for the indifferent many.

The changes ensuing from the rise in enrollment proved baffling and painful. As I indicated at the end of chapter 4, they brought about the disappearance of the people's college as the country's most successful educational institution. They also initiated the transformation of what had been called "practical" education into the high school programs of manual training and provoked the reaction of educational traditionalists in the Committee of Ten to try to settle—unsuccessfully, as it turned out—the many disputes over the purposes of the American high school and to define for the country a set of courses that would constitute the high school curriculum.

The Death of the People's College

During the 1880s and 1890s the people's college fell victim to the democratic imperative. To attract the largest possible number of students, high schools designed their curricula for a variety of purposes and almost always included a college preparatory course. Even in large urban centers high schools would no longer commit their resources single-mindedly to the preparation of graduates for leadership in the commercial and industrial life of their communities. Not to provide for college preparation, not to augment a common curriculum with parallel courses, was considered undemocratic, especially when universities broadened their entrance requirements to admit graduates of all academic high school courses. The "brief and shining moment" of the people's college came to an end. A self-sufficient high school with a single common curriculum for all students, responsive to local needs and largely oblivious to class-biased concerns, was no longer acceptable in a developing bourgeois society. The result was a high school that ceased to have clearly defined objectives and repudiated its emergence from a tradition of common schooling by trying to serve all members of its varied clientele with differentiated course offerings.

We find examples of this development as we return to Somerville, Massachusetts, and follow the history of its high school during the century's last three decades. In 1870 the school diversified its curriculum and introduced two college-preparatory sequences. One of these stressed Latin and Greek; the other substituted science for Greek. In addition, the school continued its former people's college curriculum with a mercantile or English course designed for the student "who is looking forward to a Bank or Counting-room for employment." The course included such subjects as accounts, penmanship, algebra, geometry, trigonometry, and chemistry. Several years later a separate business course was introduced but soon absorbed into the English course. An even more radical innovation came with the extension of the divided curriculum back into the elementary grades. In Somerville, common schooling for all was no longer the reigning educational idea.[6]

From the mid-1880s to the mid-1890s Somerville's citizens debated whether the diversified high school curriculum might not be better served when offered in two separate buildings. They envisaged a new English high school, which, like the former people's college, was to prepare its students for commercial, industrial, technical, and scientific employment through instruction in chemistry, biology, commercial arithmetic, technical mathematics, and industrial shopwork. The new edifice was not to house a commercial school, pure and simple, but would retain the character of a public high school by also offering work in literature, the modern languages, history, mathematics, and social studies. When it opened in 1895, it stood next to Latin High School, which now could devote itself exclusively to college preparatory work.[7]

In Philadelphia we encounter a similar story, yet, given rather different circumstances, one with a quite dissimilar outcome. Philadelphia Central High School, whose early years as a people's college we discussed in chapter 4, had prepared its students through academic scientific study for leadership in the city's business life. Throughout its early decades, its founders and directors held fast to their original purpose, but eventually they, too, redirected their efforts and responded to varied demands with differentiated curricula.[8]

The precipitating event was the opening in 1885 of Central Manual Training School in response to the same popular pressures for advanced educational opportunities that had been at work in Somerville. Philadelphia Central's monopoly over the city's high schools for boys ended, and a vigorous debate began among its faculty members over the future of the school. The issue was whether the existence of competing nonpreparatory high schools would force Philadelphia Central, in order to preserve its standing, to add a college-preparatory sequence. When the faculty decided that it did, the school entered on a new course. By the 1890s its preparatory program included a classical, a chemical, a physical, and a regular sequence. A scientific course was added "principally for those who enter school with the expectation of remaining only one or two years." That course, however, was exchanged in 1898 for a commercial department.[9] When we then note that, as David Labaree wrote, in 1893

> 82.6 percent of the freshmen chose the college preparatory route
> [and that, by their junior year,] when students had sorted them-

selves into the remaining options (and after most of them had left),
no fewer than 90.2 percent were taking the four preparatory
courses, and classics alone accounted for more than half of the
class,[10]

it becomes obvious that, for all practical purposes, Philadelphia Central
had become a college-preparatory school.

What led urban high schools like Somerville and Philadelphia Central
to give up their role as people's colleges and to opt for separated tracks
and buildings? In Somerville there was little discussion among public
schoolmen over the implications of the abandonment of common schooling at the high school. The major reason for their adoption of separate
curricula appears to have been their desire to hold and increase enrollments and their fear that apprenticeship and private commercial schools
might drain off pupils and interfere with their desire to keep students in
high school through the entire four-year sequence.

Parental motivations were a different matter. Lower-middle-class and
artisan families and, equally strongly, white-collar parents pushed for
Somerville's separate English High School. If the former wanted appropriate education for business life, the latter sought for their children a college-preparatory education. They believed that a separate classical high
school, by devoting all its energies single-mindedly to college-preparatory
studies, would contribute significantly to a better articulation between
high school and college. Opposition to the plan, to the extent that it existed, rested primarily on financial grounds. Those against it preferred
one school with two sessions as an alternative, and managed to delay the
the English High School for several years.

David Labaree has argued that when with the addition of an academic
preparatory track in 1889 Philadelphia Central left behind the tradition
of a single common curriculum for all, it sought the prestige that went
with college work, particularly with the classics. Status desire motivated
proprietary middle-class families to raise the percentage of their children
in the school, and middle-class employees and skilled workers increasingly
tended to enroll their children in the new manual training schools.[11] At a
time when growing enrollments in secondary education began to depre-
ciate the value of a high school diploma, college-preparatory work served
to uphold and enhance a school's prestige and that of the students who
enrolled in the academic track.[12] In that track, the highest prestige accrued to the classics. Again Labaree makes the point: "Of all the academic
students in the 1900 cohort who stayed in school long enough to pick a
specialty, 51.8 percent chose Latin-scientific, 31.5 percent classical, and
only 16.7 percent selected modern languages."[13]

Curricular differentiation increased enrollments and enlarged the professional responsibilities of the schoolmen. In Somerville, the enrollment percentage of the high school "increased from 20.6 percent of high-school-age persons in 1875 to 30.7 percent in 1905," and in 1895 "was more than triple the national average of 1890."[14] And Somerville was not alone. English high schools or their curricula flourished also in other Massachusetts cities such as Boston, Cambridge, Lynn, Fall River, Newton, and Fitchburg. There, too, they had substantially increased enrollments.[15] Expansion of secondary education was in the air, and the people's college had to give way to a high school with differentiated curricula.

From Practical to Manual Education

In states with the "connecting-link" tradition of secondary schooling, schoolmen were concerned how they might accommodate the growing popular demand for practical work in their high schools. They were slow to respond, and at first sought to incorporate "practical studies" as part of the traditional scientific-academic curriculum. That was true for the New York Regents, who, as we know from chapter 5, had always been intent upon upholding academic standards. They were reluctant to concede that the academies, the academic departments of union schools, and the high schools prepared most of their students for business rather than for college, and they hesitated to accept the introduction of practical studies.

In Michigan, the demand for practical education had persuaded the state superintendent in 1877 to recommend a high school syllabus that, in addition to the scientific course that led to entry into the university's scientific program, outlined a general course for students whose academic preparation was to end with graduation.[16] This general course, still conventionally academic, was proposed for the great majority of students who were to be prepared for all aspects of life: earning a living, serving the community, and improving the quality of their personal lives.[17]

The call for a less academic high school curriculum received a similar reaction in Illinois when in 1886 Superintendent Henry Raab asked the schools to prepare their students "for the work of practical life." Such preparation, Raab wrote, should strike a balance among academic study, instruction in drawing to develop "the culture of the sense of form and technical skills," correct methods of teaching, and moral as well as physical education. It did not include manual education, which, Raab said, should be left to the family, to private schools, and to institutions like reform schools and orphan asylums, which, for their students, took the place of the family.[18]

The calls for "practical" work, however, soon went beyond academic study of practical tasks and skills such as business arithmetic, bookkeeping, and stenography and came to include manual or industrial education and shopwork. In New York such courses were introduced in the academic departments of more and more high schools during the 1880s. This had become a necessity, the Regents were told, because, unless it was done, teaching was the only employment for graduates of the academic courses who did not choose to go to college. Beyond that, these students were "effectually shut out from the rest of the world until they shall have learned . . . to use their hands in some useful industry." Instruction in the manual arts was the answer.[19] Besides, the Regents were told, in the three-year mechanical course at the College of the City of New York, manual and commercial education as an option had always shared the limelight with academic instruction. Even students in the five-year collegiate courses could sign up for wood and metal workshop work after their regular academic classes.[20]

In the agricultural states of the Midwest, the progress of manual education in the public secondary schools was less rapid. Before 1900 Michigan's and Illinois's records in these fields were unimpressive. Of the twelve Michigan cities that had introduced it, only Calumet and Flint offered regular manual training in their high schools, and Ann Arbor did so as an elective. Calumet's program was unusual because its manual training plant was established by the local mining company, and its operation was self-supporting because the company used the students' work in its production process.[12] Only in 1898 did the superintendent plead strongly for the broadening of commercial courses and the introduction of manual training and domestic science.[22] In Illinois, Superintendent Raab's successor, Richard Edwards, also was skeptical of the value of manual education. Though it had been introduced in the grammar school grades of Moline, Beardstown, and Peru, Edwards was "scarcely ready to say that a manual labor appendage should be attached to all the schools of the country or even to all the grammar schools in our cities."[23]

The most adamant resistance to the introduction of manual education arose in Wisconsin. State Superintendent Oliver Wells wrote in 1894 that there were "some tendencies . . . to be guarded against." He objected to turning high schools into commercial colleges, manual training schools, or little colleges and universities. A committee appointed by him asserted that the job of the public schools was "not to make business men, not to prepare students for the university, not to train teachers,— but to qualify citizens."[24] But during the next five years, departments of manual training were opened in ten of the state's public high schools, and the new superintendent, J. Q. Emery, expressed cautious optimism and willingness to encourage and extend the work. He authorized courses in freehand and mechanical drawing, in wood and iron work, in sewing and in cooking.[25] His successor, L. D. Harvey, nonetheless complained that high school boards "practically ignored" the legal requirement to obtain the superintendent's approval for the introduction of new high school courses.[26]

Part of the problem was that there was little agreement among schoolmen about the nature of manual education. Its history went back to the American pioneers of the kindergarten, who had stressed the handling of fabrics, paper, clay, wood, metal, and other objects. With its emphasis on motor and manual skills, the Pestalozzian movement of object teaching at the Oswego Normal School then had revolutionized the pedagogy of the elementary school. On the other end of the spectrum, at the Massachusetts Institute of Technology, Professor John Runkle had promoted manual education. Educators at public land grant universities and agricultural and mechanical colleges viewed it as an indispensable part of laboratory and field research.[27]

Another tradition of manual education, at odds with the idea of integrating it with intellectual work in elementary and higher schools, held that it was the proper education for pupils who were not ready for or unable to benefit from academic instruction. This tradition had originated in reform schools for delinquent children in which manual and moral education was to rehabilitate the young misfits and criminals. In the 1860s and 1870s it governed the schooling of pupils in special classes for the children of workers in New England mill towns. Manual education had also been the preferred approach to the schooling of Native Americans and former slaves and their descendants. At the Hampton Institute in Virginia, General Samuel Chapman Armstrong had given it widespread publicity. His student Booker T. Washington had done likewise at the Tuskegee Institute in Alabama. There it was known as industrial education, designed to stress work habits, discipline, punctuality, and, in general, behavioral aspects of industrial life.

Given these contradictory reputations, we can understand why educators hesitated to accept manual education programs in their schools.[28] Felix Adler expressed the fears of educators when he wrote that manual or industrial education "seeks to make the mass of mankind more machinelike than they already are, though with the proviso that they shall be made more perfect machines, more skillful to increase wealth and to feed the channels of the manufacturer's profits."[29] Introducing methods theretofore reserved for the education of problem children, manual education, others warned, would taint or corrupt the idea of a democratic common school.

Against these hesitations and doubts were ranged the considerations of taxpayers who believed in the community's obligation to educate all its children. These citizens held that the democratic imperative did not require a common, uniform curriculum for all students. It could be realized also when students and parents were free to choose among various curricular offerings; manual education, they argued, prepared children for employment opportunities available to them in their communities. For schoolmen, their ability to offer such opportunities promised a grateful parental clientele and broadened effectiveness and reach of their institutions. This to them was all the more important because private fee-charging commercial and vocational schools had already been active in this field. Public schoolmen felt pressed to offer similar opportunities.[30]

Manual Education Comes Into Its Own

The event that was to establish manual education in the country's secondary schools was the 1876 Centennial Exhibition in Philadelphia. The Imperial Technical School of Moscow exhibited workshops for hand labor that were designed exclusively for pedagogical purposes, they played no part in the manufacture of products for commercial or industrial use. Students received systematic instruction in turning, carpentering, fitting, and forging. John Runkle, president of the Massachusetts Institute of Technology, was so favorably impressed with the distinction "between a Mechanic Art and its application in some special trade" that he introduced this approach at his institute and recommended it for use in secondary schools. The rest, as the saying goes, is history.[31] Manual education overcame the hesitation of U.S. schoolmen and in the process changed the character of the country's high schools.

In the high school, instruction unhinged from production and beginning with design drawing and hand tooling promised to lay the manual as well as the mental groundwork for future draftsmen, engineers, and supervisors of construction and production projects. Calvin Woodward, director of the O'Fallon Polytechnical Institute of Washington University, a manual training high school that had begun its work in 1879, promoted this reasoning and came to be known as the father of manual education in the American high school. As part of the general school culture, Woodward argued, instruction in the manual arts allowed every student to discover and pursue hidden mechanical inclinations and talents. This reasoning appealed to educators, parents, and taxpayers who were critical of the narrow academic emphasis of the traditional high school and gradually overcame the initial resistance of high school administrators.[32]

There was, of course, opposition to Woodward's ideas, although it came to lose much of its force. In his home town St. Louis and on the national scene, Woodward sparred with his colleague and rival William Torrey Harris. Harris, who served as St. Louis superintendent of schools from 1868 to 1880, rejected Woodward's manual training and instead insisted on the sufficiency of mental training for all students. To this Woodward responded:

> We need to know more of the concrete, less of the abstract; more of primary knowledge, less of secondary; more personal experience, less of memory. We need more life, more action, more interest, more of the executive, and less of the passive; more of growth, less of absorption.

Manual education, as part of a general education, was to provide just that.[33] Arguing in this fashion, Woodward shifted the focus of manual education as a suitable approach to the education of future engineers—a focus shared initially by both him and Runkle—to manual education as a pedagogy for all students in secondary education. Manual education, he said, persuaded students, particularly boys in their early to midteens, to remain in school. In so doing, it became a perfect instrument for assuring the survival of the common school.

It is ironic that manual education on the secondary level began in schools that were associated with private universities. As this was true of Woodward's school, so it was true also of Chicago's Manual Training School, which opened in 1883, and of Technical School of Cincinnati, founded in 1886 by a private consortium of businessmen and civic leaders. With their academic and manual work these schools and others like them attracted a generally middle-class student body. During its first ten years, the Chicago school elevated its mathematics instruction in the technological course to allow boys who normally opted for college admission to enter the second year of engineering schools. Those who had no such intention could choose a business course. Machine shopwork was offered in either course. When the school moved to the University of Chicago, it added a four-year college preparatory course with four years of Latin and three years of Greek. Only eight students, however, made use of the latter opportunity in 1898.[34] The large majority opted for business and technical work or study. Professor Henry Hames Belfield, the school's director, nonetheless continued to insist that shopwork and drawing were additional to the traditional academic work and were meant merely to aid the student's comprehension of some of his academic studies. Belfield never wavered in affirming the general-education purpose of his school. But then he also added that there was "the additional and by no means unimportant consideration that manual training has an industrial value" and "that the graduate . . . is better fitted to enter into the struggle for existence than the boy who has had an education in books only." Belfield, it appears, shared the ambivalence of so many public schoolmen.[35]

The Cincinnati school became, for all intents and purposes, a prevocational training ground for future engineers. In his study of its graduates, Richard Lakes found them to show the

> relatively homogeneous middle-class characteristics of high school enrollees. Forty-five percent . . . entered technical fields, like drafting, machining, and engineering. Five percent . . . attained supervisory status in industry as managers or superintendents. Additionally, . . . graduates entered professional fields, such as medicine and law (2 percent); architecture (10 percent); and education (3 percent). Fifteen . . . graduates entered out-of-state engineering colleges. . . . And eighteen graduates entered family businesses.

Far from turning its back on the academic tradition of secondary schooling, the Cincinnati school merely associated with it the practical and technical applications of its scientific studies. The depression of the 1890s and accompanying low enrollments forced the school to curtail its activities and, like the schools in St. Louis and Chicago, it was then transferred to university sponsorship. In 1901 it became part of the University of Cincinnati.[36]

In public high schools the introduction of manual education, hesitant as it was, was usually complicated by local politics. As already discussed, in Philadelphia the opening of Central Manual Training School in 1885 convinced the faculty of Central High School to devote themselves to college preparation. They did so because they and the city's conservative political leaders objected to "curricular experimentation," a favorite project, they thought, of James MacAlister, from 1883 to 1890 the city's first superintendent, and Edward Steel, textile manufacturer and president of the Board of Education from 1879 to 1887.

MacAlister and Steel saw themselves as progressive educational reformers and pushed manual education as a means of loosening the rigidity of the traditional classroom. They wanted to banish the "'absurd methods' and 'mechanical drudgery' associated with subjects like spelling and arithmetic drill." Although both men regarded manual and intellectual education as equally necessary and the former as an aid to the latter, they were more impressed by social and economic usefulness and by the promise of manual education to keep students in school. They were ardent advocates of the kindergarten, of industrial arts schools, of sewing and cooking for girls, and of manual training schools.[37] Political fortunes, however, turned, and with the election in 1891 of Edward Brooks as superintendent, the progressive impulse in Philadelphia's schools slowed down and, for a short time, appeared to have subsided.

Because the retention of girls in high schools had not been a problem to administrators, little was said of manual education for girls.[38] That, however, did not mean that nothing was done, though it often appeared as a by-product of the concern for boys. In Ohio, for example, the first manual training program had been inaugurated in 1884 in Toledo's public high school with the expectation that it would raise the number of male graduates, persuade more boys to benefit from the school's academic program, and thereby alter the gender balance among the high school students in favor of boys. The school offered instruction in carpentry for boys and cooking for girls, and it included music, drawing, writing, and physical training.[39] From Peru, Illinois, we learn in the next year that girls took "plain sewing, patching, darning, etc. . . . with good results." In the same year, the principal of the Dwight Grammar School in New Haven, Connecticut, wrote that depending on their age, girls from kindergarten to twelfth grade were taught "all kinds of sewing, knitting, crocheting, embroidery, and other work suitable for girls."[40] Close to the century's end we hear from Illinois that girls were taught sewing and cooking and boys woodwork in the schools of Chicago, Moline, Champaign, and Urbana.[41] Manual education for girls also served as a convenient bridge from the traditional academic to the new "useful" high school curricula. It was supposed to facilitate the transition to industrial education, that is, an education that was to overcome distaste for manual labor and encourage work discipline.

Even with all these activities going on, manual education never gained a strong student following. In 1887 the U.S. commissioner of education reported enrollment figures in different subjects and courses for different types of schools (Table 8.1). His figures show that manual training and Greek ranked lowest in popularity among students; only in private girls schools, where manual training perpetuated a tradition of teaching the "womanly arts," did the subject have a measure of popularity. Freehand drawing, the least "industrial" and the most "academic" of the manual subjects, attracted the greatest interest.[42] By 1887 manual training had not made great inroads into either public or private high schools. Latin and the preparatory course for college and scientific school continued to hold significant proportions of high school students.

The reluctance of the schoolmen to accept manual education and the low esteem in which it was held at least by some of them is remarked upon

Table 8.1 Students in U.S. High Schools, by School Type and Subject Studied, 1887 (in percentage of total enrollment)

School Category	L	CR	F	GE	Eo	CP	FHD	MD	MT	Total (*N*)
1	37	4	11	14	37	10	25	9	1	68,672
2	13	2	3	3	80	8	9	1	3	11,331
3	13		24	9		2	23		10	15,725
4	38	16	15	20	23	32	16	8	4	18,180
5	13	3	4	7	43	7	12		3	67,207
6	25	5	9	11	18	10				181,116

Key: 1 = Schools supported wholly by public funds
2 = Schools supported partly by public funds
3 = Private girls schools
4 = Private boys schools
5 = Private schools for both sexes
6 = All classes of secondary schools
L = Students studying Latin
GR = Students studying Greek
F = Students studying French
GE = Students studying German
Eo = Students studying English only
CP = Students preparing for college
FHD = Students studying free hand drawing
MD = Students studying mechanical drawing
MT = Students enrolled for manual training

Source: Report of the U.S. Commissioner of Education . . . 1887 (Washington, DC, 1888), pp 787-791.

in the introductory paragraphs of the chapter on manual and industrial training in the U.S. Commissioner of Education's annual report for 1887–1888. "Some degree of delicacy" wrote the author, was required "to avoid giving offense either to those who are carrying on the great propaganda or to others who oppose their views." He lamented that in a conflict where at one point conservatives battled "the metaphysics of education by manual labor" and at another a "watered communism," the incompatible and contradictory statements and battle cries of the partisans permitted no display of wisdom. The fog of words was impenetrable:

> To see adopted, as a means of awakening thought, operations which have for centuries been looked upon as mechanical, using the words in its figurative sense, to hear on one hand a demand for

manual labor because the youth who go from the schools are educated against it, and on the other a demand that it shall be introduced because 90 per cent of these follow a manual occupation, to
hear on one side a demand made for manual training as a branch of
education and on the other as a branch of industry, and to find the
whole subject obscured by a cloud of words, are of themselves quite
sufficient to prevent any exertions on our part.[43]

Nonetheless, the author bravely commenced to trace the fortunes of manual education in the United States, but not very successfully. He confessed
a year later:

The Office found itself in the singular position of having collected
quite an array of statistics of a movement the philosophy of which as
far as pedagogical features were involved it did not understand. The
publications of superintendents of systems by whom statistics have
been furnished were examined for light, but in vain, for there
seemed no body of pedagogical principles that was common to all
or even a majority.[44]

What the author found was that manual education was torn between two
camps. There were those who endeavored to supplement and aid intellectual development by a training of hand and eye. There were others
who were far more concerned with political economy than with education. They appeared to push for manual education as a wedge that would
make possible the ultimate introduction of vocational education in the
high schools.

The disappearance of the people's college and the ambivalence of the
schoolmen over the introduction of manual education in the high schools
marked the last two decades of the nineteenth century. The future of the
high school was shrouded in uncertainty. Did the appearance of manual
education mean that the school was to lose its traditional academic approach? Would the clamor for more college-preparatory courses force the
high schools to "water down" their curricula? Laypeople and schoolmen
sought answers to these and other questions. The nation's best-known educators, both schoolmen and academics, would try to find the answers as
the 1890s began.

9

The Committee of Ten

The Report of 1893

At the beginning of the 1890s the National Council of Education of the National Education Association commissioned the Committee of Ten to define the nature and purpose of American secondary education. It did so against the background of the issues discussed in the previous chapters. The council asked the committee specifically to organize conferences "of school and college teachers of each principal subject which enters into the programmes of secondary schools . . . and into the requirements for admission to college." It added that the committee was to limit its investigation to the principal subjects of the secondary school curriculum that were required for admission into colleges and universities. The chief questions the committee was to answer were whether the high school's primary task was to prepare its students for life or for college, or whether high schools could accomplish both assignments at the same time. The puzzling issue of manual education was not placed on the agenda; neither was the suggestion, beginning to be made toward the close of the 1880s, to introduce vocational education.

Under the leadership of Charles W. Eliot, the longtime president of Harvard University, the ten men labored to produce in December of 1893 *Report of the Committee on Secondary School Studies*, which William T. Harris, then the U.S. commissioner of education and himself a signer, called "the most important educational document ever published in this country." For fifteen years, wrote Theodore Sizer, author of the most extensive and penetrating study of the report, the document dominated the educational debate.[1]

The committee's report set a benchmark for an era that had passed. It drew an impressive and convincing picture of secondary schooling as it had been known in Europe since the Reformation and in America from the days of the colonial Latin grammar schools and academies. It suggested that this academic program would serve equally well for preparation for college and life. The document revived the spirit of the Yale Report with its definition of secondary education as training and disciplining the mind through academic studies and argued that the approach should be retained. The committee had in fact written an epitaph instead of a blueprint for the future. With manual education already a much-discussed subject and vocational education dimly apparent on the horizon, the report could not satisfy schoolmen and parents who saw their questions and concerns ignored.

Part of the blame must be ascribed to the National Council of Education, which had barred the committee at the outset from looking into subjects not germane to college preparation. Part, also, was a result of the committee's membership, which included only two active public schoolmen: Oscar D. Robinson, principal of the public high school in Albany, New York, and John Tetlow, principal of the Boston Girls' Latin School. The two men represented schools that prided themselves on strong college-preparatory programs. Other members of the committee were university and college presidents, Eliot of Harvard, James Burrill Angell of Michigan, James Hutchins Baker of Colorado, Richard Henry Jesse of Missouri, and James Monroe Taylor of Vassar; the United States Commissioner of Education, William T. Harris; Professor Henry Churchill King of Oberlin; and a headmaster of a private preparatory school, James Cameron Mackenzie of Lawrenceville. These men had been selected by Nicholas Murray Butler, a philosophy professor at Columbia University and member of the council, not for their familiarity with public high schools—besides Robinson and Tetlow, only Harris and Baker had had classroom and administrative experience in public schools—but for their national reputations as "educational statesmen." Harris had taught and served as a superintendent of schools in St. Louis and Baker had been a public school principal in Maine and Colorado.

Given their assignment, the committee members did not analyze and solve but simply reflected the uncertainties and contradictions of the nationwide debate over the high school's purpose. They declared that

> the secondary schools of the United States, taken as a whole, do not exist for the purpose of preparing boys and girls for colleges. Only

an insignificant percentage of the graduates of these schools go to colleges or scientific schools. Their main function is to prepare for the duties of life that small proportion of all the children in the country—a proportion small in number, but very important to the welfare of the nation—who show themselves able to profit by an education prolonged to the eighteenth year, and whose parents are able to support them while they remain so long at school. . . . A secondary school programme intended for national use must therefore be made for those children whose education is not to be pursued beyond the secondary school.

Fairness demanded, the committee reasoned, that programs designed for those "whose education is not to be pursued beyond the secondary school" must nonetheless be of a quality that would allow every graduate to enter a university or college. The committee urged colleges and scientific schools, once they were satisfied with a high school's ability to offer such preparatory work, to accept "for admission to appropriate courses . . . any youth who has passed creditably through a good secondary school course, no matter to what group of subjects he may have mainly devoted himself."[2]

The committee never asked *whether* schools that saw their primary duty as preparing students for life should now develop an instructional program whose every sequence would meet the entrance requirements of colleges and universities. It took that for granted and discussed *how* a school should accomplish that. It suggested a curriculum of four courses from among which the student could choose: a classical course with two classical languages and one modern; a Latin-scientific course with one classical and one modern language; the modern languages course with two modern languages; and the English course with one foreign language.[3] The entire scheme was based on the assumption that life being more encompassing than college, preparation for life, if done as suggested, would automatically prepare for college.

In not pursuing the question *whether* the high school could prepare at one and the same time for life and for college, the committee assumed that the high school would continue the common-school tradition of American public education, albeit with allowances made for four different courses. As Colonel Francis W. Parker, principal of Cook County Normal School, pointed out, the committee had been unanimous in its conviction "that there should be no such thing as class education."[4] Its members believed that extending the common-school tradition into the high school years was the best defense against class education. By silently merging the high school's two functions into one, they hoped to accomplish this. Intent also upon bringing the secondary schools into closer co-operation with the colleges and universities and being preoccupied with the requirements for college preparation, committee members paid scarce attention to the then-current issues of the neglect of the nonacademic student and the demand for manual education. The committee's labors were, as the saying goes, "strictly academic."

Given the dominant role Charles W. Eliot played in guiding the committee's discussions and writing the report's final version, the Harvard president, too, must assume a fair share of blame for the report's faults. Much of his thinking derived from his experiences at the college. There he had broken with the tradition of a uniform curriculum for all and had introduced the elective principle. It was not necessary, he maintained, that all students had to study the same subjects. It was preferable to let them follow their own interests and inclinations, provided that each subject was marked by uniformly high methodological rigor and standards of academic attainment. Eliot then applied these views to the high school. Students need not study the same subjects, but they should study the subjects they had selected in the same way. Each subject included key topics that should be studied by all who took up that subject. It was thus possible, Eliot argued, to define criteria of method, topic, and attainment by which a curriculum suitable for all could be determined.[5] Eliot harked back to an earlier era in which secondary and collegiate studies, pursued side by side in parallel tracks, shared a common approach in the study of the liberal arts. He overlooked that by 1893 Americans had come to think of the high school as an advanced common school preceding the college, and of the college as a home for the select few. High school and college no longer were parallel institutions.

The Report and Its Critics

Critics of the report were quick to point out the committee's uncritical adoption of the theory of faculty psychology as expounded in the 1828 Yale Report. They did not accept the committee's notion that the "discipline of the mind" conferred on the subjects taught in high school "equal rank for the purposes of admission to college or scientific school." They doubted that, as the report held, the main subjects of the high school curriculum taught within the four recommended courses

> would all be taught consecutively and thoroughly, and would all be carried on in the same spirit; they would all be used for *training the powers of observation, memory, expression and reasoning*; and they would

all be good to that end, although differing among themselves in quality and substance. . . . Every youth who entered college would have spent four years in studying a few subjects thoroughly . . . it would make no difference which subjects he had chosen from the programme—he would have had four years of strong and effective *mental training.*[6]

Such doctrine, the critics said, showed little respect for individual subjects and placed emphasis exclusively on mental training.

In a minority report James H. Baker pointed out that the theory of the "equivalence of studies," which held that "one study is as good as another," would make any choice of subject meaningless. "Power comes through knowledge," wrote Baker, and "we cannot conceive of observation and memory in the abstract." The committee did not believe its own words, he suggested, because the faculty psychology it professed to believe in held that different faculties required different subjects for their training. If that was so, then it *did* make a difference which subjects students had chosen.[7]

Even harsher criticism came from those who censured the committee's concentration on subjects that were required for admission to college. Such single-mindedness, they charged, had prompted the committee to ignore drawing, music, manual training, bookkeeping, and stenography. Worst of all, it had led committee members to overlook the high school's function of preparing teachers for the elementary schools.[8] Perhaps these critics should have directed their barbs at the National Council of Education rather than at the committee, but they found in "college domination" a rallying cry they could not resist. Their most vociferous spokesman was G. Stanley Hall, eminent psychologist and president of Clark University in Worcester, Massachusetts. Hall turned around Eliot's phrase that preparing for life was the same as, or included, preparing for college and asserted that Eliot had said that preparing for college was the same as preparing for life. Referring to this inverted version of Eliot's statement as an "extraordinary fallacy" and adding to it two more—the dictum that all students, regardless of their educational plans, should be taught subjects in the same way, and the assumption that if taught equally well, all subjects were of equivalent value—Hall called on high school teachers to fight for their right to prepare their students for life, not just for college. He urged high school administrators to recognize differences in talent and conditions among their students and classify them accordingly for instructional purposes.[9]

Eliot responded that an early separation of college-bound from non-college-bound students was unfair and unjust to the students and unacceptable in a democratic society. Too few parents could at an early age foresee a student's opportunities and talents in his or her high school years. A society in which ethnic and racial integration was bound up with the common learning experience of the young could not give up the common-school ideal. And the equivalence of subjects pertained only to high school subjects considered for college admission.[10] The committee never suggested, Eliot wrote, that for that purpose Latin and, say, stenography or manual training were of equal value.

Articulation and Accreditation

The curricular questions concerning college admission having been the committee's central preoccupation, high school–college articulation and the accreditation of high schools by colleges were its central issues. Before the 1870s they had hardly mattered because roughly a little more than half of all students were enrolled in preparatory or subfreshmen classes of the very colleges and universities to which they had been admitted.[11] But institutions like the University of Michigan and the New England colleges did not have preparatory departments and admitted their students by examination. They depended for a sufficient supply and for the maintenance of their academic standards on the preparation of their students in academies and other preparatory schools. Other universities and colleges, such as the University of Wisconsin, had rid themselves of their pre-collegiate programs and were much concerned with the high schools in their states. The extraordinary increase of the public city high school population from nearly 23,000 students in 1876 to 116,000 in 1888 then made the problem even more pressing.

The problems of articulation and accreditation had become urgent when in 1870 the University of Michigan had abolished its entrance examinations for graduates of high schools that had been inspected and approved by faculty members. These graduates, when supplied by their principals with a certificate, were admitted to the university's regular college program. Other students continued to be examined for entrance in the traditional way. By 1880, 45 percent of all entering students had been admitted by certificate, and 55 by examination. By 1888 the university had accredited forty-six Michigan high schools, nineteen in Illinois, three in Minnesota, and one each in Pennsylvania, Ohio, and Indiana.[12]

In Georgia, the committee's report played a significant role in solving the problem of accreditation. In that state the nationwide debate over the high school had spurred the university's trustees to take the initiative in reasserting their institution's chartered obligation to visit and examine the state's schools and academies. As described in chapter 5, the university's concern with the state's secondary institutions had virtually ceased in 1837, and secondary education had for all intents and purposes become private. Sixty-eight years later, however, the trustees appointed a state agent "to examine the work and equipment of such high schools and academies as desire to be accredited by the University." The report of the Committee of Ten and the accreditation system, as pioneered in Michigan, were to serve as guide and example.

State agent Professor Joseph S. Stewart, appointed by the university, laid down the conditions under which an accredited secondary school must operate. A high school must offer a college-preparatory program of at least three years, following upon an elementary schooling of seven years. It had to employ at least two teachers. If it was to be accredited for science teaching, it had to be well equipped with a laboratory. If it was to offer credit work in history and English, it had to have a special library.[13] As required by the Committee of Ten, all of the three prescribed high school curricula had to include English, mathematics, and history. A student seeking an eventual bachelor of arts degree would have to take the high school classical course with Latin and Greek. A student seeking a bachelor of science degree would have to take the scientific course with one foreign language, physics, and geography, and one of the following: an additional year in a foreign language, botany, chemistry, physiology, or elementary agriculture. The third course, called the commercial course, substituted commercial instruction for Latin, Greek, or a science.[14]

Stewart faithfully followed the educational philosophy of the Committee of Ten. He assured Georgia's schoolmen that he was well aware that high schools did more than prepare students for college, and that the majority of their students followed other routes. He did not intend, he stated, "to force the high schools into mere preparatory schools." Nonetheless, they had to offer "the best possible training for all at that particular period of life and study"; that was the mental discipline approach of the Committee of Ten. Arguing that mental discipline could be applied to any subject, Stewart, like the committee before him, played down the importance of subject matter:

> The high schools will not therefore allow their curriculum to be biased by any arbitrary ironclad requirements of a college, but will seek to give the maximum amount of culture, mental power and skill and the colleges will adjust their requirements to meet the needs of the graduates of these schools.[15]

Doing this, the high schools would "improve the whole system." They would prepare better elementary teachers, who in turn would produce

113

better candidates for the high school, who, under the visiting authority of the university, would be better prepared for their university study.[16] With this pragmatic *tour de force* Stewart sought to bring Georgia's schoolmen under the sway of the Committee of Ten.

Stewart was caught in a bind that only partly was not of his making. On the one hand, he was keenly aware of Georgia's educational poverty and the university's long neglect of public education. In 1904 Georgia's public high schools prepared no more than 784 students for college; Illinois had prepared 3,900, Michigan 2,700, and New York 11,000. On the other hand, he had committed himself and the state's schoolmen to the Committee of Ten's philosophy of mental discipline. Could the suggestions of the committee report really be applied to Georgia? Would not the state's high schools have to increase substantially their overall enrollments in order to be able to support the college-preparatory work?

Stewart did not flinch from that conclusion. He advised introducing courses in agriculture, domestic art, economy, and science, and manual training. These "practical" courses would broaden the base from which could be drawn an increased number of applicants for college admission. If asked about the disciplinary value of these non-college-preparatory courses, he could point only to the Committee of Ten's passing remark that

> if it were desired to provide more amply for subjects thought to have practical importance in trade or the useful arts, it would be easy to provide options in such subjects for some of the science contained in the third and fourth years of the 'English' programme.

He did not ask how this comported with the quest for mental discipline.[17]

For members of the Committee of Ten, accreditation was the main avenue by which its proposals for the articulation of high school and college could be realized, but it was not to remain the only avenue. Columbia's Nicholas Murray Butler, moving force behind the committee's original appointment and its frequent host at Columbia University, became the chief proponent of what in 1900 was to emerge as the College Entrance Examination Board. The key concern in his effort was to move college and secondary school administrators to accept the notion of uniform college entrance requirements that could serve as yardsticks for academic standards across the nation. Although the board came to be firmly established in the northeast and mid-Atlantic states, it never did succeed in completely supplanting the certificate and accreditation system that had its strength in the Midwest and West.[18]

Challenges Evaded and Opportunities Missed

What, then, are we to conclude about the historical significance of the work performed by the Committee of Ten? By representing metropolitan and largely collegiate interests and by ignoring the concerns of school administrators and local school boards, the committee misperceived the situation in which the country's high schools found themselves. In arguing that a college-preparatory program was as suitable for the student intent upon entering business, industrial, or agricultural pursuits as for the student preparing for university entrance, committee members closed their eyes to the fact that most Americans had come to view their schools as advanced common schools and servants of community interests. The committee members had listened to their friends and colleagues in the preparatory schools and colleges and then designed all of the high school's courses for college preparation. As they sacrificed Greek for all but the classical course, they asserted that they had sought a middle ground between the classicists and the modernists. But then they let it be known that the two modern courses were "in practice . . . distinctly inferior to the other two." No wonder that their critics shouted "college domination."

The committee's key assumption, never clearly articulated, was that the American high school had to carry on its role as advanced common school in an exclusively academic tradition. But the school they envisaged was not a common school; it was designed, as they themselves had said, for an elite, and its curriculum consisted of four different courses. In their social views, committee members sought to fuse an American conception of social democracy with a European tradition of an academically educated higher bourgeoisie. If there was to be an elite in society, it was to be a meritocracy based on academic qualifications that were to embrace what the English writer C. P. Snow would later call the two cultures: the culture of modern science and the culture of the traditional humanities. Cultural democracy, then, was the committee's ideal, an ideal that meant little or nothing to those who were beginning to seek entrance to the high school and who saw the promise of American life in economic and social rather than in cultural democracy.

What the committee deliberately disregarded and excluded from its consideration was that for most Americans the battle over the high school was not one of the classics versus the modern sciences but one of academic culture versus practical training—the well-known confrontation between those who wanted to prepare for college and those who wanted to prepare for life. The committee also ignored the social and curricular implications of the growing demand of parents and schoolmen to allow an

115

ever-increasing percentage of high-school-aged youngsters into the schools. It brushed off the suggestion, often voiced by its critics, that mental discipline, while a proven approach to academic study, might not be the best educational philosophy to guide students and teachers in manual and vocational education.

Finally, despite or perhaps because of Eliot's fervid defense of an undifferentiated student body, committee members did not seriously explore the meaning and implications for the schools of specialization in modern life. Eliot had insisted on teaching subjects in the same way to all students because, he said, the European practice of classifying students as "future peasants, mechanics, trades-people, merchants, and professional people" was unacceptable in American democracy.[19] In that, of course, he was right. But as high-minded and socially responsible as this proposition was, it failed to entertain seriously the opportunities and challenges of extending secondary schooling beyond the traditional training of the mind to the training of the hand. It failed likewise to consider the differences inherent in the subject matter of manual training for woodwork, metalwork, and other media. This being the case, the committee could not come to grips with the significance of industrial specialization for education and had no way of confronting, least of all resolving, the most fundamental question that industrialization posed for American education: Was there a chance for the American common school to survive into the twentieth century and extend its reach into the high school years, or would industrialization with its attendant specialization create new, and deepen existing, social divisions in the body politic?

If the committee thought that it might contain the threat of social divisions by confining them to a choice of curricula within a common school, it would soon have to realize that the public secondary school, unlike either elementary school or college, would be confronted with the specter of many different kinds of specialized schools, both public and private, that pursued a variety of educations, only few of which could be called academic. The issue to which the committee closed its eyes was that an exclusively academic concern for the mind was to give way to a practical desire for the training of hand and body. Thus it was, as I wrote at the beginning of this chapter, that the report of the Committee of Ten reflected but did not resolve the high school's problems. It summed up the school's past, but it did not become a guide for its future.

10

From Manual to Vocational Education

The Beginnings of Vocational Education

During the first two decades of the new century, high school administrators sought to come to grips with the contradictory messages of the Committee of Ten and the advocates of practical instruction. The schoolmen's course was unsteady, their voices confused. Some defended the academic tradition so forcefully upheld by the Committee of Ten; others embraced manual training but tried to stay clear of vocational education; still others saw the former as but a platform from which to launch the latter. Most were aware that a momentous, revolutionary change was in the offing and that they were engaged in a debate that would determine the course of American secondary education for decades.

Vocational education challenged centuries of tradition. From the days of ancient Greece, academic learning in the Western world had been a labor of the mind, not of the hand. In the United States as well as in Europe, secondary schooling had rested on book learning and had concerned itself with general academic skills. Even when, as in physical and manual education, skills of body and hands were prized, they were valued for their contribution to general bodily agility and health and manual dexterity. Vocational education, however, was training for particular trades. It was not considered to be a scholastic task. It was carried out in apprenticeships and on the job.

When by the beginning of the 1920s the battle for vocational education was over, the advocates of vocational education had seen to it that in the country's public high schools commercial and trade-specific instruction had taken the place of manual training. In large cities, vocationalists had introduced public technical and industrial high schools. In many of the states, they had established new forms of school-work relationships through part-time continuation schools and cooperative programs with local industries. But hardly anywhere had these developments followed the same paths. Local traditions and current economic and social conditions had created variations on a theme. In different localities opposition from within the school systems as well as from without had led to different strategies and outcomes. And, most vexing of all, there was rarely consensus as to the ultimate or momentary success or failure of a given policy or school.

Outsiders as well as schoolmen had played a role in the propagation of vocational education. In 1902, for example, a committee of the Society for the Promotion of Engineering Education had taken up this cause. The committee expressed appreciation for the work done by public high schools in the manual and industrial arts, homemaking, commercial, and agricultural classes, and it lauded the manual training schools. Graduates of these programs, the committee said, were "well fitted to go at once into any practical trade or business and learn it quickly and effectively." But this was not enough. Monotechnic or trade schools should supplement, though not displace, manual training schools and art education in the public schools and teach students "the underlying principles of one or two trades thoroughly, as well as the most improved commercial practice." These trade schools were operated by textile industries and machine trades in connection with their industrial work. Others, like the New York Trade School, opened in 1881, and the Technical High School in Cincinnati, opened in 1886, were owned and run by municipalities; again others by public libraries, scientific, technical and trade journals, or private persons.[1] Being trade- and occupation-specific, these schools enjoyed the support of the National Association of Manufacturers, which, during the new century's first decade, became known as an ardent champion of commercial and technical training.

Concern over international trade competition, especially from Germany, had increased pressure on the public schools to add trade-specific and commercial instruction to their manual training classes and, in the larger cities, had resulted in moves to open public trade, technical, and industrial high schools. These schools, however, did not address the problem of providing vocational education for youths already at work. To meet that situation, the National Society for the Promotion of Industrial Education, founded in 1906, persuaded the National Association of Manufacturers to consider the introduction of publicly supported day and evening continuation schools on the German pattern as well as of programs of cooperative education, sponsored jointly by school systems and industries. This initiative in turn helped overcome the American Federation of Labor's opposition to trade education. The federation remained opposed "to any system of public instruction privately controlled," but in 1910 it endorsed public continuation schools, union-sponsored supplemental trade schools, and public trade schools.[2] The advocates of vocational education were on the march.

One issue that was most profoundly to influence the development of vocational education in the United States was its administration. Should vocational education be administered by local and state boards of public school systems or by separately established vocational education boards? When the debate began in the 1910s, this question quickly turned highly political. Many Americans were wary of a dual system of public education in which schools for general education were administered separately from vocational schools or other trade-related educational settings. They believed this would inevitably reflect and deepen society's class divisions. Their opponents argued that only a separately administered system could do justice to the specific demands of trade training and assure that it would be neither diluted nor sabotaged by the academic interests of public school administrators. The advocates of separate or dual control had an early advantage. Eventually, however, sentiment in favor of what was called unit control gained the upper hand, and state departments of public instruction won out over lay boards of vocational education.[3] By the beginning of the 1920s, the die was cast. Under the watchful eyes of the schoolmen, vocational education was on its way to becoming an integral part of public education.

The Douglass Commission in Massachusetts

The first step to investigate the possibilities of publicly supported vocational education had been taken in Massachusetts. In 1905, Governor William I. Douglass had appointed the State Commission on Industrial and Technical Education. In its report of the next year, the commission referred to workingmen and workingwomen as well as to "broader-minded students of education" who wondered whether vocational training, hitherto offered only to the "feeble-minded, . . . wayward and vicious children" and former slaves, could not, by "preventing as well as curing juvenile delinquency, and . . . improving the social conditions of white as well as black children" equally benefit the "higher orders of mind."

Manufacturers, the commission stated, wanted skilled workmen who possessed "industrial intelligence, . . . mental power to see beyond the task which occupies the hand for the moment." "Evidently due to a misapprehension," commission members commented, labor unions were opposed to private trade schools because they feared that their establishment might lead to lower wages. The public schools, the commissioners complained, "were too exclusively literary." Their programs of manual training were not sufficient for the purpose because they were offered as cultural subjects, "a sort of mustard relish, an appetizer . . . to be conducted without reference to any industrial end." The commission recommended that "the elements of industrial training, agriculture, domestic and mechanical sciences . . . be taught in the public schools." To avoid interference with the school authorities the committee members spoke out against establishing a separate authority to direct this activity. But they advocated the creation of industrial schools completely separate from the public school system. The commissioners thus neatly straddled the divisive issue of unit or dual control.

Aware that according to the U.S. commissioner of education's report of 1904, female students accounted for 58.2 percent of the public secondary school population, the commissioners suggested that these young women should be prepared in school "to earn a respectable living wage." Reflecting then-current notions of "appropriate" female employment, they added that "the attempt should be made to fit her [the student] so that she can and will enter those industries which are most closely allied to the home." They emphasized homemaking as "that vocation in which all other vocations have their root," and asked that instruction be given in "the laws of sanitation, in the purchase, preparation, and care of food, and in the care of children, that the home may be a home, and not merely a house."[4]

In 1906 subsequent legislation set up a state system of public industrial schools separate from and independent of local public school systems and separately administered by a newly created commission. This commission, however, soon bogged down in its labors, and three years later was absorbed by the State Board of Education. The result was that Massachusetts developed a mixed form of public education. For its state public school system it operated on a unit system, but the locally established public vocational schools preserved their separate identity. In the following years, state supported vocational schools were established that offered training in agriculture, home economics, and industrial pursuits. As the U.S. commissioner of education was to point out, these vocational schools resembled in their function the normal schools of the nineteenth century. The normal schools had been created as secondary vocational schools for prospective teachers. The Massachusetts vocational schools were to fulfill the same mission for future artisans, craftsmen, and housewives.[5]

Vocational Education and the Wisconsin Idea

When in 1902 Charles P. Cary began his nineteen-year reign as Wisconsin's superintendent of public instruction, the state was about to enter a period of hard-fought debates over the future of its high schools. Caught in the crossfire of advocates for university preparatory training and of proponents for vocational education, the state's schoolmen, by and large, followed the leadership of the conservative and outspoken Cary. Cary firmly opposed everything that detracted in one way or another from what he considered the high school's proper task of preparing its graduates for responsible citizenship. He vented his anger at the college-dominated leadership of the Committee of Ten, which, he said, had taken a one-sided view and had short-circuited the question of how to recognize the different needs of college-preparatory and other students. These leaders, he wrote in his report for 1904, were "commonly college presidents" who could not help but assume that that training is best "that best fits for the college they represent." Such narrow concentration on college preparation, Cary continued, was "almost as much to be deplored as rank vocationalism."

Cary saw vocationalism as a mistaken and disastrous outcome of years of manual training. Manual training, he said, all too easily had degenerated "into the teaching of trades, or occupations" and had produced "an oversupply of half-baked applicants for low grade positions at nominal salaries." The function of the high school was "to prepare its graduates for life, and this means a generous foundation for vocation, training for citizenship, and such beginnings of culture as four years of study upon such material . . . can bring about."[6] But four years later Cary declared that the manual and commercial training courses offered in many of the state's high schools had indeed laid that "generous foundation for vocation" he had called for. The outlook for this work therefore was "excellent," and the work itself a demonstration of "the entire feasibility of the union of industrial and academic training in the public high school."[7] For Cary, manual and commercial education had come to stay, but vocational education was to be kept outside the pale.

Wisconsin's legislators, however, did not share Cary's opposition to vocational education. In 1907 they passed a law that permitted any city or school district containing within its limits a city to establish or take over and maintain a trade school. Under this law the city of Milwaukee took over the Milwaukee School of Trades. In the meantime in rural Menomonie in northern Dunn County, the initiative of a local businessman had led to a remarkable flowering of manual and vocational training. In 1891, James H. Stout had opened the Stout Manual Training School.

When eight years later the legislature authorized the establishment of county training schools to prepare graduates of eight-year schools as teachers for rural elementary schools, Stout offered the building of the Manual Training School for this work. Teacher training thus was accepted as a form of vocational education. Two years later the legislature authorized county agricultural schools for agricultural and domestic science and general education. With the opening of the Dunn County School of Agriculture and Domestic Science in Menomonie the next year, the vocational emphasis in county agricultural schools became pronounced. As the country training school taught pedagogy, so the county agriculture school offered blacksmithing, carpentry, and horticulture. In 1908 a newly opened trade school added bricklaying and plumbing. Three years later, Stout Institute, the complex of schools founded and supported by Stout, was transferred to the state and placed under the supervision of the newly created State Board of Industrial Education.[8]

The Board of Industrial Education was the brainchild of a legislature whose members were motivated by fear of international economic competition rather than the desire to stop the dropout problem of American high schools. The legislators had charged a commission, chaired by Charles McCarthy, the head of Wisconsin's Legislative Reference Department, to investigate the vocational education systems of other American states and of Germany. In his report, McCarthy stated that Germany's success in industrial production and international trade was due primarily to its extensive system of industrial, technical, and agricultural schools. All of these schools had been designed to fit the industrial conditions of their immediate surroundings, and particularly important were the part-time continuation schools. Supplementing the apprenticeship system for youngsters who had left the public schools at age fourteen, continuation schools of various types offered industrial, mercantile, and general manual instruction for both boys and girls. They appeared to hold the key to the Germans' success.

McCarthy's commission emphasized that the Germans had placed the direction of continuation and other vocational schools in the hands of local committees of businessmen, manufacturers, and employees. Thus, McCarthy wrote, they avoided being "hampered by the theoretical standpoint which inevitably would result if the teachers or school men had it all in their own hands."[9] Impressed by these remarks, Wisconsin legislators combined elements of the German system with those of the "Wisconsin Idea" of university outreach and extension. In 1911 they established the State Board of Industrial Education, its members to be appointed by the governor and to consist of three employers, three employees, the state superintendent of public instruction, and the deans of the University of Wisconsin College of Engineering and of the Extension Division. The superintendent was to oversee curricular matters; the board kept to itself control over the allocation of funds. On the local level, industrial schools were to be governed by boards of industrial education, each consisting of two employers and two employees chosen by the city school board and the local superintendent of schools *ex officio.* The legislature had crafted a compromise between dual and unit control that was not unlike that of the Massachusetts arrangements of 1909.

By 1913 twenty-four of the thirty eligible cities had received matching grants. In the newly established continuation schools students spent half of their instructional time of five hours per week in academic subjects and the other half in vocational work. In Fond du Lac, for example, the boys were taught bench work and drawing; the girls cooking, sewing, and dressmaking.[10] The compromise over control, however, brought continued friction between Cary and the State Board of Industrial education. The board controlled the statewide administration of vocational education, but the superintendent managed to run the local schools through their teachers and administrators. As the anonymous author in the *Wisconsin Blue Book* of 1958 put it, "During the first few years the vocational school system was a disappointment because it was controlled by the same people who had failed to meet the problem prior to 1911."[11] Cary's abrasive personality and McCarthy's single-minded advocacy of an independent system did not make for a smooth cooperation.

McCarthy, who during these years made his reputation as the chief propagator of the "Wisconsin Idea," never gave up his goal of a complete separation of the two school systems. Louis Reber, dean of university extension and a member of the State Board of Industrial Education, supported him in this. Reber maintained that no instructor could "be really efficient in teaching shop mathematics . . . if he has not done shop work in a working plant." Neither he nor McCarthy placed great stock in manual arts teachers who represented the "theoretical standpoint" of the schoolmen, preferring instead that skilled workmen train in short courses for their new work as vocational school teachers.[12] On the other side, Cary repeated his charges that noneducators were incompetent to supervise education, and that manufacturers and politicians should not be permitted to control the schools. A dual system, he protested, meant a caste system and would destroy U.S. democracy.[13]

Cary, however, fought a losing battle, and the supporters of dual control gained ground in Wisconsin. When in 1917 Congress passed the Smith-Hughes Act, initiating federal aid to vocational schools, the Wisconsin legislature designated the State Board of Industrial Education as the State Board of Vocational Education. By giving the board sole power over the distribution of federal funds, the legislature granted it complete administrative autonomy from the public school system. John A. Callahan, the state's director of vocational education, replaced Cary as the Board of Vocational Education's executive officer. To make matters even more painful for Cary, four years later Callahan defeated him in his re-election bid for the superintendency, largely because Cary had antagonized the state's vocational educators.[14] Wisconsin had become one of the few states in which vocational education was administered and directed independently from the system of public schools.

The Battle in Illinois

In Illinois, the takeover in 1897 of the Chicago Manual Training School by the University of Chicago had signaled the acceptance of manual education by the university world. State Superintendent of Public Instruction Joseph H. Freeman now encouraged manual training in the public schools. There was, he wrote "such a harmonious blending of the useful and practical with the higher intellectual culture as to make manual labor an aid in disciplining and energizing the intellect and character."[15] His successor, Alfred Bayliss, was not so sure. In 1904 he expressed discomfiture with the high school's "vague" and unresolved curricular situation, which was characterized, he said, by a search for "a common center of studies about which may be grouped electives so as to provide well organized plans of study various enough to meet the needs of all high schools and some of them so arranged that the colleges shall suffer no loss."[16]

In 1912 Superintendent Francis G. Blair suggested that the high schools go beyond manual training for boys and beyond the household arts and commercial subjects for girls and introduce vocational education. Manual training had not stemmed the drain of students from the classrooms, and vocational subjects, "useful for practical purposes," now were needed. "In no other way," so read a committee report, "can the higher phases of public education hold their own against the competition of the trade school." The committee recommended vocational courses for the speaking and writing professions, for science and medicine, for farming, for building trades and manufacturing, for business, and for "the affairs of the well-ordered home."[17]

One year later, two years of vocational courses were offered in sixteen of Chicago's twenty-one high schools.[18] In the state, the picture was mixed. Manual education still dominated in nearly one-third of all high schools that offered classes in commercial subjects and in the roughly one-fifth that offered home economics. Vocational education in the form of agriculture could be found in ten percent and normal work in 7.5 percent of the state's high schools.[19]

It was not Illinois schoolmen but Chicago's powerful business men of the Commercial Club who had taken the first steps to introduce vocational education in the public schools. In 1911 they hired former Chicago school superintendent and then-member of a textbook firm Edwin G. Cooley as their educational adviser and sent him to Europe, especially Germany, to report on the progress there of vocational education. Upon his return, Cooley submitted an urgent plea for the establishment of vocational schools under auspices separate from the public schools and "in closest possible relation to the occupations." Males and females from fourteen to eighteen years of age should attend compulsory part-time continuation and two-year full-time vocational, commercial, homemaking, and agricultural schools. Cooley emphasized that this would require extension of the compulsory education period beyond age fourteen, and that these schools were to supplement, not replace, the current public schools. To convince his audiences that these schools were not to be devoted to narrow hand and technical training, Cooley pointed to the Munich vocational continuation schools, under Superintendent Georg Kerschensteiner, which were public schools independent of and supplementary to the general public schools. They offered specific trade training together with general and citizenship education. Cooley urged that Chicago establish such schools to offer an education that "should aim at developing the man as well as the worker."[20]

The members of the Commercial Club readily adopted Cooley's views. They were already acquainted with Kerschensteiner through Harvard education professor Paul Hanus, who had highly lauded the German's emphasis on the combination of "good general education, good technical education, and good education in the rights and duties of citizenship."[21] The club had hosted Kerschensteiner prior to Cooley's return and, impressed by his presentation, had had his speech published in the *School Review.* Kerschensteiner had argued that just as it was the duty of the state to assure the general academic training of those ready to benefit from it, so it was also the state's duty to offer vocational training to its hand-minded youngsters and citizens. Neither general academic nor vocational training could be left to private industry and business. This was the German version of dual control in public education: a system of public schools for general and academic education from the elementary schools to the *gymnasia* and universities, and a parallel system of public vocational training leading from the continuation schools to technical schools and technical universities. Contrary to what many Americans assumed, Ker-

125

schensteiner emphasized, this was not a class-bound structure but a double-track system that in each track permitted attainment of a university-level education.[22] Except for the reference to higher education, this was also the kind of education Cooley proposed for the public schools of Chicago.

The supporters of vocational education in Chicago took comfort from the apparent success of the vocational system in Wisconsin. There, as we just saw, continuation schools had opened in several cities and, of the four types of vocational schools, had drawn the greatest amount of attention. Chicagoans recognized that part-time continuation schools were less expensive than full-time general schools, that they could supply industry with skilled and disciplined labor, and that dual control would prevent the sacrifice of practical training to general education. With the Commercial Club as their spearhead, Chicago's business interests came out in full support of Cooley's proposal, which was introduced as the Cooley bill in the legislature in 1913.

In the political battles that followed, the Chicago business community faced labor and various reform groups. At issue was dual control. For labor and reform groups such as the City Club, it signified the creation of clear and explicit class lines in public education. A separate vocational education board composed of "practical men and women" meant the subservience of public education to industry. It brought a divided school system in which the vocational part would teach its students only how to work, not how to think.[23] When, after its initial defeat in 1913, the Cooley bill was reintroduced two years later, John Dewey observed that the difference between the two parties "is not so much narrowly educational as it is profoundly political and social."[24] He warned against "the increasing tendency toward stratification of classes in this country" and protested that "few have dreamed that the day was already at hand when responsible and influential persons would urge that the public-school system should recognize the separation as an accomplished fact."[25]

David Snedden, the Massachusetts commissioner of vocational education, entered the fray and replied that dual or unit control was "not fundamental at all." The real issues concerned the aims, methods, organization and administration of vocational education:

> Such so-called dual control, as one finds in Wisconsin or as it existed in Massachusetts from 1906 to 1910, simply represents an attempt to put in immediate charge of a special form of education a group of persons who are primarily interested in its successful development, and who may be able to bring it to the point of view of practical men in that field.[26]

Dewey brushed Snedden's words aside. He spoke directly to the educational issue that concerned him.

> I object to regarding as vocational education any training which does not have as its supreme regard the development of such intelligent initiative, ingenuity and executive capacity as shall make workers, as far as may be, the masters of their own industrial fate. . . .
> I am utterly opposed to giving the power of social predestination, by means of narrow trade-training, to any group of fallible men no matter how well intentioned they may be.[27]

In the battle over vocational education the key question was whether vocational instruction should be introduced as part of a program of general education or as specific activity separate from the main academic curriculum. Conducted in the language of unit versus dual control, the issue was easily understood by politicians as well as educators.

The battle was fought and decided on political grounds. Here, Dewey's words added luster to the effective lobbying of the Chicago Federation of Labor, the Illinois State Teachers Association, the Illinois State Federation of Labor, and the City Club. These groups defeated the bill again in 1915, and once more in 1917. When in February of that year, Congress passed the Smith-Hughes Vocational Education Act and established a separate Federal Board of Vocational Education, it nonetheless left to the discretion of each state whether it would adopt unit or dual control. Eventually, thirty-three states adopted unit control and placed the administration of their vocational education programs under state boards of education. Fifteen states opted for various forms of dual control; they either appointed a separate board of vocational education or enlarged the state education board to form a board of vocational education.[28] Of the dual-control states, Wisconsin was to remain the most outstanding example of a successfully operating system.

Maxwell's Fight in New York City

In New York, schoolmen took their cue from the resounding silence of the Committee of Ten on the subject of manual education. Melville Dewey, the Regents' secretary, predicted undesirable consequences would follow the introduction of manual work in the schools. He shared Charles W. Eliot's worries about the growing tendency to place students in specialized curricular tracks. In 1893 he seconded the Committee of Ten's recommendation not to segregate college-preparatory work from other

127

programs. He warned the Regents that to ask students to commit themselves to a particular high school program would only turn them away from school; rather, students should be able to enroll in courses best suited for them and to leave such courses at any time without loss of credit. The present system, Dewey told the Regents, resembled railroad tracks walled off from each other, the one leading from New York to Philadelphia, the other from New York to Washington, forcing the passenger headed for Philadelphia to go back to New York if he changed his mind and decided to go to Washington instead.[29] John Kennedy, superintendent of schools in Batavia, New York, agreed and argued that the non-college-preparatory parts of the high school curriculum, however great their practical value, were but "tid-bits at the table," and should not be accepted as part of college preparation.[30] But the contributors to a symposium on business education maintained that for the 95 percent of students who did not intend to go to college, it was essential to have available a serious, substantial, and academically demanding program of business education, including instruction in bookkeeping, shorthand, typewriting, and domestic science.[31]

Faced with these conflicting views, the Regents decided by 1900 to include business subjects and manual training in their examinations. Five years later they reported that "more than 40 high schools had established four-year commercial courses and more than 70 had incorporated into their academic curriculum not less than five of the business subjects outlined in the syllabus."[32] In 1907 the New York State Department of Public Instruction began to establish separate industrial and trade schools under its supervision.[33] Practical education for business and industry had by then become an accepted part of secondary education.

In New York City, Superintendent William Henry Maxwell, serving in that post from 1898 to 1917, fought a similar battle of opposition and eventual accommodation. He insisted strenuously that high schools existed to prepare students "for the higher intellectual walks of life." If they were to offer commercial courses at all, he argued, these had to be, as the Committee of Ten had demanded, on a college-preparatory level. Aware that the tide was running against him and anxious to preempt a takeover by the vocationalists, in 1902 he organized two specialized high schools, the High School of Commerce and the Girls Technical High School. These schools, Maxwell expected, would offer a curriculum of four years of commercial arithmetic and law, banking, insurance, modern languages, international commerce, finance, and markets, and a fifth college-level year as well. It would be more demanding than the two-year commercial courses in stenography, typing, and bookkeeping of the city's regular high schools. Public schools, he stated, should not "assume the burden which for three thousand years has been regarded as the duty of the manufacturer—the training of his artisans." Nor should they listen to "the semicharitable views of the philanthropists . . . who deprecate the all too prevalent ambition [of the children of the poor] to enter clerical pursuits or the professions" and assign these children to industrial or vocational instruction. Public high schools should stick to their own expertise and teach academic subjects and train intellectual skills.[34]

But Maxwell could not hold the line forever. With the opening of public vocational schools after 1907, vocational educators went on the offensive. They tried to discredit the manual training schools as "cultural" or "highly technical or semi-professional." They rejected the term *industrial school* because it implied a "penal disciplinary character."[35] Maxwell made the best of what was for him a bad situation. He protested that manufacturers and philanthropists took credit for trade schools and vocational education. Instead, he asserted, "the educators, who for twenty years, through good report and bad report, through ridicule and 'detraction rude,' have fought for manual training in the schools, are the logical advocates, the true pioneers, of industrial education."[36] Maxwell wanted to persuade New Yorkers that vocational or industrial education was not the antithesis of manual education but its natural outgrowth.

Unavoidably, dual versus unit control became an issue in Maxwell's battle. Maxwell disliked the vocational educators' allies, the "manufacturers and philanthropists" who served as spokesmen for the National Association of Manufacturers. He accused them of regarding public school trade and vocational education under dual control as but a means of assuring for themselves an adequate supply of skilled labor at no or little expense. The National Association of Manufacturers did not dispute these points. Its spokesmen said that they saw in trade education in the public schools under dual control an acceptable alternative to the dying apprentice system and a preferred way of "properly protect[ing] [business] from the withering blight of organized labor."[37] This, Maxwell knew, also explained their support of private trade schools, which had strongly upheld the right to work and, in labor circles, had acquired the reputation of training strikebreakers. None of these objectives, Maxwell knew, could be supported on pedagogical grounds.

Maxwell's pedagogical principles kept him from openly applauding the educational policies of the association's great antagonist, the American Federation of Labor. The federation had strongly resisted the introduction of vocational or trade education under dual control, though in 1908 it expressed its willingness to listen to

great educators, representatives of organized labor and persons engaged in general social service, who advocate industrial education
as a common right to be provided by general taxation and kept under the control of the whole people. They suggest a system that will
make the apprentice a skilled craftsman in all the branches of his
trade.[38]

One key provision of any such scheme was that it had to fall under the
unit system of control. Maxwell could not but agree with and sympathize
with labor's position.

The 1910s, then, witnessed the integration of vocational education into
New York's school system. The National Society for the Promotion of Industrial Education took the initiative. Representatives of the American
Federation of Labor and of the National Association of Manufacturers
joined efforts with Maxwell; Andrew Sloan Draper, the State commissioner of education; Mayor John Purroy Mitchell; Nicholas Murray Butler,
president of Columbia University; Dean Herman Schneider of the University of Cincinnati; and Charles A. Prosser of the National Society for
the Promotion of Industrial Education. The final agreement provided a
compromise: representatives of the American Federation of Labor and
the National Association of Manufacturers were to advise city educational
authorities, which they began to do in 1915. By this time, a concerted effort was already under way to devise a comprehensive program of vocational education that would include continuation schools and cooperative
plans as well as the commercial, home economics, and vocational classes
in regular and specialized high schools. Vocational education had become a permanent part of New York City's public schools. Maxwell had
yielded as gracefully as he could.[39]

11

The Legacy of Vocational Education

Continuation Schools and Cooperative Programs

The vocational education movement reached its full strength when it began in a substantial way to introduce continuation schools and cooperative plans. As we have seen in the case of New York City, by 1915 vocationalists had managed to gain the cooperation of erstwhile opponents among secondary school educators with manufacturers and labor leaders. There and in other cities and states opponents of vocational education in the public high schools preferred continuation schools and cooperative programs of schools and industry. Such arrangements freed the public high schools from installing shops, kitchens, and other specialized working space. Even more to the point, artisans, master craftsmen, and others experienced in their trade were the instructors, and high school teachers could concentrate on academic and citizenship education.

Continuation programs had gained their first toehold in Cincinnati, Ohio, where in 1906 they had grown out of apprentice training begun in several manufacturing establishments. The apprentices received supplemental shop instruction in public school evening classes. This arrangement, however, suffered from high dropout rates because the apprentices gave their primary loyalty and effort to their employers rather than to the schools. The school system hence looked for an alternative, and in 1909 initiated a daytime continuation school program under the supervision of the school board appointed Committee on Continuation Schools. When the Ohio legislature in 1910 passed a compulsory-attendance child labor law, the continuation program began to thrive. This happened even before Georg Kerschensteiner visited the city, though the friends of continuation schooling had long been familiar with his published writings.[1]

Besides having inaugurated one of the earliest continuation programs, Cincinnati also had pioneered with the introduction of school-industry cooperation. Enrollments in the manual education classes of the city's public high schools, in shop work for boys and in cooking for girls, threatened to outpace the city's public school budget. Superintendent Franklin Dyer, looking for a less expensive and more effective way of high school vocational education, adopted a plan Professor Herman Schneider had devised in 1906 at the University of Cincinnati. Schneider's engineering students alternately studied and worked half-days in local factories. That cooperative arrangement had caught national attention and had been copied for high school use in 1908 in Fitchburg, Massachusetts. There, after staying the first year at school, for the next three years students spent half of their time at paid work. In 1909 Dyer adopted the plan for the Cincinnati high schools, and added it to the continuation school program that had begun in the same year.[2]

In Pennsylvania, vocational education had begun as early as 1869 in evening classes with the opening of the Philadelphia Artisans' Night School. Its curriculum supplemented that of the elementary schools with an academic-scientific program for apprentices and journeymen of eighteen years and older, and was in turn supplemented in 1885 and 1890 with the daytime manual training high schools of central and northeastern Philadelphia. By 1897 Artisans' Night School had added an extended academic program and was renamed Evening High School. Nine years later the daytime Philadelphia Trades School and its two evening cousins were in full swing. Minimum age for students was fifteen, and far more chose to enroll in the evening than in the day schools. These public trade schools, rather than the manual training schools of 1885 and 1890, then, marked the beginnings of specific vocational training on the secondary level in Philadelphia.

Regular daytime continuation schooling, however, did not get underway until 1916, when Pennsylvania passed its child labor act. This law made attendance at continuation schooling for at least eight hours a week mandatory for children between the ages of fourteen and sixteen who had left school and gone to work. Those of high school grade attended their continuation classes in the trade school. It was the compulsory school attendance feature of the child labor law that had brought about the switch from evening to daytime continuation schooling.[3]

A Victory of Sorts

With the passage of the Smith-Hughes Act in 1917 vocationalists had won their battle for nationwide recognition of vocational education as a legitimate part of public secondary schooling. The victory, however, had been strongly contested by many of the country's best-known educators, particularly those in the secondary schools. The Committee of Ten had virtually ignored all practical subjects, and so had the high school educators in the tradition of the people's college. They continued to believe that a high school served local industrial and business needs best by concentrating on a heavily academic curriculum. Faculty members at the manual training high schools in Philadelphia, many of them graduates of Philadelphia Central, also placed increasing emphasis on academic subjects. Just like Central, they wanted their graduates to be prepared for college as well as for a vocation.

When, by 1898, as a concession to parents who asked for vocational training, Central had introduced a commercial course, it had done so because white-collar office work suited the sociocultural aspirations of its students, parents, and teachers. In 1912, when it absorbed Central Manual Training School and, after three more years, Philadelphia Trades School as well, it transformed the trade school's staff and students into its industrial department. By 1919 Central had managed to absorb vocational education as one curricular track among several. Together with academic, commercial, and mechanic and commercial arts education, industrial education was now a minor and the least prestigious part of Central's work.[4]

In all these instances vocational education suffered from what Fritz Ringer has called the "generalist shift,"

> the observable tendency of newly established "practical" or "applied" educational programmes and institutions to take on a more generalist and academic character, largely in response to the sociocultural aspirations of teachers and parents.[5]

When that happened, the more academic ambiance of the home economics and clerical-commercial subjects tended to pull many students away from the shops of the industrial programs, and high school educators tended to support that trend. California provided an example of this kind. Traditional high school educators sought to undercut or at least delay the vocationalists' plans by advocating clerical education. With clerical training they expected to prepare boys for business careers. By the turn of the century, however, when rapidly increasing numbers of girls took courses in the routine skills of shorthand and typewriting, clerical education lost some of its academic and managerial luster. Educators replaced it with commercial education and hoped thereby to attract more boys with classes in salesmanship and retail occupations. Vocational reformers did not appreciate these sentiments and, as Harvey Kantor reports, "even refused to acknowledge commercial education as an important part of the vocational movement."[6] Many California educators also remained loyal to the recommendations of the Committee of Ten that a high school education—any high school education—prepare its students for college entrance. Thus in the state's polytechnic high schools, they offered not only manual and commercial instruction but also a more practical education in scientific and technical subjects as preparation for university entrance.

Given these reservations, it was not until 1915 that a vocational high school opened in the city of Oakland. Even then, reluctance and hesitation characterized public reaction, and eventually, by the 1920s, educators joined in the national movement toward the comprehensive high school. Except for its commercial classes, vocational education in California had not been a smashing success.[7]

The thinness of the margin of victory is borne out also by the relatively few students who enrolled in vocational education classes. In Illinois, for example, Superintendent Francis Blair complained in 1918 about the "the indifference of the school authorities" toward the State Board of Vocational Education.[8] Blair pointed out that from 1913 to 1916, the proportion of vocational graduates to all high school graduates never exceeded more than 15 percent, though during this period it had doubled from its 7.5 percent in 1913. Girls at 8.7 percent outranked boys at 5.23 percent. The same lopsided results in favor of girls show up in the increased percentage of high schools offering instruction in commercial classes, a little more than 11 percent; in agriculture, 10.5 percent; and in home economics, 8.5 percent. In contrast, the increase in schools giving manual and technical instruction, mainly meant for boys, was 4 percent.[9] In the regular public high schools girls, rather than the hoped-for boys, appeared to be the main beneficiaries of vocational instruction.

The story was different in evening high schools and evening trade schools; there vocational studies attracted far more boys than girls. From 1913 to 1916 the boys' percentage rose from 12.5 to somewhat more than 17, and that of girls from a little less than 6 to a little more that 13. The lesser ability of the day high school to attract boys to manual, technical, and industrial classes justified the schoolmen's fear of private and evening schools, which had greater success in that respect.

The passage of the Smith-Hughes Act in 1917, then, made little difference in Illinois. By 1925 the percentage of public high schools receiving financial support for their vocational education program reached 22.5. At the same time, the percentage of high schools offering commercial classes declined from 42.5 to 39.3; of schools offering technical training and agriculture remained nearly stationary; and that of schools offering home economics rose from nearly 27 to 38. Again, the most obvious beneficiaries of the federal largesse were female students. Because vocational educators had praised home economics or domestic science for its nonvocational quality as appropriate education for future mothers and homemakers, and only incidentally as preparation for a wage-earning vocation, this development was especially ironic.[10] Given this imbalance in the gender distribution of vocational students in the high schools, it is not surprising that in subsequent years vocationalists, aided after 1918 by the compulsory education law for employed fourteen- to sixteen-year-olds, favored part-time continuation schools, part-time cooperative trade programs, and the evening trade extension courses. Because these were meant to give additional education to working youths, they more nearly corresponded to the aims of the vocational educators for industrial and trade training.

National data on public high school enrollment show the same picture for selected years from 1890 to 1928 (Table 11.1). Students enrolled in practical subjects (see the table's shaded lines) were outnumbered by students taking such academic standbys as English, algebra, history, Latin, civics, and geometry. Those taking practical subjects consistently outnumbered only those taking trigonometry and psychology. In 1910 and 1915 they also outnumbered those taking Spanish, and after World War I, those taking German. The practical fields—whether we classify them under manual or vocational education—did not fare very well. American high school students continued to regard their schools as first and foremost academic institutions.

What about the educators' assertion that vocational instruction was the answer to the dropout problem and would keep boys in school? In 1910 home economics (a subject taken mainly by girls) and agriculture (a subject usually taken by boys and girls in fairly even numbers) were the leading fields. From 1915 to 1928, home economics continued as the single most popular practical field. When in 1922 the commercial subjects of typewriting and shorthand appeared, they together with home economics showed a combined percentage of 36.3 for mainly female subjects. The male fields of industrial education and bookkeeping mustered a combined percentage of only 26.3. At the time of the next count, 1928, the pattern was the same: female subjects, 40.4 percent; male subjects, 24.2. The vocationalists' hopes had been dashed once more. The American public high school remained a basically academic institution that attracted more girls than boys.

Table 11.1 Public Secondary Day School Enrollment, by Subject, Selected
Years, 1890–1928 (in percentage of total enrollment)

Subject	Year					
	1890	1900	1910	1915	1922	1928
English		38.5	57.1	58.4	76.7	93.1
Algebra	45.5	56.3	56.9	48.8	40.2	35.2
History	27.3	38.2	55.0	50.5	18.2	24.9
Latin	34.7	50.6	49.0	37.3	27.5	22.0
Civics		21.7	15.6	15.7	19.3	20.0
Geometry	21.3	27.4	30.9	26.5	22.7	19.8
Home Economics			3.8	12.9	14.3	16.5
Typewriting					13.1	15.2
French	5.8	7.8	9.9	8.8	15.5	14.0
Industrial Subject				11.2	13.7	13.5
Bookkeeping				3.4	12.6	10.7
Spanish			0.7	2.7	11.3	9.4
Shorthand					8.9	8.7
Chemistry	10.1	7.7	6.9	7.4	7.4	7.1
Physics	22.8	19.0	14.6	14.2	8.9	6.8
Agriculture			4.7	7.2	5.1	3.7
German	10.5	14.3	23.7	24.4	0.6	1.8
Trigonometry		1.9	1.9	1.5	1.5	1.3
Psychology		2.4	1.0	1.2	0.9	1.0

Source: Historical Statistics of the United States, Supplement (Washington, DC: U.S. Bureau of the
Census, 1957), pp. H 262–326.

What can enrollment and graduation figures tell us about the democratic imperative, which, according to so many vocational educators, had demanded the introduction of vocational education into the high school classroom? In the crucial years between 1900 and 1920 the American high school did indeed respond to the democratic surge (see Table 11.2). Enrollments more than tripled, and graduates nearly quadrupled. But the percentage of graduates preparing for college rose from 30.28 percent in 1900 to 36.56 percent in 1916, and the percentage of those actually going to college or university rose from 3.60 to 4.84 percent. Although vocationalists could note that the traditional high school route to college, the classical or scientific course, had lost popularity—the percentage of students following that route dropped from 10.82 in 1900 to 4.87 in 1914—the growing strength of the democratic imperative had not seriously slowed the tendency of young Americans to use the high school as an avenue to higher academic education.

Table 11.2 Enrollment, Graduation, and College Attendance of Students in U.S. Public High Schools, 1900–1920

Year	Enrollment N	Graduates N	Graduates %	Graduates Attending College N	Graduates Attending College %	Graduates Prepared For College %	Graduates Prepared For College in Classical or Scientific Course %
1900	519,251	61,737	11.89	18,693	3.60	30.28	10.82
1901	541,730	65,696	12.13	20,540	3.79	31.27	11.15
1902	550,611	66,262	12.03	21,018	3.82	31.72	10.66
1903	592,213	69,991	11.82	22,887	3.86	32.70	9.82
1904	635,808	75,476	11.87	25,801	4.06	34.18	9.53
1905	679,702	79,597	11.71	28,296	4.16	35.55	9.46
1906	722,692	85,449	11.82	30,414	4.21	35.59	9.13
1907	751,081	87,385	11.63	28,185	3.75	32.25	9.59
1908	770,456	90,232	11.71	28,895	3.75	32.02	7.89
1909	841,273	100,496	11.95	34,841	4.14	34.67	6.02
1910	915,061	111,363	12.17	37,811	4.13	33.95	5.58
1911	984,677	119,961	12.18	41,392	4.20	34.50	5.66
1912	1,105,360	137,880	12.47	48,421	4.38	35.12	4.98
1913	1,134,771	148,074	13.05	51,920	4.58	35.06	5.67
1914	1,218,804	160,606	13.18	55,776	4.58	34.73	4.87
1915	1,328,984	176,056	13.25	63,124	4.75	35.85	
1916	1,456,061	192,810	13.24	70,483	4.84	36.56	
1917		208,588		58,508			
1918	1,645,171	224,367	13.64				
1919							
1920	1,857,156	230,902	12.43	64,479	3.47		

Source: Annual reports of the U. S. commissioner of education.

Public school vocational educators did, however, manage to bring to a halt the loss of male public high school students to independent manual and industrial training schools. The loss peaked in 1910, when 13.3 percent of all high school students were enrolled in such schools; thereafter the introduction of manual and industrial training in public high schools reversed that movement. From 1900 to about 1914 the percentage of students in the commercial studies classes of public high schools was lower than that of students in private commercial and business schools; thereafter the differences become negligible (see Table 11.3). Though the scarcity of data and irregularities in their gathering caution against too great reliance on them, the numbers indicate that public school administrators had successfully faced up to the competition of the private industrial and commercial schools.

Table 11.3 Enrollment in Schools for High-School-Age Students, by School Type, 1900–1920

| Year | All High Schools (N) | Independent Manual and Industrial Training Schools | | | | Private Commercial and Business Schools | | | | Students Taking Commercial Studies in Public High Schools | | | | Year |
		Male (N)	Female (N)	Total (N)	Percentage of Total High School Enrollment	Male (N)	Female (N)	Total (N)	Percentage of Total High School enrollment	Male (N)	Female (N)	Total (N)	Percentage of Total High School Enrollment	
1900	519,251	15,819	8,897	24,716	4.76	58,396	33,153	91,549	17.63	33,133	35,757	68,890	13.27	1900
1901	541,730	18,928	10,053	28,981	5.35	68,519	41,512	110,031	20.31	39,787	44,625	84,412	15.58	1901
1902	550,611	18,771	10,736	29,507	5.36	81,344	55,903	137,247	24.93	35,762	41,032	76,794	13.95	1902
1903	592,213	20,170	12,892	33,062	5.58	79,175	58,804	137,979	23.30	36,320	42,887	79,207	13.37	1903
1904	635,808	20,701	15,979	36,680	5.77	80,596	57,767	138,363	21.76	39,464	45,849	85,313	13.42	1904
1905	679,702	25,571	17,626	43,197	6.36	84,621	61,465	146,086	21.49	42,636	47,673	90,309	13.29	1905
1906	722,692	31,153	17,457	48,610	6.73	74,366	55,719	130,085	18.00	45,000	50,000	95,000	13.15	1906
1907	751,081	30,434	13,860	44,294	5.90	75,589	61,775	137,364	18.29					1907
1908	770,456	37,388	21,115	58,503	7.59	82,921	72,042	154,963	20.11	28,519	31,116	59,635	7.74	1908
1909	841,273	46,672	24,096	70,768	8.41	78,652	67,636	146,288	17.39	34,796	37,459	72,255	8.59	1909
1910	915,061	75,880	45,516	121,396	13.27	72,887	61,891	134,778	14.73	35,155	46,094	81,249	8.88	1910
1911	984,677	78,500	48,630	127,130	12.91	82,775	72,469	155,244	15.77	51,603	59,322	110,925	11.27	1911
1912	1,105,360	78,076	49,409	127,485	11.53	72,258	65,532	137,790	12.47	58,323	70,654	128,977	11.67	1912
1913	1,134,771					82,775	77,782	160,557	14.15	69,135	84,907	154,042	13.57	1913
1914	1,218,804					85,432	82,631	168,063	13.79	68,600	92,650	161,250	13.23	1914
1915	1,328,984					94,870	88,416	183,286	13.79	92,226	116,379	208,605	15.70	1915
1916	1,456,061					99,134	93,254	192,388	13.21	105,142	138,043	243,185	16.70	1916
1917														1917
1918	1,645,171					96,449	193,130	289,579	17.60	104,418	173,857	278,275	16.91	1918
1919														1919
1920	1,857,156					139,551	196,481	336,032	18.09					1920

Source: Annual reports of the U. S. commissioner of education.

The Challenge of Vocational Education

During the last two decades of the nineteenth century, manual education had prepared the way for vocational education. But although manual education added training of the hand to training of the mind, it remained within the century-old conception of preparatory education as general education, whether for life or for college. With vocational education, however, the American secondary school broke in fundamental ways with what until then had been a common Western tradition of secondary schooling as exclusively a general training. Because its curriculum now included specific training for particular trades and employment, vocational education played a crucial role in defining the comprehensive high school. As we shall describe in the next chapter, this school began to offer academic as well as vocational classes side by side in the same building. It blazed a path for secondary education that, until after the middle of the twentieth century, had scarcely any parallels in Europe. Vocational education supplied the crucial element that enabled the comprehensive American high school to usher in a new age for secondary education.

Even while agreeing that a fundamental change had taken place in American secondary education, contemporaries and later historians did not always describe it in the same terms and did not always emphasize the same developments or events. Daniel Rodgers and David Tyack wrote in 1982 of a "vocational transformation" that extended schooling to children who previously would have gone to work; expanded vocational education from classes in white-collar pursuits to blue-collar on-the-job training; heavily involved urban working-class boys; created a vocational curriculum that was promoted by business, labor, and reform groups; introduced vocational guidance; and put into place a new cadre of vocational education teachers. Focusing less on the school and its history and more on the relationship of schools to the world of work, Rodgers and Tyack spoke of vocational education as a "call to refashion the schools into a comprehensive set of bridges to work" over which "young people could be propelled from childhood through schooling to work, all with an unprecedented efficiency and concentration of effort." They held that it gave secondary schooling a new mission.[11]

Earlier, in 1955, Lawrence Cremin had placed that new mission in the wider context of American social, economic, and political history. He had pointed to industrialism, immigration, and progressivism as forces outside the school, and to dynamic sociology, child study, and an activist psychology within. All these forces in combination, argued Cremin, had opened the doors of secondary schools and even colleges to all who expected to benefit from them. Progressive education, of which vocational education

139

was but a part, produced the decisive shift in the conception of the school's goals and responsibilities.[12]

Martin Trow, writing six years after Cremin, foresaw what he called a second transformation in American secondary education, a sequel to Cremin's first. Cremin's revolution had set as its goals for the American high school a curriculum that offered either academic or vocational preparation for those who desired it and a general terminal education program for all. As we shall see in later chapters, by 1945 the American high school had become, for all intents and purposes, a terminal school for the majority of its students. Trow now foresaw a transformation that would change the high school from a mass terminal to a mass preparatory institution with terminal education for only a minority of its students.[13] He took his cue from changes in the country's occupational structure and the related expansion of mass higher education. These developments, he argued, would force the high school to change its priorities from terminal to preparatory education. Other changes were likely to follow. The most important would be, as we shall discuss in later chapters, a call for a reevaluation of the comprehensive high school as the nation's standard model for public secondary education. In Trow's view the transformations spearheaded by the appearance of vocational education continue and are going to be with us for decades to come.

There is agreement, then, that vocational education set in motion developments whose consequences are still being played out. But I doubt that we can say with Rodgers and Tyack that the introduction of vocational training and the bridging function that this imposed upon the schools constitute the full measure of the transformation. Nor can we subsume vocational education, as Cremin did, as but one of many factors in the matrix of American progressivism. By 1900 vocational education already was flourishing in many European countries as part of their public education systems; it was far from being a uniquely American innovation. But Europeans distinguished clearly between general education and specific training, and conducted the one in their general public schools and the other in separate public institutions specifically designed for that purpose. Americans, however, although they had similarly created private and public vocational schools in separate buildings, and although they were to pay a great deal of attention to separate day and evening continuation schools, nonetheless remained uncomfortable with this division. During the 1920s they created the comprehensive high school to overcome the split. Locating vocational education in the comprehensive high school and placing general and specific education in one and the same building completed the process that had begun with the appearance of manual education in the high school and that was to mark most of the twentieth-century history of American secondary education.

12

Toward the Comprehensive
High School

The Commission on the Reorganization
of Secondary Education

After the turn of the century, secondary education became part of common schooling. No longer was it governed by the basic assumption of the Committee of Ten that it concerned only "that small proportion of all the children in the country . . . who show themselves able to profit by an education prolonged to the eighteenth year."[1] Americans now believed that all, or at least nearly all, young people could and should benefit from high school attendance.

It was the Commission on the Reorganization of Secondary Education that developed the blueprint that gave definitive expression to this philosophy. In doing so, the Commission brought up-to-date or—which in this case amounts to the same thing—overthrew the work of the Committee of Ten. It radically revised the curricular philosophy of secondary education and prepared the ground for the comprehensive high school as the institutional expression of that new philosophy. It also departed from the time-honored path of nineteenth century committees that had asked what should and ought to be, and had set purposes and goals. Instead, the commission asked what was, inquired of the needs of students, and derived its curricular objectives from the current practices of society. It asked what were the tasks of everyday life and suggested that the secondary schools prepare their students for those tasks. Despite its insistent rhetoric to prepare youths for the tasks of the future, it kept its eyes on the demands and needs of the present.

Unlike the members of the Committee of Ten, most of whom were academics, the members of the commission were "new men": high school teachers, supervisors, and principals; normal school teachers and presidents; educational administrators; representatives of state departments of education; and professors of education in colleges and universities. Spokesmen for the college point of view and for college and university subjects were not entirely absent, but they were in the minority. The commission's executive committee, or, as it was called, reviewing committee, consisted of the U.S. commissioner of education; three faculty members of Columbia University's Teachers College and two of the Chicago Normal School; one education professor from Harvard University and three from various state universities; one state university and one private college president; one principal of a technical high school; one associate superintendent of schools; one state high school supervisor; a dean of a school of art; two subject specialists from different high schools; a representative each of the Ethical Culture School in New York City and of the International YMCA, two officials of the U.S. Bureau of Education; one member of the U.S. War Department; one specialist each in music and physical education; and its chair, Clarence D. Kingsley, a state high school supervisor from Massachusetts.

The reviewing committee represented almost to perfection the new educational hierarchy that had taken over from the old oligarchy of university presidents and professors, and school superintendents.[2] Only one woman was among its twenty-six members, and she represented the Committee on Household Arts of the U.S. Bureau of Education. There was not one representative of a racial or ethnic minority group. Although the reviewing committee could not be charged with "college domination," it did not include a still-practicing classroom teacher. It was a male administrative elite from the nation's public school systems and the associated teachers colleges and schools of education, together with representatives of outside groups, that now set to work to direct the curricular fortunes of American secondary education.

Clarence D. Kingsley, who in 1910 had been a mathematics teacher at the Brooklyn Manual Training High School, was known as an ardent proponent of high school curricular reform. He had pushed the High School Teachers Association of New York City to ask the colleges to reduce their foreign language entrance requirements and accept high school credits for practical and vocational work. The National Education Association's Committee on the Articulation of High School and College, of which he was the chair,[3] asked for a relaxation of high school curricular requirements to accommodate community needs without at the same time jeopardizing student chances for college admission. This was a drastic shift away from paying primary attention to issues of college preparation. Now, Kingsley stated in 1913, curricular specialists "shall think in terms of the development of the boy and the girl rather than in terms of subject matter."[4] Following his recommendations, the National Education Association in 1913 created the Commission on the Reorganization of Secondary Education by merging the Committee on Articulation of High Schools and Colleges with its ten existing and two newly appointed subject subcommittees. The commission's reviewing committee consisted of the chairmen of all subcommittees and ten members at large. During the years from 1913 to 1922, this commission issued sixteen subject and other reports, of which the reviewing committee's *Cardinal Principles of Secondary Education* (1918) was by all odds the most significant. Kingsley had parlayed his New York campaign regarding college admissions into a thoroughgoing national reform of secondary education.

The New Philosophy: Democracy and Efficiency

Cardinal Principles was the third major report within less than a hundred years to give definitive shape and direction to the curriculum of American secondary education. The first, the *Yale Report* of 1827, had been an *apologia* for the college whose name it bore, but it came to serve for all secondary and collegiate institutions throughout the remaining decades of the nineteenth century as a beacon of liberal education. The second report, issued in 1893 by the Committee of Ten, had done little more than to reaffirm the academic values expressed in the *Yale Report*. Like that document, but quite unlike the pronouncements of the Committee of Ten, *Cardinal Principles* was to prove its staying power for many decades. It furnished and still furnishes the basic curricular guidelines and the institutional framework for the public secondary schools.

The heart of *Cardinal Principles* was Kingsley's concept of democracy. Kingsley defined the purpose of democracy as "so to organize society that each member may develop his personality primarily through activities designed for the well-being of his fellow members and of society as a whole." In a democracy schools should be organized such that "the individual and society may find fulfillment each in the other."[5] When discussing their mutual curricular accommodations, schools and colleges should subordinate their demands to this concept and meet the needs of individuals, localities, and the national community. To make this possible, a clear conception of the meaning of democracy, Kingsley wrote, must guide education in the United States.

143

Making democracy the philosophical centerpiece of his document, Kingsley did no more than reflect the "democratic imperative" in secondary education. He appeared to echo John Dewey's 1916 statement in his *Democracy and Education* that

> [a] democracy is more than a form of government; it is primarily a mode of associated living, of conjoint communicated experience. The extension in space of the number of individuals who participate in an interest so that each has to refer his own action to that of others, and to consider the action of others to give point and direction to his own, is equivalent to the breaking down of those barriers of class, race, and national territory which kept men from perceiving the full import of their activity.[6]

However, Kingsley spoke in rather general terms and avoided any reference to such specifics as "the breaking down of those barriers of class, race and national territory" that Dewey had mentioned. *Cardinal Principles* was silent on the nation's most pressing social problems.[7]

In April of 1917 the currency of the word *democracy* was to receive a strong boost through the formation of George Creel's Committee on Public Information. This committee presented World War I as "the war to make the world safe for democracy," and addressed youngsters through the *National School Service*, a bulletin distributed to the schools. In collaboration with the Red Cross, the YMCA, the National Security League, and the League to Enforce Peace, the Creel committee hammered home the message that if Americans were to give their lives to bring democracy to the rest of the world, they had better learn to live it at home.[8] Again, like Kingsley's commission, this national propaganda campaign for the most part refrained from addressing directly the issues of racial and ethnic discrimination, but it helped to make democracy a defining issue for the nation's schools.

If democracy was *Cardinal Principles'* main theme, efficiency was its twin. The fulfillment of the democratic ideal, wrote Kingsley, "demands that human activities be placed upon a high level of efficiency."[9] Kingsley had adopted efficiency as a major criterion of curriculum planning from his mentor, David Snedden. As commissioner of education in Massachusetts and education professor at Teachers College, Columbia University, Snedden had been a prime mover in the development of vocational education and scientific curriculum building. According to him, curricula were to be constructed from small, concrete objectives that corresponded to specific activities that particular adults performed in their lives. Educational efficiency consisted of matching as exactly as possible actual instruction in specific activities with particular people who were expected to engage in these activities. This, of course, presupposed that the teacher knew which student would need which skill later in life, and that teachers agreed that it was neither necessary nor desirable to teach a student anything beyond that. To do so, as Herbert Kliebard acidly remarked, "was simply wasteful."[10] Efficiency in education meant to find the most perfect fit between instruction and what were considered the needs of students and society.

With these needs in mind and with efficiency as its guidepost, secondary education in a democracy had to come to grips with the teaching of values and ethical behavior. In *Cardinal Principles* Kingsley demanded that efficiency was to be balanced with "an appreciation of the significance" of the activities the school encouraged and by "loyalty to the best ideals involved." But Kingsley never said wherein this significance lay and what constituted the best ideals. Subsequent passages, however, suggest that work and vocation were the activities whose significance was to be appreciated, and social service provided the occasion where students could demonstrate their loyalty to the best ideals. If the school succeeded in getting the student to "choose that vocation and those forms of social service in which his personality may develop and become most effective," it had succeeded in its task. By providing the main testing ground of a student's character, vocation had moved from being a curricular sideline to a major *raison d'être* of the school. If the school could also inspire a student to a commitment to social service, it would have prepared him not only to "find his place" but also to "use that place to shape both himself and society toward ever nobler ends."[11] The American school fulfilled its moral obligation when it prepared its students for work and social service. That was the ethical message of *Cardinal Principles*.

The Seven Cardinal Principles

With the above theoretical guidelines in mind, Kingsley's subcommittees turned to the task of curriculum planning and specifying the principles or objectives that were to direct the curricular mission of the American high school. As Kingsley put it: "In order to determine the main objectives that should guide education in a democracy it is necessary to analyze the activities of the individual."[12] This was the essence of "scientific curriculum building." One wonders whether Kingsley was ever struck by the incongruity of arguing, on the one hand, that the high school needed a curriculum that took account of the ongoing changes in society and in the character of the high school population and the sciences on which education claimed to be based, and, on the other hand, of devising a curriculum for tomorrow's adults that was derived from the experience of their parents. Kingsley's emphasis on present activities was intentional because this represented for him the break with the academic tradition of the past. But he did not seem to realize that that very present-mindedness did not prepare his students for future developments in industry, commerce, and in the labor market. If vocationalists applauded him in 1918, they were bound to be disappointed a decade later.

For Kingsley, however, these considerations were not relevant. He surveyed the activities of his contemporaries and found that they served his purpose. The first "cardinal principle" he enunciated was health. Health is indispensable for everyone, "hence health education is therefore fundamental." All else, "the vitality of the race and . . . the defense of the Nation" depend on it. To ensure that health received proper recognition in the high schools, teachers had to be able "to inculcate in the entire student body a love for clean sport"; school boards had "to furnish adequate equipment for physical activities"; and schools had to "conform to the best standards of hygiene and sanitation."[13]

Second on the list Kingsley placed the "command of fundamental processes"—by which he meant the traditional three Rs. "While not an end in itself, [it] is nevertheless an indispensable objective." It was to be pursued not through formal reviews but by application to new material. "Instruction and practice must go hand in hand," and "only so much theory should be taught at any one time as will show results in practice." No longer should college entrance requirements determine high school instruction. Languages and mathematics were not to be pursued as disciplinary studies but to be regarded as skills that could be adjusted to each student's abilities as shown in daily practice. This demotion from discipline to be acquired to skill to be performed at the level of one's ability lay behind that mysterious formulation of the "command" of "processes" that was no longer an end in itself but a "nevertheless . . . indispensable objective."[14]

Because individuals were members of families and of vocational and civic groups it followed, wrote Kingsley, "that worthy home-membership, vocation, and citizenship, demand attention as three of the leading objectives." Traditional subjects like the social studies, literature, music, and art should be called upon to aid a student in becoming "a worthy member of a family." But because teaching specific curricular fields often called for separation of the sexes, the "worthy home-membership" objective required a coeducational family setting that would "exemplify wholesome

146

relations between boys and girls and men and women." This coeducational school, a "home away from home," was to teach its students how to live at home. Boys "should understand the essentials of food values, of sanitation, and of household budgets." Girls should be prepared for "their lifelong occupation" as home makers.[15]

Kingsley and his colleagues recognized that not all girls sought preparation for homemaking in the school, and that many wanted to prepare themselves for wage-earning occupations and for higher education. The high school should press these girls to pay major attention to the household arts because, Kingsley warned, for them, too, "home making becomes their lifelong occupation." He could not understand, he added, "how society can properly continue to sanction for girls high-school curriculums that disregard this fundamental need [for home making], even though such curriculums are planned in response to the demands made by some of the colleges for women."[16] There rings in these words an unmistakable undertone of resentment against the remaining vestiges of the college-preparatory curriculum and against the schools or colleges that preferred to remain academic institutions and refused to see themselves as family homes.

Kingsley's comments on vocational education were a blend of recommendations for schools to prepare students academically for vocational life and to train them for a specific vocation. He stressed vocational guidance through which "the pupil explore[s] his own capacities and aptitudes, and make[s] a survey of the world's work, to the end that he may select his vocation wisely." Further, classwork should consist of

> an appreciation of the significance of the vocation to the community, and a clear conception of right relations between the members of the chosen vocation, between different vocational groups, between employer and employee, and between producer and consumer.

All of these topics could well be taken up in the history, sociology, or economics classroom, but Kingsley did not mention this. He simply insisted that "these aspects of vocational education . . . demand emphatic attention."

Kingsley remained noncommittal about the vocationalists' chief concern to train students for a specific trade or vocation: "The extent to which the secondary school should offer [such] training depends upon the vocation, the facilities that the school can acquire, and the opportunity that the pupil may have to obtain such training later." For Kingsley, practical instruction was not one of the school's priorities. When, how-

147

ever, a high school undertook this task, "those proficient in that vocation should be employed as instructors and the actual conditions of the vocation should be utilized either within the high school or in cooperation with the home, farm, shop, or office."[17] Such efforts required considerable expense and threatened to move the school further away from Kingsley's image of it as a home. As vocational education inevitably involved specialization, it also threatened his ethical-social ideas of the school as community; specialization could prevent a student from exploring the other cardinal objectives. Kingsley therefore devoted a separate paragraph to warn against the separation of vocational education from training in citizenship. "The commission," he wrote, "enters its protest against any and all plans, however, well intended, which are in danger of divorcing vocation and social-civic education."[18] Both Kerschensteiner and Dewey, each from his own different point of view, could happily approve.

Judged by the amount of space devoted to the subject in *Cardinal Principles,* civic education received the lion's share of attention. Kingsley set forth these essentials of good citizenship:

> A many-sided interest in the welfare of the communities to which one belongs; loyalty to ideals of civic righteousness, practical knowledge of social agencies and institutions; good judgment as to means and methods that will promote one social end without defeating others; and as putting all these into effect, habits of cordial cooperation in social undertakings.

Kingsley suggested classroom activities that bore a decided collectivist stamp. For geography, history, civics, and economics, he recommended assignments that required cooperative solutions and socialized recitation in order to train collective thinking and a sense of social responsibility. The social studies should be presented not as so much information but as matters of current relevance revealing human interdependence and involving local agencies and issues, such as child-welfare organizations and consumer leagues. A similar emphasis on social ideals, conditions, activities, movements, and needs should pervade the teaching of English. From primary attention paid to local conditions it was to be extended to the study of the nation and

> other nations also. . . . Such a study of dissimilar contributions in the light of the ideal of human brotherhood, should help to establish a genuine internationalism, free from sentimentality, founded on fact, and actually operative in the affairs of the nation.

This was Kingsley's recodification of the democratic imperative as it took on collectivistic and international overtones under the drumbeats of the Creel committee's publicity efforts "to make the world safe for democracy."[19]

The sixth principle or objective, likewise derived from scientific curriculum making, was "the worthy use of leisure." The reduced time spent working for a living, Kingsley argued, made it ever more mandatory to prepare people for leisure activities that could occupy from hours and days. There was an "unworthy use of leisure" that impaired health, disrupted home life, lessened vocational efficiency, and destroyed civic-mindedness. The schools could forestall its spread by teaching youths to utilize "music, art, literature, drama, and social intercourse together with . . . avocational interests." Unfortunately, the school had not done so in the past because it "so exclusively sought intellectual discipline that it has seldom treated literature, art, and music so as to evoke right emotional response and produce positive enjoyment." This "right emotional response" the school should now foster by providing recreation within itself and "other proper agencies in the community."[20]

The seventh and last objective of *Cardinal Principles*, "paramount among the objectives of the secondary school," was ethical character: "conduct founded upon right principles, clearly perceived and loyally adhered to." The individual who possessed it was a "sterling character," who substituted principles for impulses in the discharge of his duties. Kingsley never defined those principles but only suggested that they might be developed through

> the wise selection of content and methods of instruction in all subjects of study, the social contacts of pupils with one another and with their teachers, the opportunities afforded by the organization and administration of the school for the development on the part of pupils of the sense of personal responsibility and initiative, and, above all, the spirit of service and the principles of true democracy.[21]

One would assume that the "sterling characters" who wisely selected content and methods of instruction and arranged for the social contacts within the school lived and worked by principles that, in turn, they had imbibed from sterling characters who had wisely selected content and method of instruction. Neither the circular argument nor the fog of generalities appears to have bothered Kingsley and his colleagues. It seemed all to be part of the general appeal to democracy, efficiency, and goodness.

The Comprehensive High School: Specialization in Command

With the seven principles or objectives Kingsley and his commission members had defined separate functions that the individual performs during a lifetime. They then had constructed curricular objectives to match these functions. Of necessity there resulted a curriculum in which specialization and separation of curricular paths and of the students who followed them played dominant roles. Kingsley was uncomfortable with this separation and, as we shall see later, sought to provide balance by emphasizing the unifying features of the comprehensive high school. But as the school developed, the divisive effects of specialization persisted and grew stronger.

Vocational education exemplified specialization and separation at their most intense level. This process had begun already with the introduction of manual training and accelerated with the switch to vocational training. Students could choose among agricultural, business, clerical, industrial, fine arts, and household arts curricula. Kingsley did his best to stop the trend. As we have just seen, he warned against the separation of vocational education from training in citizenship. He spoke out against cooperative programs, continuation schools, and every kind of specialized or neighborhood high school that isolated students from exposure to all of the cardinal objectives. Within the comprehensive high school he opted for vocational information and guidance rather than for specific trade training.

Subsequent developments bore out Kingsley's fears. In what is to date the only general history of the comprehensive high school, its author, William G. Wraga, writing of the school's first twenty years, stated that "in practice the specializing function received wide support as the unifying function was neglected."[22] In 1926 George S. Counts connected specialization with the issues raised by students of different ability levels. In the past, interest and vocational expectations had been used to separate students. Now, mental testing had come to use intellectual ability as a criterion and had created homogeneous grouping. Principals and teachers, Counts reported, generally expressed themselves "as pleased with the experiment," and expected that new composite subjects requiring "less intellectual power" could be used as substitutes for traditional ones. Composite or general mathematics could take the place of algebra, and practical arts that of academic fields. "While a certain amount of this must be done," wrote Counts, "care needs to be taken lest certain subjects come to be regarded merely as places of refuge for the mentally incompetent." He left no doubt that he disapproved of this "solution," which later generations have come to know as tracking. He also indicated that some kind of sorting of students was a necessary and

150

inevitable facet of the comprehensive high school and its specializing function.[23]

Several years later, in a report first prepared in 1930, the U.S. Office of Education called homogeneous grouping and special classes for the gifted and the slow "core elements in a typically successful program to provide for individual differences."[24] In "The Horizontal Organization of Secondary Education," the office sketched out the segregating effects of the comprehensive high schools' vocational programs. As these expanded,

> the different lines of education have been divided into curriculums, each representing a grouping of subjects preparatory for some line of activity, usually occupational. In some communities, the different sections of the program have been further divided by providing separate schools for each of the major divisions. The college preparatory pupils may be enrolled in one school, the commercial pupils in another, the trade pupils in another, and the technical pupils in still another. Sometimes separate schools are also provided for the pupils who attend school on a part-time basis.

It is hard to imagine a more thoroughgoing splintering of the student body than here described. Homogeneous grouping, classes for the gifted and the slow, and the vocational program stand out as the marks of specialization and separation.[25]

Leonard V. Koos, the editor of the 1930 government report, was uneasy about the questions it raised. He mentioned "some persons" who believed that "segregation of pupils in specialized schools . . . accentuates the development of distinctions and class loyalties in society." Koos countered that comprehensive schools were free of these defects. They promoted "social integration, mutual understanding, and cooperation of the different groups." Teachers had told him, Koos wrote, that separate schools discouraged vocational pupils from participating in social activities and that comprehensive schools had good effects on the vocational students. But even so, the same teachers said, the group spirit and morale of vocational students in separate schools were higher than those of students in comprehensive schools. In the latter, industrial students came "to regard their own group of pupils and subjects less highly and the academic pupils and subjects more highly."[26] Though these results were tentative and stood in need of qualifications, Koos warned, they once more underlined the problems of specialization within the comprehensive high school.

Koos's final words on the subject came in his findings on the preparation of teachers for the various schools and subjects:

The teachers of academic subjects on the average reported as much
as 9 years of formal education beyond the eighth grade while the
teachers of industrial subjects reported only 6.8 years. The teachers
of commercial subjects have less education than the academic
teachers but more than the teachers of household and industrial
arts. Also, academic teachers in general and academic schools have
more education than academic teachers in trade schools; the same
advantage in training exists for the industrial arts teachers in the
comprehensive and academic schools. The reverse relationship exists in regard to experience in occupations other than teaching.
That is, the percentage of such experience is higher for the industrial arts teachers in the trade schools than for the same teachers in
the comprehensive schools.[27]

There clearly existed a hierarchy of prestige among students and teachers
in the various specialized branches of instruction the high school provided. In comprehensive high schools administrators continued to prefer
academic teachers and were less interested in vocationally well prepared
industrial arts or vocational teachers. The academic program remained
the school's priority.

The Comprehensive High School: The Priority of Academics

If the authors of *Cardinal Principles* had hoped to break the academic character of the American high school quickly, they could not but be disappointed. What Koos found in 1930, George S. Counts had encountered
four years earlier. In his high school study of 1926, Counts stated that the
urban schools he had visited had not kept pace with the radical changes
demanded by the rapid increase in enrollments: "The basic traditions and
practices of the high school remain essentially unchanged." In the comprehensive schools, the traditional college preparatory academic curriculum enjoyed superior social prestige and continued to dominate. As a
result, the school

> often generates attitudes of social inferiority in those who do not
> pursue the favored curriculums. . . . [T]he great motive back of
> high-school attendance is the belief on the part of both pupil and
> parent that the high school is a means of gaining access to preferred
> occupations and to favored social position.

For that purpose, only the academic program was viable.[28]

152

Two years later an investigation directed specifically at the country's high schools of fewer than one hundred students arrived at similar results: "the basic academic subjects" met the six "life objectives" only indirectly and made "their major contribution to the seventh objective—that of vocational training—when interpreted to include preparation for college." Expressed less obliquely, this meant that only the academic program fulfilled the function it was designed for. The nonacademic studies for the non-college-bound student were so limited that their effect was small. To soften this unfavorable assessment, the schoolmen classified their college preparatory work as vocational and thus saved face. A sad comment, indeed, on the curricular situation of small high schools.[29] But what is even sadder is that Kingsley had all but asked for this travesty. In his section on the vocational objective in *Cardinal Principles* he had written: "Provisions should be made also for those having distinctly academic interests and needs."[30] Apparently, his antipathy to the college preparatory function had led him to disqualify it altogether as an objective in its own right, and to reintroduce it as but one of many vocational objectives. How ironic that in the small high schools the academic program turned out to be the only viable one that schoolmen had to camouflage as vocational in order to make their schools look good.

The Unifying Function of the Comprehensive High School

For Kingsley and his colleagues, the winning argument for the comprehensive high school was that by bringing its students together in one building, the school made real the American ideal of *e pluribus unum*. It was the chosen instrument of the American melting pot.

> Through friendships formed with pupils pursuing other curriculums and having vocational and educational goals widely different from their own, the pupils realize that the interests which they hold in common with others are, after all, far more important than the differences that would tend to make them antagonistic to others. Through the school assemblies and organizations they acquire common ideas. Through group activities they secure training in cooperation. Through loyalty to a school which includes many groups they are prepared for loyalty to State and Nation. In short, the comprehensive school is the prototype of a democracy.[31]

Yet, as we shall see, Kingsley's inspired rhetoric could not insure that reality always corresponded to his vision.

Kingsley and his commission members identified the unifying elements of the curriculum as "*constants*, to be taken by all or nearly all pupils," and distinguished them from "*variables*, peculiar to a curriculum or to a group of related curriculums," and "*free electives*, to be taken by pupils in accordance with individual aptitudes or special interests, generally of a nonvocational nature." The most important constants were academic subjects like the social studies and English language and literature. They entered the curriculum through all the objectives, except for vocation and the worthy use of leisure. The social mingling of pupils and their participation in common activities, were to supplement the constants. Kingsley expected that these subjects and activities would allow the school to act as "the one agency that may be controlled definitely and consciously by our democracy for the purpose of unifying its people."[32]

Kingsley believed that in the comprehensive schools even vocational activities would counteract isolation. Here, students were not bound to one particular trade but had the opportunity to pick from, explore, and, if necessary, change from one to another vocational program. They gained

> contacts valuable to them vocationally, since people in every vocation must be able to deal intelligently with those in other vocations, and employers and employees must be able to understand one another and recognize common interests. Similarly, teachers in comprehensive schools have a better opportunity to observe other curriculums and are thereby better able to advise pupils intelligently.

The vocational program in the comprehensive high school proved its superior value over that of specialized schools because of its scope and variety.[33]

The worthy use of leisure provided other opportunities to bring students together. In its leisure activities a high school that was no longer serving the narrow sector of academically interested youth could "establish bonds of friendship and common understanding that can not be furnished by other agencies." It could promote a classless society.[34] The extracurriculum offered even better unifying opportunities. In 1926 George Counts had paid special attention to "those numerous activities and interests which, during the past half-century, have sprung up spontaneously in the high school." Principals and teachers approved student clubs and organizations, student government, athletics, and journalism. They believed these activities fostered school spirit, desirable recreational habits, and capacity for leadership, higher scholarship, and citizenship.

They helped develop finer social sensibilities, promoted health, and advertised the school's good name. Counts suggested that these "enterprises . . . may possess educational value even superior to that possessed by some of the more formally organized work of the school."

But Counts and other observers realized that not everything that glittered was gold. Counts remained skeptical of the schoolmen's "better school spirit" argument:

> [U]ndesirable recreational habits may be formed; the powers of leadership may be devoted to antisocial or narrowly social purposes; an undue amount of energy may be drained away from the other work of the school; and evil civic tendencies may be established.[35]

In their 1924 study of the schools of Muncie, Indiana, Robert and Helen Lynd seconded Counts. The Lynds described the high school with its extracurricular activities as "a fairly complete social cosmos in itself . . ., [a] city within a city," where "the social sifting devices" of adult society— "money, clothes, personal attractiveness, male physical prowess, exclusive clubs, elections to positions of leadership—all are for the first time set going."

> This informal training is not a preparation for a vague future that must be taken on trust, as is the case with so much of the academic work; to many of the boys and girls in high school this is "the life," the thing they personally like best about going to school.

"Education is a faith, a religion, to Middletown," wrote the Lynds. But when Muncie's parents spoke of education, they did not refer to the curriculum but to the symbolic value of their children's participation in "the life." Working class people desired it "as an open sesame that will mysteriously admit their children to a world closed to them." Members of the business class cherished it "as a heavily sanctioned aid in getting on further economically or socially in the world."[36] Counts and scholars like the Lynds felt uneasy about these aspects of the school's unifying function.

To ensure that education became a "unitary and continuous process," the Commission on the Reorganization of Secondary Education recommended for each student an uninterrupted passage through six years of elementary school and three years each of junior and senior high school. If funding permitted, the junior college could then extend the secondary program for another two years.[37] A student's promotion from elementary to secondary school should take place strictly according to age. Colleges and universities were obliged to admit and instruct students "whose needs are no longer met by the secondary school and [who] are disposed to continue their education." "Higher institutions of learning are not justified in maintaining entrance requirements and examinations of a character that handicap the secondary school in discharging its proper function in a democracy."[38]

The schoolmen's perception of individual needs and capacities should have precedence over traditional academic standards and requirements in all levels of schooling. Kingsley and his commission asked the nation to see to it "that every normal boy and girl will be encouraged to remain in school to the age of 18, on full time if possible, otherwise on part time." Should this encouragement not suffice, then

> a sound national policy dictates the urgent need for legislation whereby all young persons, whether employed or not, shall be required to attend school not less than eight hours in each week that schools are in session until they reach the age of 18.

When he wrote this, Kingsley did not think of continuation schools, which he dismissed as a "custom in less democratic societies." He wanted part-time schooling to be carried out in the comprehensive high school where "the part-time students and the full-time students may share in the use of the assembly hall, gymnasium, and other equipment provided for all."[39] This was Kingsley's most ambitious vision of the comprehensive high school's unifying function: to serve as catch basin for all youth of high school age; to thrive as a compulsory educational monopoly in the hands of the public schoolmen.

13

The High School Under Siege

The Comprehensive School's First Decade

By 1920 the publication of *Cardinal Principles* and the incorporation of vocational education in the programs of the comprehensive high schools had put American secondary education on a new course. The high school set out to transform itself from a school for a selected few into a home for the many. At the end of the decade the U.S. Office of Education certified success: secondary education was being democratized. Public high school enrollment had climbed to 46.6 percent of the age cohort. Additional thousands were reached through vocational programs in regular high schools and continuation and evening classes. In junior high school classes the replacement of traditional academic subjects such as arithmetic or algebra with "general mathematics" for all brought students of various interests and abilities together. The same unifying effect was at work in high school choruses, glee clubs, bands, and orchestras, in courses in art appreciation, and in interscholastic contests of various kinds.[1]

The Bureau of Education report, however, did not mention—as George Counts had done in 1926—that general courses usually required "less intellectual power" and that the school was still a primarily college-preparatory institution in which the addition of the vocational programs served to heighten, rather than to lessen, social distinctions.[2] Other studies showed that although *Cardinal Principles* had "contributed much to the cause of reform," and had gained the endorsements of many "educational leaders," its principles were "by no means fully conformed with" in school practice. A 1928 survey carried out for the Department of Superintendence of the National Education Association added that the Cardinal Principles "have received wide acceptance in theory; only gradually are they modifying practice in the schools."[3]

Another investigation, also sponsored by the Department of Superintendence, showed that high schools of more than 250 students had adapted better than small ones to the objectives of *Cardinal Principles*, but even in those schools compliance had not been universal. There, courses had been "more strongly socialized and more closely connected to community interests" and had been "somewhat revised to handle better the spread of pupil abilities." In freshman English, homogeneous grouping provided for "classes for accelerated, normal, and slow pupils." Principals who had made changes in curriculum had most frequently added commercial and social studies, industrial arts, physical and biological sciences, and home economics, and had most frequently dropped Latin, ancient history, French, and advanced mathematics. Yet even so, the report admitted, "43.9 per cent of the more than twelve hundred principals who responded to the questionnaire had not attempted any reorganization in line with the recommendations of the *Cardinal Principles*." Most of these principals asserted that the document had never been called to their attention; of those who had read it, "slightly fewer than one-third (336 out of 1025) . . . had undertaken no reorganization."[4]

Matters were not helped by the onset of the Great Depression at the end of the decade. In the schools, the nationwide economic distress and dislocation accentuated the dividing lines of social class, and budgetary retrenchment affected the varied curricula quite differently. Even though, as Edward Krug pointed out, foreign language instruction was almost everywhere curtailed, the traditional academic programs, mainly utilized by middle-class students, were least affected.[5] Vocational education, often reserved for the academic low achievers, suffered the most. In Chicago the school board eliminated the city's junior college, the junior high schools, the bureaus of curriculum and vocational guidance, all elementary school vocational and home economics training, all athletic teams and coaching, half of kindergartens, and all but one of the district's continuation schools. There was no money for school bands and orchestras, and the board dismissed fourteen hundred teachers, among them all elementary physical education teachers. It increased the high school teaching load to seven classes a day. What made these cuts all the more galling to school people were the satisfied remarks of James B. McCahey, the board's president, that the retrenchments were not temporary crisis measures but desirable revisions that would increase rather than decrease the schools' effectiveness.[6] The Chicago example showed what was true in other cities as well: the retrenchment program concentrated on the aspects of schooling that had been introduced or emphasized in *Cardinal Principles*.[7] In the parlance of the day, these activities were the "fads and frills" that, according to one Chicago journalist, were "anything in the school system which was not there thirty years ago."[8] It looked as though *Cardinal Principles* had been discarded.

Educational Progressives and the Comprehensive School

As the 1930s rolled on and businessmen were in control of most of the nation's school boards, they became the target of schoolteachers' and school administrators' anger. The protesters were a diverse body. There were the high school faculty members of the Progressive Education Association who shared with the mainstream educators in the comprehensive high schools a distaste for a discipline-bound classroom but remained committed to a college-preparatory curriculum. There were the militant teachers in Chicago who condemned "the cabal of rich 'entrenched interests' bent on destroying the schools that seemed 'immune to prosecution for their criminal activities.'" And there were university presidents, like Wisconsin's Glenn Frank, who excoriated a "discredited economic leadership" for trying "to shift the blame for the depression to the shoulders of government." There were others who, like school administrator Edward Elliott, indignantly insisted that the public school systems had "an inherent right to be exempted from the invidious classification as a bureaucratic part of government."[9] The very diverseness and incompatible outlooks of the protestors militated against their effectiveness, and the generally conservative and nonassertive natures of schoolteachers and administrators made any concerted political action on the part of the nation's public school establishment illusionary.

This became very evident when George Counts, professor of education at Teachers College, Columbia University, and spokesman of what came to be called educational reconstructionism, sounded a trumpet blast for teachers to assume leadership in the battle to change the course of American civilization. On February 18, 1932, he addressed the Progressive Education Association and challenged its members "to pay the costs of leadership: to accept responsibility, to suffer calumny, to surrender security, to risk both reputation and future." This was a tall order, particularly when Counts went on and asked teachers to emancipate themselves from "the viewpoint of the members of the liberal-minded upper middle class" and fashion "a compelling and challenging vision of human destiny." Teachers were to become "less frightened" of "the bogies of *imposition* and *indoctrination*."[10]

Counts's reconstructionism had originated among a small group of faculty members at Columbia University's Teachers College who subsequently became known for their journal *Social Frontier*. As he had addressed the National Council of the National Education Association and the Department of Superintendence, Counts had carried his message also to the mainstream teachers and administrators in the comprehensive high schools. But neither they nor their colleagues in the Progressive Education Association took up his challenge. The social-frontier ideology did not speak to either of them. In part this was due to Counts's infelicitous choice of words. Teachers, by and large, did not agree that imposition and indoctrination were mere "bogies" and could properly be used as teaching devices. They knew local school boards would not tolerate teachers who were to "impose" their views of the country's destiny on their communities' students. Edward Krug put it succinctly: "What alienated the school man from reconstructionism was precisely its lack of prospects for success. . . . Reconstructionism was visionary romanticism, and the voice of the school man in the land in the late 1930s proclaimed that it wouldn't 'work.'"[11] Reconstructionism, in short, was all very well for tenured faculty members at Teachers College; it had nothing to offer to the country's high school teachers.

The Progressive Education Association, however, had an agenda of its own that it pursued throughout the 1930s. Its leaders resented traditional college entrance requirements, which they felt unduly stymied both private and public progressive schools in their curricular experiments. Accordingly, they initiated the so-called Eight-Year Study to find out how their graduates compared with those of the conventional college preparatory programs of the comprehensive high schools. Although many questions were raised about the design of the experiment, the results appeared to show that non-traditionally-prepared students suffered no disadvantage in their college careers. This pleased the members of the Progressive Education Association, but it also gave, by indirection, comfort to the supporters of the comprehensive high school. They could take from it assurance that a high school, in order to successfully prepare its graduates for college, need not be of the traditional, subject-matter-bound type.

But could valid inferences for public high schools, which had to be equally concerned for all their students, be drawn from an inquiry conducted in schools with predominantly college-preparatory students? The investigations undertaken by the Eight Year Study in the Des Moines school system cast doubt on the matter. The report on the city's Theodore Roosevelt High School found that "the most significant change that came about during the entire course of the experiment was the shift from subject matter to pupil needs as the criteria for the selection of content." This passage may sound as though the school had taken to heart the many similar admonitions of *Cardinal Principles*, but in fact it reflected the vocabulary of the Progressive Education Association. In the Eight Year Study the passage was linked not to "the needs of democracy" but to "the child-centered school" and the "experience curriculum." It reflected the association's key belief in the teacher's role as "stimulating, guiding or counselling rather than dictating, directing, judging." What made a comparison with a comprehensive high school even more questionable was that at Theodore Roosevelt High School only a limited number of students and teachers—those in the college-preparatory program—participated in the experiment centered on student needs. As a result, teachers in the "regular" part of the school program were "jealous" and thought of themselves as second-rate.[12] The progressive school reformers in the Des Moines experiment held conceptions of student needs that were quite different from those espoused in *Cardinal Principles*.

Similar results, highlighting again the concerns of parents and schoolmen for the college-preparatory students, were obtained by the Lynds when in the mid-1930s they returned to Muncie, Indiana. There the college laboratory school provoked the same rivalries and jealousies as did the experimental program in Des Moines. Parents of children in other schools resented the departure of able teachers to the laboratory school; parents of students in the laboratory school complained of lack of discipline and solid learning. Teachers in the school felt themselves regarded as "pedagogical royalty" and remarked that their "success" derived not from the changed methods of teaching but from the small class sizes. What the critics in Muncie resented most was that the progressive experiments were restricted to the laboratory school and contrasted starkly with the trend toward bigness and efficiency in the city's other high schools.[13] Like Theodore Roosevelt High School in Des Moines, the laboratory school in Muncie shared little more than progressive rhetoric with the comprehensive high school as portrayed in *Cardinal Principles*.

But what about progressivism and Muncie's regular comprehensive high schools? The Lynds noted that as far as the pronouncements on the purposes of education were concerned, in Muncie the progressive flavor of educational reform was visible. The Department of Educational Research of the Muncie public schools declared in 1933 the aim of education to be "to enable every child to become a useful citizen. . . . We believe in the doctrine of equal educational opportunity for every child to develop according to his abilities, interests, and aptitudes."[14] In daily practice, the Lynds noted, the new policies had brought a displacement of traditional factual courses with exploratory work. "Mathematics" had become "shop math."[15] Because parents demanded that education assure for their children better jobs and opportunities to earn more, ability grouping and guidance programs had made their appearance. Academic guidance, however, was parceled out at ten minutes a student each semester. How useful could it possibly be? Vocational guidance, the Lynds wrote, was no more than "rudimentary" and reflected badly on the effectiveness of the school's unifying role. Guidance, the Lynds were told, had first been developed for what Muncie's school people called "our" children; then it had to be modified for "their" children, "marginal persons who are going into high school because they cannot get jobs" and who came from the "wrong" side of town.[16] One teacher called them "soggy intellectually and socially and usually nonparticipants in high-school life." The children themselves said they no longer used the school's front entrance "with the steps crowded with richer students looking you over. . . ."[17] The Lynds never mentioned the absence of minority students, although they made clear that many lived "along certain outlying, poorly paved or unpaved streets" on the South Side.[18] It is safe to assume that there were no minority students in the high school.[19]

The divisive tendencies nurtured by the extracurriculum, first noted by George Counts and the Lynds in their respective volumes of the 1920s, had grown stronger in the 1930s. In Muncie they were propelled primarily by the illegal sororities of business-class girls. Depression or not, the social pace continued, and not even mothers' attempts to curtail their daughters' spending brought any results. The school itself was powerless to deal with the issue: because it could not officially recognize the existence of illegal fraternities and sororities, it could not make rules against them. Churches and country clubs further nurtured the social distinctions. Social standing in sororities depended in large measure on the Sunday school attended: membership in the Presbyterian Church conferred the highest prestige.[20]

Teachers complained about the plethora of commissions and committees fostered by a growing bureaucracy of educational administrators and specialists. Flooded with reports and ordered to committee meetings, one Muncie teacher exclaimed: "If we could only take a day off to teach!" The steadily rising attendance, too, made many teachers uneasy. In 1890 there had been in Muncie one high school graduate for each 810 residents; in 1920 the ratio was 1:320; in 1930, 1:154; and in 1934, 1:120. More worrisome to some teachers was that of the entering class of 558 students at Central High in 1931, 200, or 36 percent, tested with an IQ of 90 and below. Summary figures for the school years from 1925/1926 to 1934/1935 showed an increase in enrollment in Muncie's entire public school system of 27.6 percent. This contrasted with a rise of teaching and administrative staff of 1 percent, and with declines in total operating expenditures of 1.7 percent and in per-pupil costs of 23 percent.[21] Squeezed as they were by increasing enrollments and decreasing budgets, Muncie's teachers had few reasons to cheer.

The Lynds also observed that all the emphasis on educating for individual differences as spelled out by national as well as local reports could not overcome deep-running contrary tendencies toward conformity. The depression with its resulting restricted labor market and its necessity to plan for economic relief and development did not encourage tolerance for diversity. It placed a premium on directed planning, common enterprises, and evaluation of educational performance by the yardstick of financial efficiency. Never before, wrote the Lynds, had the local business leadership "been in a mood to tolerate so little dissent."[22] The progressive rhetoric of individualism was at odds with a reality characterized by conformity.

The New York Regents' Inquiry

The New York Regents' Inquiry into the curriculum and the experience of students provided another glimpse of the reality of high school life in the 1930s. Organized by Francis T. Spaulding, an education professor at Harvard University, the inquiry was carried out through 1936 and 1937 and resulted in a book-length report, *High School and Life*. Ever since the nineteenth century the Regents' list of subjects required for Regents' diplomas and the examinations based on that list had guaranteed a certain amount of curricular uniformity for the New York State system. This uniformity still existed in the 1930s and was reflected in the statement that "*more than three-fourths of all the work which boys and girls were 'taking' in New York State high schools in 1937 was academic work or work in music and art, and most of the remainder consisted of training for business.*"[23] Their work consisted mainly of general academic subjects necessary for college admission, business and skill courses like typewriting and shorthand for commercial work, and household arts for girls in home economics. It relied heavily on "*drill on technical skills and memorization of a kind of factual material*" and could not, wrote Spaulding, "be expected to produce scholarship in any real sense." In business and home economics, too, drill limited to clerical and specific tasks predominated. General understanding of business and economic trends was not part of the program. The same emphasis on mechanical skills ruled the work in household arts. Its vocational part stressed domestic applications and service; its general education part emphasized family life.[24] Progressives as well as traditionalists found little to cheer in New York State.

But advocates of the academic program were dismayed about more than the emphasis on drill. The high schools did not offer any special challenges for the academically gifted student; their work was tailored for the academic average. In education for citizenship—a field schoolmen considered to be of primary importance—the schools guaranteed satisfactory results only for their graduates, especially of the 10 percent who intended to go to college. Of the nongraduates, the schools considered only two-thirds to have been adequately prepared. Spaulding viewed the nongraduates as "a group largely adrift, cut off from adult assistance." They had been "schooled in academic facts" and recognized "their rights as free citizens," but they were "unconcerned about civic responsibility."[25] The graduates who planned to go on to college generally satisfied the inquirers, though Spaulding conceded that college entrance requirements tested the ability to pass systematic courses and left unchecked the students' capacity to learn on their own.[26] The schools' greatest failures lay with their nongraduates, who constituted the majority. These young people, wrote Spaulding, "flounder with extraordinary aimlessness and lack of understanding in their efforts to adjust themselves to out-of-school conditions."[27]

The worst performance, however, took place in the vocational programs. There were few of them to begin with, though they increased markedly during the depression years. Spaulding thought the information handed out about educational careers and opportunities to be without merit. Few students, he wrote, had vocational plans for the future. Those who did had *"plans which are quite out of line with their own demonstrated abilities and with opportunities for employment."* They left school ignorant of their vocational aptitudes and of the conditions of employment.[28] Such ignorance, Spaulding emphasized, had nothing to do with the disastrous economic conditions: it had to be laid at the doors of the schools and was a result of their miserable performance in vocational preparation.

Students, however, generally valued the vocational training because they hoped it would lead to good jobs. They favored technical education in electrical and mechanical engineering, chemistry, architecture, and construction. Technical training permitted its graduates to transfer to higher education, and it thus enjoyed a degree of social respectability that, wrote Spaulding, "the industrial curricula do not have." For the great majority, however, the most popular offerings were those in the industrial arts courses, descendants of the manual training work of an earlier day and, as such, not properly considered training for trade or vocation. Because New York lacked an apprenticeship program in cooperation with industry, much of the work in trades, industry, and agriculture took place exclusively in schools, and students, except for those in agricultural programs, had little opportunity to become acquainted with or prepared for the "real" world of work. Their vocational work carried a distinct school-room flavor.[29]

Spaulding blamed the comprehensive high schools for the ill-conceived and badly executed vocational programs, which compared unfavorably with the work done in the specialized vocational schools of the few large-city school systems. However "undemocratic" the schoolmen thought the specialized schools, they offered a realistic experience in shops and related classes; they dealt with problems meaningful to the students; and emphasized preparation for a future that the students themselves knew they were facing. They also tried and succeeded in placing their graduates in jobs.[30] The state's comprehensive high schools, by contrast, evaluated their vocational students by academic criteria that bore "*little relation to the actual success of these boys and girls in getting jobs.*" Principals rarely could recommend students for vocational skills in trades and industries because they had assigned them to the "general curriculum." Employers hired the students despite the absence of teacher evaluations, hence their jobs bore "*only a crude relation to the amount or nature of their previous school work.*" Spaulding concluded that the vocational work done in the comprehensive schools was pointless and hurt the students more than it helped.[31]

Spaulding's overall evaluation of the curriculum in New York's comprehensive high schools, though measured in tone, cut deep. He appreciated their academic endeavors, unimpressive as they were, but censured the schools for their almost total neglect of the social competencies and programs stressed in *Cardinal Principles*. The academic flavor, he wrote, pervaded even the extracurricular activities, which, in most cases, were "as scholastic as the curricular work."[32] "What the schools actually teach they teach with reasonable effectiveness," Spaulding concluded, "but they fail entirely to teach many significant things which boys and girls are quite unlikely to learn except as the schools do teach them."[33] New York State clearly had left behind the nineteenth-century college-preparatory high school and people's college. It had not discovered yet the comprehensive high school as projected by *Cardinal Principles*. In 1937 its high schools appeared to be floundering without direction and purpose.

The Comprehensive School and the Needs of Students

The reports from Muncie, Indiana, and New York State made it clear that the high schools were struggling unsuccessfully at serving the needs of all their students. Theirs was an impossible task. The needs of the students were as diverse as their backgrounds, abilities, interests, and purposes. How could schools possibly respond to them all without disintegrating into chaos? In 1938 the Commission on Secondary School Curriculum of the Progressive Education Association sought to address the problem. It rejected attempts to respond directly to student wishes without attempting to transform them, and it rejected attempts that confronted students with social or curricular demands that had no relevance to their personal situations.[34] Mainstream public school teachers and administrators expressed their views in the publications of the Educational Policies Commission, jointly sponsored by the National Education Association and the American Association of School Administrators. In *The Purposes of Education in American Democracy* (1938), the Educational Policies Commission came to essentially the same conclusions as the Progressive Education Association. It affirmed unequivocally that it did not endorse identical educational programs for everybody; it sought programs that would assure equality of educational opportunity for every student, "an opportunity not inferior *in its own kind* to that given to others."[35]

In a brilliant satirical sketch, the Educational Policies Commission contrasted the traditional school program with conditions existing in 1938. Students lived in

> a democracy struggling against strangulation in an era marked by confused loyalties in the political realm, by unrest and deprivation, by much unnecessary ill-health, by high-pressure propaganda, by war and the threats of war, by many broken or ill-adjusted homes, by foolish spending, by high crime rates, by bad housing, and by a myriad of other urgent, real human problems. And what are the children in this school, in this age, in this culture, learning? They are learning that the square of the sum of two numbers equals the sum of their squares plus twice their product; that Millard Fillmore was the thirteenth President of the United States and held office from January 10, 1850, to March 4, 1853; that the capital of Honduras is Tegucigalpa; that there were two Peloponnesian Wars and three Punic Wars; that Latin verbs meaning command, obey, please, displease, serve, resist, and the like take the dative; and that a gerund is a neuter verbal noun used in the oblique cases of the singular and governing the same case as its verb.

The point was clear: Although there were students for whom the above information was useful and relevant, "for the great majority . . . such learning [was] transitory and of extremely little value." The comprehensive high school had yet to learn how to respond to that majority.[36]

The Civilian Conservation Corps Challenges the Schools

When one institution fails to live up to the demands set before it, another will take up the challenge. This happened in the spring of 1933 when the first camps of the Civilian Conservation Corps (CCC) opened their doors. The camps were designed to provide work relief through public conservation measures. Two years later the National Youth Administration (NYA) pursued similar objectives when it provided financial aid to high school and college students whose families were on relief. These measures of Franklin Roosevelt's New Deal then led to the introduction of vocational and adult education in the camps.[37]

Because this educational program was organized initially under the overall direction of the War Department, it soon aroused the ill-will of the nation's public education establishment. Opposition came into the open in 1935 when Commissioner of Education John W. Studebaker submitted a plan to Roosevelt to deal with the youth unemployment problem through community guidance and adjustment centers under the direction of the Office of Education. But the War Department won out over the Office of Education, and schoolmen were excluded from the planning and supervision of education in the camps. The schoolmen suspected that Roosevelt had been persuaded that "federal money released to the present public school systems would simply purchase more of the book-type, the fundamental type, the non-technical type, the college-preparatory type of education."[38] Although it was, indeed, true that the educational effort in the CCC camps centered on practical and adult education, the programs of the NYA favored traditional academic education as well as practical training and did not discriminate against academic work.[39] Schoolmen, however, continued to blame their being sidelined on the president's supposed animus.

President Roosevelt was less concerned with snubbing the schoolmen than with bringing effective educational aid to underprivileged Americans. The high schools could not or did not want to provide that aid; their record had shown that. The president instead turned to nursery schools for poor children and to adult and practical education, to art, theater, and music performances in the camps of the CCC and the school programs of the NYA. He did not think that the schoolmen showed any interest in these, and he was seconded by one of their own. Charles H. Judd, the former dean of the University of Chicago School of Education, certified in 1942 that "a great many school people are suffering from acute intellectual myopia." They failed "to get any view of the vast social horizon which lies beyond their immediate selfish interests," and had been "complacently oblivious" to their failure to consider new approaches to vocational

167

and adult education. Judd spared no words to confirm Roosevelt in his antipathy toward the "school crowd," as the president had called the public education establishment. The CCC and the NYA were to be the New Deal's answer to the failures of the schoolmen.[40]

The "new deal" in education addressed itself primarily to high-school-age youths whose needs the public schools had failed to meet. Enrollees in the CCC were unemployed young men, usually from low-income families or families on relief. Twenty percent came from families of foreign born parents; 10 percent were African-American; and 37 percent came from broken homes. Because 70 percent lacked any significant work experience, job training was an immediate necessity. The NYA enrolled both young women and men, and provided work for them in their home communities: men on public construction projects; women as clerical workers and assistants in schools, hospitals, libraries, and social work agencies. By 1937 the program included work opportunities and vocational training in agriculture, home economics, and industrial and mechanical occupations.[41]

The programs of both the CCC and the NYA were designed to respond to the needs of individual students, especially to those less academically inclined and excluded from the middle-class social set of the high school. In their own way, these programs sought to provide the life and growth experience that schoolmen had promised in the rhetoric of *Cardinal Principles* but had been unable to deliver. As David Tyack wrote, "In comparison with the elaborate bureaucratic structure of high schools—the grades and credits, the required courses and hall passes—the educational program of the CCC camps was flexibility incarnate." Students could choose from among vocational, academic, remedial, and avocational offerings. Their instructors came from all walks of life and thus could offer work- and life-related education. In short, this "new deal" education tried to be "progressive" and responsive to needs in the way the ordinary high school had never been able to attain.

Did the CCC and the NYA succeed where the schools had failed? The school people did not address this question because they were opposed on principle to the New Deal educational programs. They objected to the disciplinary approach of the army and the army's authoritarian style of citizenship education. Most of all, they bitterly resented the federal government's intrusion into what they considered their own sphere. As the American Youth Commission put it; "The concern of the school people has arisen out of fear that we were developing a federal system of education which would undercut and eventually displace the established public high schools of state and local school systems."[42] Except for a few individuals like Judd, quoted above, schoolmen were not likely to evaluate the experiment fairly.

The American Youth Commission, a group of prominent leaders in business, labor, government, higher education, journalism, and culture, found the schoolmen's fear of a federal takeover of the schools groundless. They pointed out that the CCC camps, located in areas distant from large high schools, had no choice but to develop their own educational programs. The NYA, active in urban and rural communities, frequently delegated its educational work to the local school systems, though, the commission admitted, such attempts at cooperation did not always succeed. Its resident centers, the commission judged, could easily be turned into state vocational schools or, if serving youths from several states, be administered by the federal government. Apparently thinking of the Danish folk high schools, the Commission suggested that these centers could become "a uniquely American type of folk school, one in which a co-operative self-help program can be provided for oncoming rural youth who have no adequate opportunities for employment or education in their home localities."[43] The commission's overall characterization of the educational "new deal" amounted to a recognition that so long as it offered educational opportunities as an integral part of its primary task of providing public work opportunities for the unemployed, it constituted a workable alternative to a standard high school education for the country's most underprivileged youth. The commission warned, however, against any "establishment of competitive and duplicative public educational services."[44]

As the 1930s drew to a close and World War II brought the country a second time within the century to embark on a program of preparedness, the issues of the 1920s and 1930s faded from view. The schoolmen considered their options. Another war for democracy rekindled their faith in the "Cardinal Principles" and in the comprehensive high school. They concluded that another attempt to translate programs and rhetoric into reality was in order. It was hoped that the 1940s would bring about what the 1920s and 1930s had failed to accomplish.

14

The High School in Search of Itself

General Education

For schoolmen of all persuasions the 1930s had been a time of disappointment, and they resolved to do better in the 1940s. The mobilization for war raised their hopes for the disappearance of the Civilian Conservation Corps and the National Youth Administration and with it for an enlargement of their own professional authority over all facets of public educational activities. Other interested groups did not hesitate either to announce their views about the future of the high school. The American Youth Commission looked for ways in which the lessons of the two New Deal agencies could be incorporated into the schools. It suggested programs of work and general education for students who had been most neglected by the schools' vocational and academic programs. The schoolmen in the National Education Association and its Educational Policy Commission, however, wanted general education for *all* American young people. Even Harvard's faculty joined the cry for general education, though the professors naturally understood it as a program of studies designed for academically trained youths. There was, then, no agreement as to just what general education might be, how general or specific it should be, and for whom it was meant to be the proper academic fare. But whatever it was or might be, general education became the desired goal.

The campaign began in 1940 with the American Youth Commission's call for a general education program for boys and girls of low ability, low motivation, and low interest who responded to neither a preprofessional academic nor a vocational education designed for highly skilled trades.

171

Such youngsters were the majority, the commission's Committee on the Secondary School Curriculum noted, and it was their right that the school take their needs and situations into account. For them, general education could be thought of either as "that common body of experience which all pupils should have" or as "that adjusted intellectual material which is introduced into the curriculum for pupils not now well served by existing courses."

Thus a new and ambiguous concept of general education was born. General education students were to be instructed in reading throughout the high school years, though teachers should be careful not to slow or halt the students' interest by demanding excessive textual analysis of the material. Students were to spend part of the school day in manual operations, though not vocational education; they were to be reintroduced to the manual training of the turn of the century and to actual work outside the classroom. As future citizens, they were to be instructed in the social studies, and as homemakers they were to be given a course in personal problems covering physical and mental health and family life. The Committee urged that history as a chronological account be replaced with social studies based on topics of current concern on which students could form "wise judgments based on knowledge of facts." General education was to equip students "to gain wisdom by absorbing independently the experience of the race on every subject on which this experience has lessons of importance to teach."[1] Still, the committee left unresolved whether general education was to be part of every student's program or whether it was meant for those who did not engage in either vocational or academic studies.

When in 1942 the American Youth Commission published *Youth and the Future,* it explained, however indirectly, its preference for work experience and manual training over vocational education. It had been impressed by the effectiveness of the federal government's initiatives in work relief and vocational training through the Civilian Conservation Corps and the National Youth Administration. These New Deal measures provided lessons for the schools, the commission observed, and showed how meaningful work had produced beneficial educational results for the students. This was all the more important now because Congress had closed the CCC camps and a year later terminated the NYA. Educators in their professional organizations now would be able to feel secure again in their undisputed hegemony over the affairs of the nation's youth. The war was providing a breathing space, but when peace returned they could expect the resumption of unemployed youths' crowding into classrooms and reviving the problems the schools had experienced in the 1930s. During the war was the time to get ready to meet the critics and prepare the ground for a vigorous comeback.

Educators, however, remained silent on the nation's most persistent social problem, the country's shameful record of segregation and discrimination against its minority citizens. As David Tyack pointed out, though
there was no lack of statistical data and sociological studies elsewhere, in
the schoolmen's publications African-American and minority students
simply did not exist. Not only was segregation legal in the southern states
but segregation stalked the schoolmen's own professional organizations.
At its conventions the National Education Association, the nation's largest
professional teachers organization, segregated members by race and pa-
raded racial stereotypes in its floor show. Even liberal professional leaders
like John Dewey and George Counts often relied on no more than democratic rhetoric to protest the racism of their colleagues.[2]

The Views of Schoolmen and Professors

Not to be outdone by the American Youth Commission in its professed
concern for the general education of the less able and unmotivated student, the National Education Association in 1944 cast its net far more
widely. Through its Educational Policies Commission it presented its conception of the high school under the provocative title *Education for All
American Youth*. The program presented therein was not to be a limited
one for any special group but a comprehensive approach to include all
young people of high school age and, as we shall see, beyond.

The commission took its readers to two imaginary localities, Farmville and American City. In each was to be found the kind of high school
the historian of 1950 would describe. In a repetitious, unctuous, and
saccharine narrative, the authors portrayed a galaxy of wise and competent schoolmen, eager and pliant students, and agreeable and applauding parents and citizens. Schooling was a community affair, the
book repeated on nearly every page. From the foreword and the first
chapter onward it is clear that the urgency driving the writing was the
authors' paranoid fear of "a federalized system of secondary education
. . . to compete with and ultimately replace the traditional American system of state and local control. . ." They called instead for "a wisely
planned and vigorously implemented program for the improvement,
adaptation, and extension of educational services to youth . . . by the local and state educational authorities." If such authorities would do their
part, "it will be neither necessary nor desirable for the federal government itself to operate educational services for the youth of the nation."
With the help of local and state boards, the school establishment could
do it all.[3]

What, then, were the high schools to accomplish? The commission gave its readers a slightly revised version of *Cardinal Principles*. All students should be vocationally prepared, readied for citizenship and family living, and exposed to health education, art and cultural appreciation. They should be intellectually curious, know how to pursue happiness, and have learned to think rationally and appreciate ethical values. The public school would now extend its tutelage from the junior high schools' seventh, eighth, and ninth to the senior high schools' tenth, eleventh, and twelfth grades and then include grades thirteen and fourteen for out-of-school youths and adults. As the commission put it for the case of Farmville,

> The entire period of youth is thus encompassed within a single institution. Within the school, one finds no hard-and-fast divisions, but rather a continuous program suited to boys and girls from twelve to twenty, changing with the changing needs and interests of maturing youth, and sufficiently flexible to permit adaptation to students who differ somewhat from the average.

The junior high school would stress the common areas of learning: in the later years differentiated instruction would appear in occupations, intellectual pursuits, and recreation. For the transition from mainly common to differentiated education the school's guidance program would become of primary importance; it was considered the school program's "keystone."[4]

For American City, the commission placed greater emphasis on vocational education. In the urban context this should include "work experience under employment conditions." Teachers would now be more ready to accept this because the accusations of the past that the high schools "had failed in their duties to millions of boys and girls" had "shaken many a teacher out of his accustomed routine of subject teaching." Because there were three high schools in American city, each should be comprehensive in its programs but differ in specific vocational assignments. All three should offer instruction in business, distributive, and homemaking education, but programs in agriculture and cosmetology, in domestic, hotel or restaurant occupations, in airplane or automobile mechanics, in the building, electrical, machine, metal and printing trades should be offered in one high school only. In American City people would think of the junior high school as the lower secondary school, of the senior high school as the middle secondary school, and of a new community institute as the advanced secondary school. Because the institute was to supply liberal and practical education for full- and part-time students, it was thought best that it be closely aligned with the local schools. The relationship would also keep it out from under the specter of "college domination."[5] The schoolmen, whether locally or on the state level, wanted to make sure that post-high-school education would remain under their control.

Not only schoolmen but also university faculties had become concerned over the future of the high school. During the war, the Harvard College faculty decided to devote part of its self-study to the education its freshmen received in the high schools. With the wartime democratic rhetoric ringing in their ears, the professors could hardly do otherwise than endorse the general progressive concerns of the schoolmen for the comprehensive high school, but they were not willing to permit academic training and intellectual pursuits to be pushed to the sidelines. In their famed Redbook of 1945, *General Education in a Free Society*, the Harvard faculty members viewed a liberal education as the appropriate academic fare for students in high schools and colleges. They reminded high school teachers that the schools had to educate the one-fourth of their students who intended to go to college along with the three-fourths who did not. They urged the teachers to preserve the best of tradition and join it to the newfound concern for "the common man" and his children. The teachers would have to find a middle way between academic and practical education, between schooling for the few and the many, and between showing concern for individual students and for all.

In practical terms, the Harvard committee reverted to the general education concept first introduced in 1940 by the Special Committee on the Secondary School Curriculum of the American Youth Commission. That concept, the reader may recall, was anything but clear: it had described general education at times as a common body of experience for all students and at others as intellectual material that was "adjusted" so that it could be understood by the slow as well as the fast learner. The Harvard committee did not make the concept any clearer. It did not spell out just how that concept resembled or differed from its concept of a liberal education but simply suggested an academic core curriculum of social studies, English, science, and mathematics. The committee recommended that the same material be taught to gifted and slow students by different methods and at various levels of difficulty, and that practical courses be used to "meet students on their own grounds."[6] This was Harvard's way of dealing with a problem that had been around since *Cardinal Principles* had first been discussed. One reviewer was prompted to write sarcastically, "The fact that 'much of yesterday's wisdom is today's banality and tomorrow's baloney' does not trouble the framers of this report."[7] The great majority of critics, however, missed or ignored the cavalier way in which the Harvard faculty had dealt with the issue of general education. According to their own positions, they condemned or praised the report for its emphasis on academic subject matter. After all, that was what most people expected to hear from Harvard.

Life Adjustment

While the schoolmen and the Harvard professors debated general education, the Vocational Education Division of the U.S. Office of Education had begun an inquiry of its own. Old-line vocationalists had always felt uncomfortable with comprehensive school-based vocational education. They felt that it was too often guided and overseen by professional schoolmen who had no personal experience and often no sympathy with the "real world of work." Schools lacked the feel of the "factory floor" and could not afford the necessary up-to-date machinery and tools. Thus instructors shifted the emphasis from practical training to general theoretical matters that were more appropriate for students who intended to go on to higher technical schools. Matters were not helped when vocational guidance and information were often spotty and incomplete. This left many youngsters adrift and without incentive to stay in school. In 1945 the vocationalists thought they had found an answer to these problems.

At the closing session on June 1, 1945, of the national conference Vocational Education in the Years Ahead, Charles A. Prosser, former secretary of the National Society for the Promotion of Industrial Education and then director of the Dunwoody Institute in Minneapolis, presented a summarizing resolution. He asserted without statistical studies to back up his numbers that vocational schools were able to prepare 20 percent of the nation's secondary-school-age youths for entrance into the skilled trades. The high schools, he said, did well for another 20 percent in preparing them for college. But, he added,

> We do not believe that the remaining 60 percent of our youth of secondary school age will receive the life adjustment training they need and to which they are entitled as American citizens—unless and until the administrators of public education with the assistance of the vocational education leaders formulate a similar program for this group.

Thus was launched a new concept and a new program that would make headlines for years to come and, as the vocationalists hoped, would finally set vocational education on the right path.

The Prosser resolution was remarkable. Greeted with enthusiasm at the conference for its call to yet another schoolmen's crusade, it was at the same time by indirection a terrible indictment of the failure of the comprehensive high school. Prosser, perhaps the country's best-known vocationalist, not only did not mention the vocational programs of the comprehensive high school when he spoke of "the vocational school of a community" that would educate 20 percent of its youths but also ignored the comprehensive high school altogether. As he would subsequently spell out in his *Secondary Education and Life*, he did not see much point for specific vocational training in the high schools and would rather have it replaced by a program of general education.[8] He had always believed that the comprehensive high school was not the most suitable home for vocational education, and that vocational education, to be effective, had to be specialized and conducted in close collaboration with trades or industries. The comprehensive high school performed only one function well: serving a minority of its students in preparing for college. Other parts of the school's curricula had failed; it had done next to nothing for 60 percent of its students and would do nothing unless schoolmen came up with another program altogether. The Prosser resolution was a damning indictment of the comprehensive high school. That the schoolmen nevertheless managed to turn this virtual death sentence into a platform for a high-powered public relations campaign on behalf of life adjustment stands as testimony to their remarkable capacity for self-deception and their manipulative ingenuity.

What was life adjustment? In the words of U.S. Commissioner of Education John W. Studebaker, it was meant to be an aggregate of programs designed for "the educationally neglected youth [who] are retarded in school and who even though they make lower than average scores on intelligence and achievement tests, we cannot conclude that they are inferior."[9] This grammatical monstrosity of a sentence spliced together sentiments from previous pronouncements in *Cardinal Principles*, in bulletins of the U.S. Office of Education, in statements of the Educational Policies Commission and the American Youth Commission, and in *Education for All American Youth*. And sure enough, when in 1947 the Commission on Life Adjustment Education for Youth, called into being by Studebaker, defined life adjustment education as "that which better equips all American youth to live democratically with satisfaction to themselves and profit to society as home members, workers, and citizens,"[10] the schoolmen's appetite for self-aggrandizement had within two short years expanded Prosser's 60 percent of American youth into the Educational Policy Commission's *all* American youth. Interestingly enough, Prosser was not a member of the Commission on Life Adjustment Education for Youth. One wonders what he thought of this gratuitous inflation of his concept.

Life adjustment as the latest program of general education amounted to a rewording of *Cardinal Principles* with added phrases from the various conceptions of core curricula and general education programs then in circulation. Because the antiacademic bias of the life adjustment spokesmen was pronounced, Harvard's version was rarely mentioned. Life ad-

177

justers wanted to break loose from the service of an intellectual elite, and, as one schoolman put it, in the name of democracy and common learning scuttle the elective system "run rampant."[11] Academic subject matter became a scorned concept. To be taken up, curricular materials had to meet the tests of student interest and functional relevance to every student's life and situation. Now everything could be made a part of the high school's curriculum as long as it promised to keep students in school.

In this newfound ideology schoolmen saw the tool with which they could expect to do away with low-academic achievement scores among students from low income families and among students from racial and ethnic minority families. With it they could also expect to defeat the rising high-school-dropout and juvenile crime rates. What none among these schoolmen seems to have noticed was that a campaign prompted by the needs of quite specific groups within the high school population would produce a watered-down program aimed at the lowest common denominator of the entire population.

The Academic Counterpunch

Life adjustment education set the tone for much of American secondary education during the late 1940s and into the mid-1950s. But a countermove propelled by events of the Cold War and the worldwide efforts to achieve technological breakthroughs in the arms race and space exploration began during those years. Scientists, scholars, and military leaders pressed the schools to improve their academic and scientific training to guarantee U.S. world leadership in science and technology. Their campaign received the support of the academic progressives and old-line traditional academics who had watched the democratic posturing of the life adjusters with growing exasperation. The comeback of the academics now turned the tables on the schoolmen who in the early postwar years had succeeded in stamping out any vestiges of "college domination." Within a few years and quite abruptly, the life adjustment boom collapsed. The high school was off on a new tack.

The "academic rearmament," if we may call it that, had begun in 1950 with the creation by Congress of the National Science Foundation. Initially, the foundation directed its efforts toward the universities, but in 1956 it funded the Physical Science Study Committee at the Massachusetts Institute of Technology to prepare a revised high school physics curriculum. A similar university study group, the Committee on School Mathematics, had begun work in 1952 at the University of Illinois and produced what became known as "the new math." Private foundations also joined the effort. In 1953 the Ford Foundation's Fund for the Advancement of Education launched the Advanced Placement Program for high school seniors; two years later the foundation set up the National Merit Scholarship Corporation and, for high school teachers, the John Hay Fellowships. Other initiatives of similar kind issued the "new physics" and the "new social studies." All of these efforts received added impetus when in 1957 the Soviet Union's sputnik appeared in the skies and, as the cartoons had it, asked in German where its American counterpart might be found. That it was nowhere in sight most Americans blamed on the high schools and their neglect of academic studies.

Neotraditionalists, who, in many instances, could trace their lineage back to the old-line academic schoolmen in the Progressive Education Association, blasted what they considered the curricular inanities and absurdities of life adjustment. In *And Madly Teach* Mortimer Smith charged that the life-adjusters had deserted Thomas Jefferson and Horace Mann. Four years later, Arthur Bestor, himself a graduate of Lincoln School, the progressive laboratory school of Teachers College, Columbia University, wrote that life adjustment

> is the philosophy which asserts that the public schools must "adjust" a majority of our children . . . to the bitter fact that they are good for nothing but undesirable, unskilled occupations, and that intellectual effort is far beyond their feeble grasp.[12]

Bestor and like-minded neotraditionalists maintained that the schoolmen had bungled the educator's most crucial task: to awaken and raise in students the power of thinking to its highest possible potential. With life adjustment, the neotraditionalists charged, the mainline progressivism of *Cardinal Principles* had reached a dead end.

As life adjustment, the latest of the schoolmen's gospels collapsed, and as the sputnik scare and the Cold war–fueled clamor for scientific and technological expertise provided the needed stimulus, academic progressives and neotraditionalists sought ways of resuscitating the academic liberal arts tradition of secondary education and of restoring it to its central place in the schools. They found them in the theories of Jerome S. Bruner, spelled out in his small book of 1960, *The Process of Education*. Thirty-five natural scientists, mathematicians, psychologists, and other scholars and educators had gathered at Woods Hole in Massachusetts in 1959 to review the curricular reform efforts of the preceding decade and to discuss how to improve the teaching of science and history in the elementary and secondary schools, how "to present subject matter effectively." The psychologists in the group stressed the future benefits students ought to be able to

179

derive from learning, benefits that would flow from the ability to recognize future problems as special cases of an idea originally learned. Thus learning, once begun, could continue through a transfer of principles, which transfer would depend for its success on earlier student mastery of subject matter: "the most fundamental understanding . . . that can be achieved of the underlying principles that give structure to [a] subject."[13]

Teaching the structure of subject matter by going back to fundamental principles and ideas was the key to successful teaching. And these basic principles and ideas, Bruner wrote, "are as simple as they are powerful." Their very simplicity allowed him to maintain that the teaching of the liberal arts and sciences was possible at any level. It need not be set aside for the "academically gifted" or for the more advanced and older student. Bruner's hypothesis stated that "any subject can be taught effectively in some intellectually honest form to any child at any stage of development." In Bruner's words:

> If one respects the ways of thought of the growing child, if one is courteous enough to translate material into his logical forms and challenging enough to tempt him to advance, then it is possible to introduce him at an early age to the ideas and styles that in later life make an educated man.

The Woods Hole conference sought to delineate a roadmap, with the help of which American schools might once again point their students in an academic direction.[14]

It was much to Bruner's credit that he recognized the dangers inherent in such a redirection of effort. For forty years the schoolmen had emphasized the social rather than the intellectual life of the high school, had encouraged the cooperative rather than the competitive leanings of their students. Now, just after the life adjustment drive had played itself out and Americans seemed overawed by the demands of science and technology and the threat of Soviet power, high schools were about to throw the rudder around and concentrate on the academically gifted students who were to be rewarded with fellowships and careers. The sudden about-face, Bruner warned, was fraught with danger. It was likely to lock young people into a meritocratic system in which high school scholastic success or failure was to determine the course of a lifetime. In the hands of inexpert teachers, an emphasis on science and technology would lead to a devaluation of literature, history, and the arts. A system whose energy was fueled by competitive examinations would soon degenerate into rote book learning—exactly the opposite of what the academic revival with its emphasis on discovery learning and basic understanding of structures desired. The answer lay in advanced planning to stimulate a vigorous pluralism of academic school life in which "the theater, the arts, music and the humanities" would be equal partners with the sciences and technology, and rote was banished by discovery learning.[15] Bruner's concern, however, extended only to the academically gifted students; he had nothing to say of the students in the vocational and general education classes.

The Conant Reports

At about the same time that Bruner and his colleagues met at Woods Hole, there appeared the first volume of the Carnegie Corporation–sponsored study, *The American High School Today*. It was followed two years later by a supplementary volume, *Slums and Suburbs*. The author was James Bryant Conant, formerly president of Harvard University, high commissioner to the U.S.-occupied zone of Germany, and ambassador to the Federal Republic. Conceived before sputnik sent shockwaves through American society and published after that event, Conant's studies represented a grand effort at resuscitating the dream of *Cardinal Principles* as reformulated in the Educational Policies Commission's *Education for All American Youth* and at synthesizing it with the general education theories of the American Youth Commission and the Harvard *General Education in a Free Society* report. Conant's commitment to the comprehensive high school and to academic rigor for the academically able student left no room for the "functional relevance" of life adjustment, and his studies sovereignly ignored that sorry interlude. Instead, he focused on the comprehensive high school of *Cardinal Principles*, which he regarded as the quintessential school of American democracy, unique and without equal in the world.

The school's program, Conant wrote, "corresponded to the needs of *all* the youth of the community." The question that he wanted to answer was whether this school could

> at one and the same time provide a good general education for *all* the pupils as future citizens of a democracy, provide elective programs for the majority to develop useful skills, and educate adequately those with a talent for handling advanced academic subjects—particularly foreign languages and mathematics?

Conant's answer was yes. "No radical alteration in the basic pattern of American education is necessary in order to improve our public high schools."[16]

The comprehensive school's most salutary effect on American society, and in Conant's view its chief redeeming value, was its unifying function.[17] It was most in evidence in the school's homeroom program. Homerooms, containing a "cross section of the school in terms of ability and vocational interest," elected representatives to the student council, and so became "significant social units." Conant believed that homerooms, like the social studies class for graduating seniors, helped develop mutual respect and understanding among students across lines of social class and academic and vocational pursuits.[18] After forty years of homerooms and their beneficial effects, Conant thought, the comprehensive high school of *Cardinal Principles* had proved its worth.

Even so, Conant held that the high school's academic program was deficient, particularly in the teaching of foreign languages and in its guidance services for academically capable girls. Everywhere, he wrote, the

> academically talented student, as a rule, is not being sufficiently challenged, does not work hard enough, and his program of academic subjects is not of sufficient range. The able boys too often specialize in mathematics and science to the exclusion of foreign languages and to the neglect of English and social studies. The able girls, on the other hand, too often avoid mathematics and science as well as the foreign languages.

What distressed Conant even more was that not all U.S. high schools fit the model of the comprehensive school. Separate specialized schools lacked the unifying features of the comprehensive school, and too many small high schools—74 percent of the total—had graduating classes of fewer than one hundred. These small schools had to disappear; elimination by district reorganization was to be a priority.[19]

In large cities, the specialized schools Conant so disliked were vocational and academic high schools; in affluent suburbs, the latter were college-preparatory high schools without vocational and commercial programs. In some states, federal support under the Smith-Hughes or the George-Barden acts for separate vocational schools deprived the comprehensive schools of their vocational offerings. In all these instances specialized schools robbed their students of the social interaction with peers of different backgrounds and interests. Comprehensive schools should so improve their academic work, Conant suggested, that separate high schools would become unnecessary. He particularly deplored the stress on the college-preparatory function to the detriment of the vocational in wealthy suburban areas, railing against "the overambitious parent who wants his offspring to go to a particular college, even if the pupil has less-than-average academic ability."[20] Conant implied that Americans should know better than to let such parents have their way.

Even worse was the situation of schools in the slums of large cities. As Conant turned to these in *Slums and Suburbs*, he exhorted the schoolmen to devote their best efforts to their improvement. He encouraged them to work for a racially integrated teaching force; to appeal to the voters to end the inequality of opportunity attendant upon the lesser allocation of money to inner-city schools; to assume responsibility for educational and vocational guidance of out-of-school youths up to the age of twenty-one; to expand work-study programs for slow learners; and to put their energies into improving schools for African-Americans, into sending more teachers into slum schools, and into enlisting the support of parents rather than simply seeking cross-town busing for minority students.[21] He warned that the present situation allowed "social dynamite to accumulate in our large cities," and called attention to the root cause of slum deterioration: the permanent unemployment of minority youths and its ineluctable consequence, a lack of conviction on their part that there was a way out of their predicament.

Conant and the schoolmen knew that these were matters beyond the capacity of the schools to deal with in any effective way. No amount of curricular manipulation, whether through general education or vocational education programs, could cope with near-permanent unemployment and hopelessness.[22] Accordingly, he called on the federal government for relief and endorsed initiatives that were in part similar to those of the National Youth Administration of the 1930s. He pointed to the draft of President John F. Kennedy's federally subsidized Youth Employment Act of 1961 and to the job-training and public-service-employment opportunities it provided. "[W]ithout a drastic change in the employment prospects for urban Negro youth," he asserted, "relatively little can be accomplished." But he also was aware that to educators federal help in the form of work-study relief was as much a threat as promise. The schoolmen still carried with them their suspicions from the New Deal era, and they were reluctant to act. Conant knew that. He was hoping he could appeal to an aroused public sentiment to live up to the challenge of equality of educational opportunity.[23]

The Elusive Promise

Seen in historical perspective, Conant's reports asserted that the high school could live up to the democratic aspirations of *Cardinal Principles*, function again as a nineteenth-century people's college for its employ-

183

ment-bound graduates, and bring back to life the academic training the Committee of Ten had asked for. But he also pointed out that for forty years the school had been unable to accomplish these goals. The 74 percent of all high schools that had graduating classes of fewer than one hundred students did not meet Conant's criteria for a well functioning school. From the remaining 26 percent—which furnished 68 percent of all twelfth-grade students—we should have to subtract all specialized vocational and academic schools, as well as the schools in wealthy suburbs and inner-city slums to arrive at the percentage of schools that did meet Conant's criteria. They amounted to probably less than 20 percent of the total.[24]

Conant's equal emphasis on vocational and academic preparation brought him close to the educational philosophy of the nineteenth-century people's college. For the vocationally inclined students, he recommended gender-based programs. For boys, they would provide training in trades and industries; for girls, in typing, stenography, home economics, distributive education, and, in rural areas, agriculture. To face the world of modern industry with confidence and to be prepared for changes and shifts in future employment, students in any of these programs were also to take English, social studies, and other courses required for graduation.[25] Conant was aware that these recommendations would offend the sensibilities of ambitious parents and liberal ideologues, and that "some professors of the liberal arts will denounce [them] as dangerously heretical." But so convinced was he of the necessity of strong vocational training that he charged critics proposing a purely academic high school curriculum with making "a suggestion dangerous to the security of our nation."[26]

In his concern for the highly gifted and academically talented students—the former he defined as those in the top 3 percent of their class and the latter as those in the top 15 to 20—Conant resembled his predecessor at Harvard, Charles W. Eliot of the Committee of Ten. Conant advised that schools make special arrangements for the highly gifted already in the seventh or eighth grade and enroll them in an advanced placement program when they entered the twelfth grade. The academically talented should be encouraged to study advanced mathematics, science, and foreign languages, and should be protected from interference with their homework. Communities should deemphasize "basketball, football, and marching bands," and see to it that the students' home study time was not constantly interrupted by "club meetings, junior lodge meetings, dramatic and music rehearsals, [and] athletic events sponsored by community organizations." "It is in the national interest," Conant added, "to have them [the academically talented] develop their capacities to the full and to start this development as early as possible." In these words it was quite evident that for Conant the motivating spur and sustaining thrust of the academic revival lay in the country's Cold War need for academically trained people.[27]

With *The American High School Today* and *Slums and Suburbs* Conant had documented once more that the comprehensive high school remained an elusive promise, its realization across the length and breadth of the country far from accomplished. In addition to the observations already recorded, his many other comments illustrated how far the school still had to travel. Conant urged that it create a properly trained staff of counsellors who could avoid the rigidities of a tracking system and assure individualized programs for each student through subject-by-subject ability grouping. He called for a remedial reading program and "simple vocational work" for the slow readers, for academic honor lists and summer schools for both slow and bright students.[28] His suggestions all pointed to present inadequacies and were meant to bring closer to reality a comprehensive high school that would justify everyone's dreams for a school that accomplishes it all: educates all youths together for their different destinies, with equal opportunity for each and discrimination toward none. But there obviously was a long, long way to go.

15

End of an Era

New Horizons

During the 1960s, the spotlight shifted from curricular to social concerns. What happened in schools, how their curricula evolved and how their policies were shaped, became grist for the mills of politicians. Educational policy entered the halls of Congress. The schoolmen's debates were overshadowed by state and national legislation that substituted social, economic, and racial policies for curricular and pedagogical considerations. The traumatic events of the decade were in large measure responsible for this shift. The strains of the Cold War and of the war in Vietnam were creating social and racial unrest at home. The civil rights movement, highlighted for educators by the aftereffects of the 1954 *Brown v. Board of Education* decision, spread racial ferment far and wide. The nationwide discrepancies in income and health standards added fuel to the conflagrations that broke out in cities from Watts in California to Newark in New Jersey. University students went on the rampage from Berkeley to Madison to New York. The assassinations of President John F. Kennedy in November of 1963 and, five years later, of civil rights leader Martin Luther King and of the slain president's brother Attorney General Robert F. Kennedy deepened the traumatic impact of the decade. When in 1970 university students were killed by gunfire and bomb blasts at Kent State, Jackson State, and the University of Wisconsin–Madison, it became clear to the last doubter that the developments in the country's educational institutions were intertwined with the larger destiny of the nation.

In *The Comprehensive High School: A Second Report,* James Conant in 1967 reaffirmed his predilection for federal action. He attributed the dearth of well-functioning comprehensive high schools to the reliance on local financing and the unwillingness of the schoolmen to call for state and federal assistance. As a result, wrote Conant, "the American ideal of equality of educational opportunity is far from being realized."[1] The comprehensive high school had quite obviously not succeeded in unifying the high school population. Adolescents were scattered into all sorts of schools: comprehensive, slum, and suburban high schools, and the many different specialized and private schools. The absence of nationwide common practices, "let alone a national policy," made it impossible to assure a common educational platform. Huge differences in per capita expenses for students and in the instructor-to-students ratio among and within states made a mockery of the equality of educational opportunity.

Conant therefore again recommended state and national financial initiatives. Though he did this as cautiously as he could—avoiding citing dollar figures, and using instead the discrepancies in the staff-student ratio among states—he aroused anxiety and ill-will among the schoolmen, who still feared a revival of the federal depression-era programs that they had detested so much.[2] But legislators did begin to move. Following up on the *Brown* decision of 1954, the Civil Rights Act of 1964 instructed the U.S. Commissioner of Education to survey efforts made to assure equal educational opportunity and to assist localities in desegregating schools. The most momentous development, however, occurred the next year when Congress passed legislation enabling federal aid to education. The Elementary and Secondary Education Act of 1965 assigned federal funds according to the number of poor children in a given school district. Because the formula benefited the inner-city schools, the act may be seen as a direct congressional response to Conant's pleas. At the same time, however, it had little to say about his concerns for insufficient academic and vocational instruction. For all practical purposes, the events of the 1960s aborted the "academic rearmament" that had begun in the 1950s. As Diane Ravitch put it, "The expected pedagogical revolution in the schools was not to be. . . . It was swept aside by the onrush of the racial revolution. . . . [T]he pedagogical revolution was no revolution at all."[3] Priorities had once more been changed, and this time they were driven by forces outside the schools and academia.

Protesters, Social Scientists, and the Schoolmen

Although Congress and the state legislatures had seized the initiative, a multihued band of rebels and protesters highlighted the pedagogic inadequacies in academic and vocational instruction. They underscored Conant's disturbing accusations of inequality of opportunity rampant in the public education system and held up to public view the evidence of segregation and discrimination in the schools. In *How Children Fail*, John Holt proposed to resurrect the child-centered school of the 1920s. Paul Goodman in *Compulsory Mis-Education* attacked the idea of compulsory education as an oxymoron and professional schoolmen as "a vast vested interest" who kept "more than a million people busy, wasting wealth, and pre-empting time and space in which something else could be going on." Edgar Friedenberg accused Americans of ignoring what happened to adolescents in the classrooms. His *Coming of Age in America* argued that adolescents were given "the full nineteenth-century colonial treatment," infantilized in schools and kept out of the adult world. Five years later Charles Silberman's *Crisis in the Classroom* described the high school classroom as "grim, joyless . . . oppressive and petty," subjected to a rigid and inhumane school bureaucracy. Although these critics and others like them did not all center their complaints on the high schools, their accusations—especially those that questioned the schools as the only place for youths to be educated—contributed to the unease that pervaded the world of the professional educators.[4]

The real bombshell, however, exploded in 1966: James S. Coleman's *Equality of Educational Opportunity*. This book has been described as the single-most-significant contribution made by social science research to the debate over the nation's schools. In it Coleman provided statistical evidence for Conant's accusations: minority students, especially lower-class African-Americans, had less access than white students to physical facilities and curricular and extracurricular programs, though the difference was not as marked as had been thought. But more important, academic achievement appeared to be related more to family background than to school quality. Only for minority students, whose academic achievement declined progressively as they moved from grade to grade, did school quality and social-class and racial composition of the student body make a difference. Coleman therefore concluded that they would benefit academically if they were brought in closer contact with more students of nonminority and middle- and upper-class backgrounds. The dispersal of minority students, and their integration into schools with a majority of nonminority students thus appeared to many as a desirable policy.[5]

The subsequent report in February 1967 of the U.S. Commission on Civil Rights, *Racial Isolation in the Public Schools,* pursued the argument and helped shift policy away from concentrated compensatory instructional efforts in predominantly black schools to busing of minority students into schools with a majority of white students.[6] The eventual result was the backlash of a movement for black pride and community control. Many

189

African-Americans objected to the denigration of minority schools implied in the integrationist policies of busing and dispersion of minority students. Integration as a policy was further weakened when in 1972 Christopher Jencks, a Harvard social scientist who had earlier advocated resort to nonschool institutions as well as to alternative schools, warned against too great a reliance on school reform as a means to social reform. Equalizing educational opportunities and racial desegregation in schools had not been shown to bring about changes in educational attainment.[7]

Three years later James Coleman threw another bombshell when he warned against the policy implications that had been drawn from his 1966 report. The policy of busing, he pointed out, far from having improved the school performance of minority students, had prompted the phenomenon of "white flight" from the inner cities.[8] The schoolmen, it appeared, could expect little firm and reliable guidance from social scientists. As two of the latter confessed in 1977, social science research resembled "a dialogue—rather than a problem-solving exercise."[9]

While protesters and social scientists filled reams of paper with accusations and advice, while politicians debated in Congress and state legislatures, and while the public, reacting to the evidence of poverty, destitution, racial strife, and unrest in the classrooms, began the flight from public into private education, the schoolmen showed signs of losing their sense of direction. Because they wanted to hang onto their vision of the comprehensive high school and also to do justice to the changing temper of the time, they responded by seeking to make the high school ever more inclusive in its programs. In 1962 the Educational Policies Commission, for example, added the ability to think to the canon of objectives. The same educators, who since the end of the war had seen in education for democratic citizenship the core of the high school's efforts for all American youth, now borrowed their language from Jerome Bruner and declared rational inquiry to be the school's most important task. They spoke glowingly of astronomers, biologists, and historians and held them up as models for high school students.[10]

Such bending to then-prevailing curricular winds, however, did not do away with the accumulating evidence of instructional failure in the comprehensive high schools. Unease characterized the 1967 convention of the National Association of Secondary School Principals. There they learned from Ralph Tyler—like Coleman, one of the nation's foremost social scientists—that the association's National Committee on Secondary Education had been able to find only 4,850 truly comprehensive public and private high schools in the country. This compared with 17,850 noncomprehensive schools of various kinds. Harold Howe II, U.S. commissioner of education, pointed out that the recent emphasis on academic subjects and rational inquiry had had an unbalancing effect on the curriculum, as had the increasing number of separate vocational schools. None of these developments strengthened the comprehensive high school. To Howe and to most of the principals at the gathering, that was a pity. Howe summed it up quite concisely when he called the comprehensive high school "an ideal we may never reach but which gives us a goal to seek."[11]

Other educators showed their insecurity by endorsing many different and often diametrically opposed curricular approaches, in the hope that each could benefit some student. Harl R. Douglass, who in 1937 had been a staunch supporter of *Cardinal Principles,* now endorsed with minor modifications Conant's recommendations of subject-matter study, and even found some, though limited, merit in a national curriculum and a standard system of instructional methods. At the same time, he announced that dropout and terminal students needed a curriculum that "will fit their needs in life."[12] B. Frank Brown, a former high school principal, upset his colleagues when in *New Directions for the Comprehensive High School,* he declared that "the seven Cardinal Principles and their resulting guidelines served their purpose well for half a century, but they are now hopelessly out of date." Brown advocated student choice and educational alternatives; attacked the monopolistic and self-aggrandizing drift of the school establishment; and accused his colleagues of wanting to keep every aspect of adolescence under their authoritarian control. He recommended the abolition of all general education programs and their replacement with career education, a newly developed version of vocational education that I shall discuss presently. He favored out-of-school learning activities, which were to include community service, work study, part-time employment, independent study, and field work. He angrily repudiated Conant's suggestion for school counselors and suggested instead that the traditional counseling system "be replaced by a system using . . . a consortium of teachers and business personnel." As Brown's case shows, there were heretics, even among the ranks of the faithful, who were ready for a radical restructuring of the high school.[13]

Not long after Brown's book appeared, the National Association of Secondary School Principals combined their members' insistence on undisputed control over their domain of schooling with a demand for authority to refer to other agencies the young people who resisted their efforts. The association asked that the "delivery of rehabilitative services . . . be by youth-serving agencies," but that schoolmen retain overall control over the assignment of students and the coordination of the agencies. Schoolmen remained in control, though other agencies were to carry out the work.[14] But the association meant to go further and extend into adulthood the schoolmen's claim over individuals who sought instruction. Under the heading "Compulsory Education," the association spoke of an individual's involvement "with a structured program of learning under the guidance of the school," "until requirements for the high school diploma are completed"—this could happen before or after the student had reached the age of eighteen. As the statement put it in its honey-sweet language: "[p]ersons who do not qualify for graduation upon reaching legal adulthood at age 18 should be allowed and encouraged to pursue the diploma at public expense until the diploma is achieved, regardless of age." The 1975 task force report represented the schoolmen's most extended claim over the direction of youths and adults. It embodied in its phrases a concept of "total education" that had antecedents in modern times only in the educational proclamations of modern totalitarian societies. Needless to say, the association offered this proposal in the language of a democratic society's responsibility for offering all youths an equal opportunity for education.[15]

From Vocational to Career Education

One of the recurring problems the schoolmen faced was to find an educational program for students who, as Prosser had once put it, were served neither by academic nor vocational instruction. In the 1940s educators had tried to shelter them under the blanket of life adjustment education; in the 1950s general education became the new gospel. With its bland offerings usually reduced in academic quality to the lowest common level, it had not been able to hold the vocational education dropout students either. In the 1960s, prompted by the new concern for disadvantaged youths, vocational educators began to speak of them as "youth with special needs." They suggested that with the help of subject matter specialists they could prepare such young people for the increasing complexity of the economy and of technology. As the authors of *Education and the Disadvantaged American* wrote, "The long-range solution is an increase in the length and effectiveness of schooling."[16] But the vocational educators did not say how a school that had not been able to solve the problems of the disadvantaged students through life adjustment and general education was now to do so with a combined program of vocational and academic education of increased length. Those students, after all, had been barred from or had deserted the very academic and vocational education to which they were now again to be assigned at a higher level of intensity and for a prolonged period.

The vagueness of these proposals notwithstanding, Congress responded to the pleas of the vocational educators and in 1963 passed another vocational education act. Following President Lyndon Johnson's general outlines for the war against poverty, Congress extended federal support for the vocational instruction of men and women of all ages in high schools and in community or junior colleges. It provided funding for part-time employment for youths, for people seeking employment or wishing to upgrade their skills, and for the educationally handicapped—as the disadvantaged were now called. Because funds were available for the construction of area vocational and residential vocational schools, the comprehensive high school no longer received favored attention.[17]

As time passed, nobody was very satisfied with the results. W. Norton Grubb and Marvin Lazerson pointed out that

> students never flocked to vocational education courses; they rarely found jobs in the area for which they had been trained, and many did not even stay in school long enough to complete their training. In terms of status, income, job mobility, unemployment, and job satisfaction, vocationally trained students did no better and often did worse than students in academic programs.

Congress, which had funded the initiative, had reason to be dissatisfied as well. In 1965 vocational enrollment in the schools in home economics and agriculture accounted for 55 percent of total enrollment. But these two fields were not where the country was experiencing its greatest need for trained persons, and the training they provided was not very helpful for those in search of employment. Something else needed to be done.[18]

That something else was career education. Introduced in 1971 by U.S. Secretary of Education Sidney P. Marland, career education was the schoolmen's response to the detractors of vocational education and to the protesters who had charged that secondary schooling had become a soulless, routine-driven, and overadministered business. More specifically, it was to help vocational educators escape from the frequently heard taunt that their instruction was reserved for students of low academic ability and from the somewhat contradictory accusation that they had raised entrance requirements to keep these students out of their programs. It was to bring to an end the practice of crowding the student "who cannot fit into a general pattern of studies . . . into an educational no man's land" of the general education track.[19] Career education was to blend the protesters' Deweyan plea for recognition of the adolescents' curiosity, interest, and search for relevance with the public's late-twentieth-century concern for an efficient public school system that served the economic welfare of both the individual student and society.

Because the percentage of high school graduates finding employment had become the key indicator of a school's success or failure, preparation for employment was now defined as the central task of schooling. It had to begin in early elementary grades and be carried through until graduation from high school. All curricula, whether academic, practical, or general, had to be built around the concept of "career." As Marland put it, there was need for a new orientation of education, "that would expose the student to the range of career opportunities, help him narrow down the choices in terms of his own aptitudes and interests, and provide him with education and training appropriate to his ambition." Even though Marland spoke exclusively of male students, career education was meant for every boy and girl in every one of the schools' programs. Marland referred to occupational clusters that covered any conceivable occupation, from work in business and marketing, to the media, manufacturing, the professions, fine arts, and humanities. Career education took in the older components of vocational education from information about vocations to counseling and training. It would involve field trips to factories, businesses, and offices, and it would bring visiting speakers from the world of work into the schools. It would give focus to all the other academic and nonacademic subjects of the curriculum and the activities of the extracurriculum. Everything taught in school had career implications, said Marland, and these made schooling relevant and motivated the student to stay in school.[20]

Alas, the very school-centeredness of the program proved to be its weakness. Only students in the traditional vocational education programs and in a few experimental arrangements experienced the reality of the workplace, and through that experience were sometimes aided in finding employment after graduation. Those in academic and general programs, however, felt themselves "on the receiving end of a series of repetitive, standardized 'pep talks,'" as a Rand corporation report put it. They were given little encouragement from teachers, who in their customary concentration on their particular subject, were either not able or not willing to provide the "focus on careers" that the program demanded. In 1976 the report summed up its impressions:

> Career education still has not found a permanent home in the programs of most high schools. The flurry of innovative activity tends to die down when the federal grant dollars are spent, particularly in secondary schools, and usually leaves little trace of permanent change.[21]

It did not seem likely that career education was to provide a workable answer to the troubles and travails of vocational education.

Alternatives for Youth

Sidney Marland's manifesto for career education entered the public discourse at just the wrong time. A wave of doubt concerning public education swept over the nation, and more and more people questioned whether the public schools, and particularly the secondary schools, were the only and the chosen institutions for the education of young people. Many Americans began to think that the "school problem" was at heart a "youth problem." Several social scientists and official commissions and committees urged that the schools be relieved of part of their all-encompassing responsibility for youth. As early as 1964 Christopher Jencks had presented his proposals for alternative school organization, for allowing students and their parents choice among public schools, and for offering adolescents nonschool educational opportunities in the armed forces and in CCC-like new federal- and state-sponsored organizations.[22] In 1973 the Kettering Foundation appointed its National Commission on the Reform of Secondary Education under the chairmanship of B. Frank Brown. As one might expect from his 1972 book, Brown showed little patience for the comprehensive school and instead endorsed student choice and alternatives. Under his leadership, the commission remained skeptical of the wisdom of many traditional school practices and suggested that the school-leaving age be reduced to fourteen and that employment opportunities for young people include on-the-job training.[23]

In the same year the Panel on Youth of the President's Science Advisory Committee presented *Youth: Transition to Adulthood.* Headed by James S. Coleman, the panel argued that "environments for youth" should neither be defined by nor limited to schools. Education as the central concern of adolescents comprised more than schooling. Echoing the report of the National Commission on the Reform of Secondary Education, the panel found that secondary schooling suffered from large-scale organization and from a fast-growing self-conscious adolescent youth culture. The comprehensive high school had turned into an instrument of "separation of the young from the rest of society; separation of age strata within the ranks of the young; and segregation by culture and race within the general population." The panel did not think much of the "minor forms of American secondary education." Catholic and other private schools were declining in numbers, as were specialized academic schools. In public vocational education, "little has gone well," and separate vocational schools had often become "a dumping ground for poor students." The more recent alternative schools also had "not gotten very far."[24]

Against this background of failures and insufficiencies the panel proposed that comprehensive high schools should give way to specialized and alternative schools, and large schools should be replaced with small ones or broken up into small units within the larger one. This was a refutation of the central concept of *Cardinal Principles* and of Conant's condemnation of the small high school. The panel further suggested that older students be used as teachers to tutor younger ones, and that students be allowed access to cooperative programs and public-service activities. The panel supported career education and part-time schooling and work, including delegating educational functions to nonschool agencies and employers.[25]

Given that it had been appointed by the U.S. commissioner of education, the National Panel on High School and Adolescent Education surprised the public when in its report it agreed with many of the points made by the other panels. It asserted that the comprehensive high school had weakened the academic character of secondary education without having strengthened its ability "to meet the needs of contemporary adolescents." It repeated the charge of the protesters that high schools "lack creativity, emphasize conformity and obedience to rules, are intellectually dull and joyless, and . . . inhibit staff, student, and community participation in determining operational conditions." It charged vocational education with not having fulfilled its promises. It lamented that "large high schools . . . have tended to be inflexible" and had separated adolescents "from significant contact with older adults." Schools prolonged young people's dependence and had become "aging vats" that retained control "more in keeping with the costly custodial care of masses of children in large institutions than with developing the potentials and increasing maturity for self-direction of young adults." Decentralization of the school establishment was imperative, the panel members concluded. It appeared that even the Office of Education had given up defense of the existing school bureaucracy and now supported the attack on the comprehensive high school.[26]

But not everyone joined in the chorus. In 1976 the Rand Corporation, a private think-tank, was commissioned by the United States Department of Health, Education and Welfare to review and discuss the policy implications of the three reports just discussed. Its *Youth Policy in Transition* asserted that the reports' authors had been unduly influenced by the student unrest of the 1960s and had interpreted as "trends" what should be seen as "responses to transient events." Many of the reports' conclusions were "somewhat overdrawn" and, although "largely sensible," "unaccompanied by evidence of effectiveness" and considerations of "costs or feasibility." The authors of the Rand report brushed off their colleagues' policy suggestions with the disparaging remark that "tinkering with our institutions will not buy youth productive lives, happy marriages, and

196

lovely children." Overall, the Rand report concluded, "many things 'are not as they seemed'—either to the reports' authors or ourselves."[27]

The authors of the Rand report identified the nation's schoolmen as the source of greatest and most effective resistance to the policy proposals made by others. They maintained that the schoolmen's strategy was to agree with many of the reform proposals but to reject them as soon as they threatened their own monopolistic suzerainty over the nation's youth. A 1975 report of the National Association of Secondary School Principals was cited as an example:

> On close examination . . . it becomes clear that the NASSP has cut and fit the proposed reforms in ways that assure that high school managers remain in the driver's seat. They believe workplace and other off-campus educational activities should remain under their control, with beefed-up, highly specialized guidance staff. Community involvement should be defined and managed by secondary schoolmen, and community policy inputs will be more advisory than participatory in nature. Alternative programs and accelerated college courses should be created *within* the structure of the large high schools. The unburdening of social missions is conceived of mostly as the transfer from the high school to unnamed locations of those students who are unable to function educationally in the re-oriented high school programs.

Unless reforms "begin to create competitors to the high school or otherwise loosen the high school's grip on the process of secondary education," the Rand authors concluded, the schoolmen's defensive and self-protective attitude would always condemn the reforms to infeasibilty.[28]

The Rand evaluation of the comprehensive high school and its vocational education efforts was marked by ambivalence. It was "ultimately unknowable," the group wrote, how well the schools had prepared students for working life, but that "without doubt they could do better." Any kind of suggested vocational training was of necessity a "retreat from comprehensiveness," and such retreat had "important potential consequences for the attainment of equity in American society." But school-centered vocational training was of questionable value.[29] Workplace education, on the other hand, did "nothing to change the pool of jobs in the economy," a point earlier critics of vocational education had made repeatedly. It therefore could not touch the chief cause of failure in vocational education: low expectations that it would lead graduates into rewarding jobs. Worse, it shifted the schools' custodial function to the employer, who might have no incentive or interest in assuming it. It tended to displace adult workers, most generally female and minority workers, and it threatened union members with possible replacement. This would bring about predictable adverse reactions of labor unions. Thus the Rand group questioned "the political feasibility of the proposals." In the minds of its members, all of these considerations led to more questions than answers, and they concluded that more research was required—a response always safe and nonarguable.[30]

The High School in the 1980s

As the 1980s began, another of the by-now-predictable changes of course in the debate on the high school occurred. The wave of proposals of protesters and social scientists was replaced by a "back-to-academics" movement. Mortimer Adler's *The Paideia Proposal* of 1982 led the parade. It proposed "a one-track system" of liberal arts schooling for all. The next year, the National Commission on Excellence in Education issued its *A Nation at Risk*. Now the negative trade balance and the importation of Japanese automobiles and electronic appliances triggered the alarm, as the Cold War and the appearance of sputnik had done in the 1950s. Hyperbole characterized the language of the manifesto: "If an unfriendly foreign power had attempted to impose on America the mediocre educational performance that exists today, we might well have viewed it as an act of war." The report summed up many of the familiar complaints, chief among them that students deserted both academic and vocational programs in favor of the "general track": "The proportion of students taking a general program has increased from 12 percent in 1964 to 42 percent in 1979." Not to be outdone, politicians and businessmen, finding similar fault in the public school system, recommended partnerships between businesses and schools to bring the academic and skill achievements of high school students up to internationally competitive levels.[31] The theme of the 1980s rang clear and loud: bring the academic standard of students graduating from American high schools back to that of ninety years ago, the years of the Committee of Ten report.

While commissions, panels, and task forces suggested, recommended, censured, insisted, and pontificated, a few scholars and reporters were actually going to the high schools to give the public an up-to-date series of eyewitness reports. In 1983 Ernest L. Boyer's, *High School: A Report on Secondary Education in America* appeared. Boyer, president of the Carnegie Foundation for the Advancement of Teaching, had drawn recommendations for the future of public high schools from a number of eyewitness reports. In the same year Philip A. Cusick, a professor at Michigan State

University, published his observations of the students and teachers in three comprehensive high schools. His book was complemented two years later by Arthur G. Powell, Eleanor Farrar, and David K. Cohen's *The Shopping Mall High School: Winners and Losers in the Educational Marketplace.* In 1984 John I. Goodlad published *A Place Called School: Prospects for the Future,* in which he discussed elementary as well as secondary schools. I shall refer to it in the next chapter. There were several other such volumes, among them Theodore R. Sizer's *Horace's Compromise: The Dilemma of the American High School. Horace's Compromise* was a heartfelt plea to Americans to desist from the endless debates over the dead and deadening paraphernalia of education and to concentrate their attention on the teachers and students at the center of the educational process.[32]

Boyer insisted in *High School* that Americans begin by clarifying the goals and purposes of secondary education. Quoting approvingly Arthur Bestor's observation of 1953 that "the idea that the school must undertake to meet every need that some other agency is failing to meet, regardless of the suitability of the schoolroom to the task, is a preposterous delusion that in the end can wreck the educational system." Boyer identified as secondary education's goals the individual's capacity to think critically and to communicate effectively; to have gained knowledge of self and of the human heritage; to be prepared for work and further education, and to be ready for fulfilling social and civic obligations through school and community service. In line with his general emphasis on academics, Boyer emphasized the liberal arts and modern communication. A one-semester seminar on preparation for work was to replace vocational education. The remaining aims of 1918—health, home membership, citizenship, leisure, and ethical character—were swept up in the readiness to fulfill social and civic obligations. Boyer had taken seriously Bestor's warning: in his curricular proposal he had trimmed down the high school's overloaded agenda to what he considered "a clear and coherent vision of what the nation's high schools should be seeking to accomplish."[33]

Cusick's analysis of three comprehensive high schools threw a brilliant light on the degree to which the guiding assumptions of American schooling were inextricably intertwined with the dominant ethos of American society. Cusick was puzzled about the seeming incongruity between the teachers' and administrators' concern with discipline and order and their willingness, even commitment, to permit students as well as teachers the greatest possible latitude in choosing for themselves what and how they wanted to learn and teach. These observations were confirmed in *The Shopping Mall High School,* a study of fifteen comprehensive mainstream public high schools. The study's authors explained Cusick's observations as accommodations or treaties between school and students, which promoted mutual goals or kept the peace. This dominant pattern of accommodation appeared to have the tacit support and encouragement of the community in which the schools existed.[34]

Cusick found the answer to the incongruity he had observed in the pervasive ethos of egalitarianism that pervaded society and the comprehensive schools and gave the schools he had visited their common structural elements:

> The central concept around which that structure centered seemed to be the obligation of the schools to take, retain, and instruct all possible adolescents in the hope of teaching them whatever they needed to know to participate in the life of our society on a relatively equal basis. Just as it became clear that there was a common structure, so it seemed that the linchpin of the structure in all three schools was just that commitment to the egalitarian ideal.[35]

Powell, Farrar, and Cohen called attention to the schoolmen's never-ceasing readiness to accept any task and any function that society chose to assign to them. Educators did this, as I have pointed out, because of their attachment to the democratic imperative and in service of their professional self-interest. Powell and his colleagues added that the educators' indiscriminate acceptance of any and all tasks stemmed from their own lack of a clear sense of direction.[36]

During the 1970s and 1980s, the civil rights revolution, war, social unrest, and the growing gap between poverty and wealth had set the parameters for developments in the high schools and for the accompanying debates. Direction over educational policy had slipped from the hands of the schoolmen into those of politicians in the halls of Congress, gubernatorial offices, and state legislatures. Once-sacrosanct institutions like the public school system and the comprehensive high school were openly being questioned or, what was even more painful to old defenders, were being ignored and dropped from discussion. The era of *Cardinal Principles* appeared to have ended. What to the schoolmen must have been the most doleful aspect was their own inability to supply direction to the new initiatives. The one theme they had fallen back on again and again—the claim to "total education," that all matters concerning young people ought to come under their exclusive purview—was obviously unacceptable to most Americans. Apart from that, the schoolmen's contributions were often no more than a rehash of old ways of schooling, variations on a theme, but no fresh departures. Schoolpeople seemed to have forgotten that education was more than schooling. They had lost their bearings.

From the Twentieth to the Twenty-First Century

School Choice

While during the 1980s the professional leadership of American secondary public education was losing its bearings, parents and politicians in cities and suburbs turned to the school-choice movement for relief. School choice, as Paul Peterson has pointed out, had begun in the 1950s, slowly expanded in the following decades, and emerged as a politically potent movement in the 1990s in the "segregated, bureaucratized, expensive, ineffectual central-city schools."[1] In these schools the concept of comprehensiveness had become a mockery and a farce because it was the comprehensiveness of the ghetto of low-income, disadvantaged, and mainly minority students. School choice had initially been employed by southern segregationist and northern well-to-do parents to pull their students out of integrated schools and schools with low academic standards. In the inner cities, it had by the 1990s become a preferred rescue operation for poverty-stricken and minority families. In Milwaukee, one of the centers of this movement, parental approval stressed the disciplined learning environment choice schools provided.[2] It made little difference whether choice schools were privately sponsored or were parts of the public school system. Their small size alone made them contrast favorably with the comprehensive schools. Demanded by parents and pushed through by politicians, choice schools torpedoed any hope public school people might have had to keep reform efforts under their undisputed supervision.

Proponents of school choice objected to the schoolmen's claim to monopolistic control over youths in the large comprehensive high schools and to the growing hold of what Philip Cusick called the egalitarian ethos discussed in the previous chapter. The schoolmen's claim to monopolistic control was easily accepted wherever schools existed in socially, racially, and ethnically homogeneous communities. But where that homogeneity could not be taken for granted, the schoolmen's zeal made them blind and deaf to the voices of diversity among parents and taxpayers who resented and resisted the schoolmen's claim to "total education." The ethos of egalitarianism offended proponents of school choice because, as Cusick pointed out, it made impossible a school program valuing achievement. The ethos had come to mean the equal right of every student to be left alone or to be taught whatever he or she wanted to be taught at the moment he or she asked for it. Under those circumstances,

> were the schools to assume a position requiring a uniformity of curriculum, standards of achievement, or consensus among the staff on how to conduct themselves and their classes, it is inevitable that they would have had to make judgments about and take actions against students which might have damaged those students' opportunity for equality. . . . The school people purposely discarded anything that could have put them or their institution in such a position.[3]

School administrators and teachers who applied such standards and criteria were condemned as meritocratic elitists, and as racists and sexists to boot. In inner-city schools such accusations could be fatal to their survival in office. Needless to say, under such conditions, educational achievement could not be one of the school's goals.

For many administrators and teachers, the egalitarian ethos served as a built-in imperative for ever-larger inclusiveness and thus as an affirmation of their own professional self-interest. Diversification and specialization, wrote Cusick, have "vastly increased the opportunities of school people for . . . increased salaries, greater job opportunities, and in general, larger and larger institutions."[4] Cusick's argument underlined the point made before: one of the greatest obstacles to a more realistic discussion of school reform was and is the self-interest of the schoolmen in an enlarged educational bureaucracy.

David K. Cohen, author of a chapter in *The Shopping Mall High School*, further confirmed Cusick's analysis. Schoolmen were being urged by their own traditional commitment to the democratic imperative and by pressures from an impatient electorate to include and keep from "dropping out" virtually the country's entire adolescent population, but teachers were being exhorted to pay particular attention to the academically interested and able student. High schools sought to meet both demands by introducing a few new academic and scientific courses for the small segment of top students and by inventing and adapting whole regiments of general courses for the great mass of nonacademically-inclined students. Cohen reported that in 1961 a little more than 9,000 students took college-level English courses, but thirty times as many—276,000—enrolled in remedial English courses. Because during the 1960s enrollment in institutions of higher education rose from 3.2 million to 7.1 million—with the bulk of the increase taking place in less selective public colleges and universities and two-year junior and community colleges—high school college-preparatory classes had fewer and fewer incentives for demanding academic work. The democratic impulse had by now become an egalitarian command, and turned the high schools into mass custodial holding tanks.[5]

In a study published in 1995, David Angus and Jeffrey Mirel confirmed Cohen's observations. They showed that beginning in the 1930s, growing high school enrollment led schoolmen to assume that it "inevitably meant increasing numbers of low-ability students" and that "the only way to approach universal secondary school enrollment is to make the high school curriculum less challenging and more entertaining." Course selections by high school students from 1930 to 1980 showed one long rather uniform trend away from academic subjects to personal development courses, such as health, physical education, and driver education.[6] Angus and Mirel attributed this trend to the schoolmen's assumption that the majority of high school students were incapable of academic or vocational work. In the 1930s and 1940s it had been still fashionable to assign the "educationally neglected" to the "general track" and keep them out of the more demanding and prestigious academic and vocational areas, but in later decades, when such practices became condemned as tracking, teachers happily permitted students to learn or not to learn whatever they wanted.[7] Whether we read Cusick, Cohen, or Angus and Mirel, the inability of schoolmen in the comprehensive high schools to come to grips with the challenge of learning for an ever-more-heterogenous school population has become starkly evident.

These developments were responsible in large measure for the rise of the school-choice movement in the 1980s. The egalitarian ethos—particularly if it drove learning and behavior to their lowest common levels—was incompatible with the hopes of ghetto parents for their children. Whether they knew it or not, advocates of school choice harked back to the professionalism of the teacher in a nineteenth-century people's college. As discussed in chapter 4, these schools had of necessity been small communities in which principals, teachers, and students knew one an-

other personally and were linked by bonds of common academic and vocational purpose. The purposes and philosophy of these people's colleges
were strikingly similar to the goals and school spirit parents and students
sought in a choice school. A relative homogeneity of social, ethnic, or
racial background made it easier to agree on and live by common standards of academic achievement and disciplined behavior. Relative small-
ness of size fostered mutual familiarity among all involved. In small-school
communities in which the questions and wishes of parents, teachers, and
students could pose an effective counterweight to the directives of a central school bureaucracy, the greatest liabilities of the urban comprehensive school were overcome.

The Twilight of the Senior High School

As one would expect, school-choice advocates criticized the high school
from a contemporary perspective. They could point for confirmation of
their charges to reports from Europe where, at an Organization for Economic Cooperation and Development meeting in the early 1980s, an assistant U.S. commissioner of education had described the American
high school as a "disaster area."[8] But would an historical assessment of
the school's development when placed in a comparative perspective
come to the same verdict? Responding to that question Angus and Mirel
wrote:

> For those who believe that the primary purpose of the school is to
> educate youth "with equal seriousness in the great areas of human
> knowledge," the curriculum changes of the middle fifty years of this
> century were a disaster. For those who see the school as responsible
> for meeting a wide range of youth needs and problems, as well as
> for "developing social and civic awareness and responsibility," the
> picture until recently has been much brighter.[9]

Angus and Mirel saw disaster in the school's academic performance but,
except for developments in the recent past, were a bit more optimistic
concerning its social mission. Television reports, newspaper accounts, and
feature articles in magazines have created a picture of truly horrendous
conditions in inner city high schools. But survey results also have told us
of students and parents in urban and rural areas who are well satisfied
with their high schools and the education they offer. Disaster has not
characterized and does not now characterize every secondary school
throughout the country. The salient point that emerges is that in school-

ing as in almost everything else, diversity of conditions and results characterizes American life.

As a general statement, it nonetheless holds true that the American high school of the twentieth century has not lived up to the dreams of its creators and has fallen far short of the expectations the nation had set for it. The discrepancy between the high sentiments announced in 1918 in *Cardinal Principles* and the dire warnings expressed in 1983 in *A Nation at Risk* is palpable and cannot be wished away. The many reform efforts we have encountered in the preceding pages have not brought the results their initiators had hoped for.

A historical and comparative evaluation will identify the incorporation of vocational education and the publication of *Cardinal Principles* as turning points in the high school's history. From the early 1920s to the 1960s, the American high school sailed on a course different from that of its European cousins. By turning part of the school into an industrial workshop, vocational education splintered its mission and purpose. This was a fatal mistake. As European, especially German, models showed, schools and workplaces have different educational tasks. They accomplish them best when each pursues them separately or in cooperation with each other. But one cannot well perform the task of the other. Vocational education carried out in schools could not, as Kantor and Tyack put it, "integrate youth into the occupational structure. . . . Vocational reformers attacked the symptoms rather than the sources of the conditions they hoped to eliminate." Teachers assigned to vocational classes assumed for themselves a task for which they were not qualified. Industrial and business specialists, economists, and managers were required, not academic teachers, to define and supply the conditions under which young people could be properly prepared for the world of work.[10]

Vocational educators did not accept the critics' verdict. It was not their job, they declared, to restructure the labor market or to reorganize the economy. They said they did no more than respond to the cry from students and their parents for practical relevance of the curriculum. Had not high school principals and superintendents stated again and again that competition from private trade schools and the ever-rising dropout figures, particularly of male students, forced upon them vocational instruction? Had not Americans demanded that every youth in the country study every subject and acquire any skill for any occupation and activity he or she might want to learn?

These questions reflected the concerns of schoolmen and their critics, but they hardly touched on the historical significance of the American experience with vocational education. A movement that had begun as a simple response to a perceived demand for practical education and as an attempt to shore up and enlarge the role of secondary schooling and the power of its managers had radically transformed conceptions of secondary education. It undermined the high school's historical mission to ground all of its students in the basic skills of the liberal arts. What could have been, and in other countries did become, a much-needed and well-functioning separate branch of popular education, in the United States served as a catalyst to redefine the meaning and to redesign the institutions of public secondary education. As Herbert Kliebard has pointed out, Americans came to see not individual growth and personality development but "economic mobility and national economic issues [as] the centerpiece of our thinking about schools."[11] This shift in perception devalued education from an end in itself to but a cog in the wheel of the nation's economy. It turned the secondary schools from being institutions of academic education into holding companies for many diverse, specific, and often unrelated training enterprises. It led to Charles Prosser's pronouncement that the high school had nothing to offer to 60 percent of its students, and to University of Chicago president Robert M. Hutchins's description of the schools as "a custodial system . . . for the nonpenal accommodation of the young."[12] These bitter comments summed up what had become evident by the 1940s: the American high school had lost its sense of identity and educational purpose.

If the introduction of vocational education was the trigger for the American experiment with the comprehensive high school, *Cardinal Principles* has been the experiment's blueprint. For the past eighty years it has supplied the high school's curricular guidelines. As the preceding four chapters have shown, the document has never been adhered to in every detail in every high school; principals did not agree on an interpretation of its meaning. But still it needs to be said that since the document's original publication in 1918 there has never been a commission or committee that, with equal backing by the educational establishment, has even attempted to draw up a paper of equal authority and impact. For good or ill, *Cardinal Principles* still guides the high school curriculum, as did the *Yale Report* during the nineteenth century and the Committee of Ten report at the beginning of the twentieth.

The great strength of the document flows from its authors' conviction that secondary schools as they existed during the 1910s had outlived their usefulness. Without thoroughgoing change, they could no longer cope with the demands placed on them by a democratic polity in an industrializing society. Kingsley and his colleagues saw comprehensive schooling as an indispensable requirement for a nation of a mixed population of native inhabitants, of descendants of forcibly imported slaves, and of immigrants from every corner of the globe. They were right in stressing the unifying function of the public schools. Their formulation of democracy and efficiency corresponded to the needs of the hour. How to introduce them into a school whose traditions had their roots in aristocracy and academic learning? Kingsley and his colleagues knew that there were no models to follow. The progressivism of European school reformers and of American colleagues in the private schools differed from their progressivism precisely because it clung to aristocracy and academic learning; *Cardinal Principles* endorsed democracy and efficiency. The country's demographic revolution, propelled by immigration and industrialization, had created conditions that European countries would experience forty years later, when, as a result, European educators, too, experimented with the introduction of comprehensive schools. The idea of comprehensive schooling was sound in the United States in 1920, as it was sound in Europe in 1960 and as it is sound in both societies today.

In Europe the issue of comprehensive schooling became a subject of vigorous debate and reform efforts in several highly industrialized countries during the 1960s. Sweden abolished its traditional parallel system in which most students at the age of ten continued in their common school for another six or seven years and then entered upon an apprenticeship and part-time continuation school. Only a minority transferred to a secondary school for another eight years and prepared themselves for mid-level white-collar careers or, after passing a leaving examination, entered the universities for professional training. Such a system, common to many European countries, reflected and contributed to a sharply divided social-class structure. The Swedish Education Act of 1962 established a basic nine-year school: the first six grades being common to all students and the final three grades allowing for differentiation among an academic, a vocational, and a general program. This new system then was complemented by upper secondary academic and vocational schools. A decade later the education ministry extended the common core curriculum of the first six grades through all nine grades. As Torsten Husén put it, "A fully integrated basic school without pre-vocational instruction had emerged."[13]

But the turn toward comprehensiveness did not stop there, and it eventually raised serious questions about its effectiveness. In Sweden the upper secondary schools were transformed from university-preparatory schools enrolling less than 10 percent of the age group into schools attended by 90 percent of the age group. These schools then offered a great variety of two-year vocational courses and three-year academic programs. The result, however, was that the vocational subjects tended to crowd out academic instruction, and that employers and teachers began to complain increasingly about the deficient preparation of their trainees and students in basic literacy skills.[14] Similar developments toward comprehensive schooling, based to some degree on the Swedish model, and similar disappointments occurred in other European countries. Why these disappointments? In European countries, as in the United States, schoolmen and legislators ran into trouble when they pushed the idea of comprehensiveness from the lower schools to the level of the senior high school. Then the curricular liabilities of comprehensiveness began to overshadow the social advantages the school had promised.

In the United States, the appeal of *Cardinal Principles* began to wane when the effects of comprehensive schooling on youths beyond the age of fifteen or sixteen became evident. The attempts to counter the separating effects of curricular specialization with emphasis on the school's socially unifying function led to inconsistencies and contradictions that gradually destroyed any chance for effective instruction and learning. It is too easy in retrospect to fault Kingsley and his colleagues for events that became evident forty years after they had concluded their work. It is pointless to charge that the ultimate triumph of separation over unification could have been predicted, and it is unfair to blame the endorsement of efficiency—whether social, industrial, or educational—for the decline of academic learning. There surely is no brief to be held for an inefficient social, industrial, or educational system. What remains as a cause of just complaint, however, is the schoolmen's rigidity in clinging to the notion of comprehensiveness for the senior high school in the face of all the accumulated evidence that that school has been in trouble for decades. Beginning with the farce of life adjustment in the 1940s, continuing with the overreaction of "academic rearmament" in the 1950s and the consequent scuttling of that effort in the 1960s, the turn to career education in the 1970s, and the uproar over *A Nation at Risk* in the 1980s, schoolmen had ample evidence that such a rudderless voyage indicated deep-seated flaws. They shut their eyes and repeated their commitment to comprehensiveness at every level. We should not be surprised that today laymen, parents and legislators, have begun to press for their own empowerment to put an end to the schoolmen's hegemony. It is time for a reformulation of the purposes and means of secondary education for youth of senior high school age in the twenty-first century.

From Schooling to Education

American education in the twenty-first century cannot flinch from its commitment to education for everyone. It will have to solve the problem of mass education that it posed for itself in the twentieth century and for which it has not found satisfactory solutions. This is especially urgent for the education of students of senior high school age. With this age group in mind, Americans will have to ask themselves questions like these: Are comprehensiveness and specialization compatible with each other in institutions for the education of senior high school students? Is the senior high school, as we know it today, the only conceivable place for adolescents to spend their time? Are there not educational activities other than schooling? Given the reports which told us what goes on in high schools today, can we any longer pretend that schooling always equals education? Is it not time to challenge the school people's claim to total dominion over adolescence? Do we have to accept as inevitable the drift of students from academic and vocational courses into the "general track"? Because custodialism is inextricably intertwined with compulsory school attendance and the latter implies that teachers can compel young people to learn or, if they cannot, can at least force the students' bodies to be present, should we not rethink the concept of compulsory education for adolescents? Do we really believe that in the absence of realistic career goals, adolescents of senior high school age can be compelled to learn?

To overcome the custodialism of schooling, we shall have to rely on a more promising view of education than the one that dominates our schools today. Although this book concerns itself in its final chapter primarily with young people of senior high school age, any successful restructuring of education at that level depends for its success on reforms of schooling in earlier grades. I take my text here from John Goodlad's *A Place Called School: Prospects for the Future.* In it, Goodlad showed convincingly how custodialism has encouraged absenteeism, truancy, and violence in our high schools. He agrees with the authors of *The Education of Adolescents* that there is little point in keeping maturing adolescents in "aging vats" when, as several of the reports cited in chapter 15 made clear, these youngsters are already old beyond their years.[15] Goodlad therefore suggested that we take into account the downward shift in the age of puberty and consider a corresponding lowering of the age for school attendance. He recommended that schooling begin at age four and end at age sixteen.[16] Such policy would encourage teachers in the preelementary, elementary, and middle-school grades to focus on an education in basic literacy and numeracy, and to introduce their students to the liberal arts. In these years of compulsory schooling teachers could accomplish the unifying task of the comprehensive school through their instruction in the arts and in music, in physical education, and in an age-appropriate career education for all students. Once compulsory schooling has accomplished its work of basic common academic and social education for all children, our young people will be ready to embark on their own individual careers in an advanced secondary education.[17] They will do this without compulsion, and they will be able to choose the education career paths they desire.

A successful transition from basic schooling to advanced secondary education requires that we do not delay unduly the termination of compulsory schooling. If we follow Goodlad's proposals, then, the period of compulsory comprehensive schooling can be finished for most students sometime between the ages of fourteen and sixteen. There is no need to require a termination age that is the same for all students. Instead, students can receive a certificate of mastery whenever their teachers and parents or other pertinent adults agree that they are ready to embark on their advanced secondary education. The certificate would signify a student's successful completion of compulsory schooling and entry into the world of responsible maturity. It would require the student to take charge of his or her own further education.

It is to our discredit that we have for so long ignored and failed to act upon the signs of the downward shift in age at which young people assert their readiness and impatience to take control of their own lives. Not only Goodlad but other observers as well have remarked upon this shift in several of the documents cited in chapter 15.[18] Had we acted upon their insight earlier, we might have prevented or at least have alleviated some of the shift's negative manifestations, such as the rampant teenage absenteeism from school, the lower achievement scores, and the increases in teenage pregnancies, motherhood, drug use, alcoholism, vagrancy, violence, and crime. The reasons for our obliviousness stem from a mixture of charitable and self-serving motives. Reformers want to protect youngsters from exploitation in the labor market. Labor unions, eager to keep jobs available for their own ranks, want to shut young people out of employment. Schoolmen and organized teachers persuaded themselves and us of the "democratic imperative," which counsels the extension of compulsory schooling to ever-advanced ages. At the same time, such policies of compulsion feathered the schoolmen's nest by herding and keeping youngsters in their classrooms.[19] I believe it is time now that in the interest of our young people, we leave these irrelevant and self-defeating arguments behind and debate the termination of compulsory education on grounds appropriate to the issue: Is a young person prepared and ready to exercise a choice of her or his advanced secondary education, an education that involves commitment to a self-chosen course of studies, training, or work? We should by now have learned that we cannot force education upon anyone against his or her own will.

The advanced secondary education of which I speak accompanies young people during their passage from adolescence into early adulthood. The curricula and programs students may choose are not part of schooling in the familiar sense of the past. Rather, they constitute the early stages of their own, self-chosen education. Although they may, in many cases, present information and convey skills that in the past have been taught in senior high schools, they may also draw on subject matter and training material from specialized academic high schools and academies, from vocational, commercial, and continuation schools, and from workshops in industry and business. They may be offered by technical institutes; by vocational, technical, and adult education colleges; and also in regular classes of community, junior, and senior colleges and of many other types of schools and colleges as well. Because all these offerings will carry their own prerequisites for entry and their own certificates of successful completion, students are free to construct their own "careers in education" and adjust them, at each step, to their desired objectives. Ultimately, if students desire education beyond the advanced secondary level, their various certificates will indicate their paths into the higher vocational and technical colleges, into institutions of adult and lifelong education, and into colleges and universities.

The choices open to students should not be limited to schools and colleges. There will also be a wide variety of institutions with educational functions that students will be free to seek out to complete their "careers in education." They could include employment as apprentice, intern-in-training, or full-fledged worker in any business, industry, or office. They could also involve service and training in the armed forces, in state and federal civil service, and in other public- and private-service and community agencies ranging from local hospitals to state or federal youth corps or the Peace Corps.[20] The options for post-compulsory-schooling "careers in education" should be numerous, and they should also be available for students of any age. They should constitute the avenues for lifelong learning adequate to the requirements of the twenty-first century. Such an approach will require a willingness on the part of employing businesses or agencies to cooperate in training and certifying and thus to become part of society's educating institutions.

Such a shift in our thinking about secondary education requires our willingness to discard familiar but outworn assumptions. That is a difficult task, and most of us tend to resist it, if for no other reason than we cling to known ways and shun the unfamiliar paths. It means that we must accept as adults the young people who have left compulsory schooling behind them, and that we must grant them the right to choose their own educational ways. That is a risk, but in my opinion far less a of a threat to our community life than the revolts and terror that have broken out in so many of our schools where students are kept against their will and, in many cases, with no clear purpose in mind. It means that we should relieve our teachers of the many and varied custodial functions they were forced to take on during the last several decades, and free them again for the educational work that is properly theirs. It means that we can dismantle part of the enormous and costly school bureaucracy that has grown up around the multifaceted activities of school authorities, and redirect these tasks to the social work, public health, and other agencies to which they belong. It means that we may safely discard, too, the assumption that everything concerning youths has to be dealt with everywhere in the same fashion throughout a uniform school system. Instead, we can allow free room for individual and collective initiative, whether this be exercised by a teacher in a classroom or by a principal in a school, by parents or administrators in their district, or by a state department of public instruction. There is no reason that in the fifty different states, educators, parents, and other citizens cannot experiment in fifty or more different ways to make advanced secondary education meaningful for each of the young people during their educational careers.

When I wrote above of "careers in education" I indicated that a far greater participation in education than formerly will be necessary by business, industry, agriculture, private offices, and public agencies. These institutions will have to cooperate with schools of various kinds in training and certifying young people in their respective activities. This is particularly important in light of 1994 legislation that focused on the school-to-work transition. In this transition, an integration of the educational and the vocational element in the student's career should take place in learning situations of any number of different and alternating combinations. In a recently circulated paper, W. Norton Grubb laid out at least five approaches to the "new vocationalism," all of which replace, as he put it, "a unitary conception of the high school with much more varied forms, a kind of 'principled heterogeneity' suited to the variety of student interest and the diversity of student backgrounds."[21] In these approaches, the non-school-based part of education will bring students the advantage of gaining the expertise and know-how of the employer. The more conventional educational program can focus on the intellectual, moral, and political purposes of education to make and keep the student adaptable to the ever-changing conditions of the labor market in the twenty-first century. In these integrated learning situations of the "careers in education" a proper balance between the educational and the vocational will have to be maintained, to avoid, on the one hand, the boredom and irrelevance of the high school's custodial approach and, on the other, the waste and uselessness of the outdated vocational program.

Summing It Up

To challenge the claim of the American senior high school to be the all-encompassing home for American youth is a radical proposal. It denies that the education of the young, beyond the successful completion of their compulsory schooling is any longer the unquestioned task of professional educators. It says that for many of the young, we can accomplish that educational task better with the help of other institutions and people. I do not submit here yet another proposal for the reform of the existing school system. Instead, I ask that we restructure that system. I believe that the institutional structure, inherited from the nineteenth century and re-formed any number of times during the twentieth, has finally reached the end of its usefulness. As a fast-developing technology has pushed our economy from the industrial age of coal and steel into a postindustrial era dominated by electronic communications, our educational arrangements will have to keep pace. The comprehensive high school will not disappear, but it will have to give up its claim to monopolistic control over youth of senior high school age. At that level, it will have to share the educational task with many other institutions within a framework that allows room for choice and banishes custodial compulsion. Education, in order to be effective, can take place only in an atmosphere of freedom. That is what this restructuring is all about.

To prepare the nation's educational facilities for the requirements of the twenty-first century is a task that transcends party politics and special interests. An effort of this kind will demand nonpartisan political leadership that is prepared to battle the opposition that is to be expected from professional interests in education and from our industrial, business, and labor establishments. The traditional recipients of federal funds in secondary and vocational education will resist any effort to redirect such resources to the new players in our educational arrangements. The latter will be wary of accepting their new tasks; they will demand to be reimbursed for the outlays their new responsibilities will bring with them. If, as was suggested by James Coleman and his colleagues on the 1973 panel on youth, students at the completion of their compulsory schooling will receive educational drawing rights to help finance their subsequent "careers in education," additional funds will have to be set aside.[22] In adjudicating all these claims and requirements, it will be up to Congress and state legislatures to keep uppermost in mind the educational welfare of youth,

213

and not to allow themselves to be swayed by the special and particular interests of the parties involved. The rewards to be reaped in rescued lives of young people, in a decline of vandalism and crime on our streets, and in a return of purposeful activity and economic productivity will more than repay the outlay such restructuring requires.

The plan here outlined derives its scope from a survey of the 350 years of American secondary education viewed in its North Atlantic setting. In this survey, the first 260 years appear as an American variant of a common history. When by 1895 American schoolmen seized upon the "democratic imperative" and broke with the notion of secondary schooling as an education of a select minority, and when twenty-five years later they launched the comprehensive high school, they departed from the common path. Their European colleagues would wait another forty years until they, too, felt compelled by demographic and industrial changes to experiment with the comprehensive high school. Now, disappointment has set in on both sides of the Atlantic with the upper grades of that comprehensive school.[23] In Europe as in the United States, many senior high schools, constrained to accept and treat equally every student, have been overwhelmed by the often chaotic social environment in which they exist, and by the unruly crowds of individuals who are kept in school against their will. At best, these schools provide custodial care and discipline. At worst, they disintegrate into lawlessness and chaos. The call for restructuring of educational systems is heard everywhere.

In the United States, restructuring can find nourishment in the legacy of what has been this country's exemplary institution of secondary education: the nineteenth-century people's college. As I wrote in chapter 4, with its academic curriculum and its "career education" program of school-workplace relationships, the people's college was democracy's finest educational institution. It was and is the "once and future school" of this book's title. This school will not return to replace the senior high school, but its democratic spirit and its purpose of providing a thorough academic and career-preparatory education can and should set the course for the variety of institutions I envisage and that I outline above. None of these new institutions will be a people's college. But each of them can play their part in reviving the people's college legacy and thus restore democracy to education in a way commensurate to the conditions of the twenty-first century.

Notes

Preface

1. See the School to Work Act passed by Congress in 1994.
2. For an overview of American education during the post–World War II period, see Diane Ravitch, *The Troubled Crusade: American Education, 1945–1980* (New York: Basic Books, 1983).
3. I have discussed the people's college in "The American People's College: The Lost Promise of Democracy in Education," *American Journal of Education*, C (May 1992), 275–297.

Chapter 1: The Origins of Secondary Education

1. See Bruce A. Kimball, *Orators and Philosophers: A History of the Idea of Liberal Education* (New York: Teachers College Press, 1986), pp. 14, 66–67.
2. On Bologna, Salerno, and Paris, see Gina Fasoli, *Per la Storia dell'Universite di Bologna nel Medio Evo* (Bologna: R. Patron, 1970); Paul Oskar Kristeller, "The School of Salerno: Its Development and Its Contribution to the History of Learning," *Studies in Renaissance Thought and Letters* (Rome: Edizioni di Storia e Letteratura, 1956), pp. 495–551, and also in *Bulletin of the History of Medicine*, XVII (1944–1945), 138–194; and Jacques Verger, "A propos de la naissance de l'université de Paris: Contexte social, enjeu politique, portée intellectuelle," in *Schulen und Studium im sozialen Wandel des hohen and späten Mittelalters*, ed. Johannes Fried (Sigmaringen: Jan Thorbeke, 1986).

3. On the beginnings of the medieval universities, see Hastings Rashdall, *The Universities of Europe in the Middle Ages*, ed. F. M. Powicke and A. B. Emden, 3 vols. (Oxford: Oxford University Press, 1936); and Alan B. Cobban, *The Medieval Universities: Their Development and Organization* (London: Methuen, 1975).

4. See Herbert Grundmann, *Vom Ursprung der Universität im Mittelalter*, Berichte über die Verhandlungen der Sächsischen Akademie der Wissenschaften zu Leipzig, Philologisch-historische Klasse, 103, no. 2 (1957), 11–13.

5. See Vern L. Bullough, *The Development of Medicine as a Profession: The Contribution of the Medieval University to Modern Medicine* (New York: Hafner, 1966), pp. 81–88.

6. See the essays in John W. Baldwin and Richard A. Goldthwaite, eds., *Universities in Politics: Case Studies from the Late Middle Ages and Early Modern Period* (Baltimore: Johns Hopkins University Press, 1972).

7. See Lawrence Stone, "The Educational Revolution in England, 1560–1640," *Past and Present*, XXVIII (July 1964), 41–80.

8. See James H. Overfield, "Nobles and Paupers at German Universities to 1600," *Societas*, IV (1974), 175–210.

9. Mark H. Curtis, *Oxford and Cambridge in Transition, 1558–1642: An Essay on Changing Relations between the English Universities and English Society* (Oxford: Clarendon Press, 1959), pp. 71–72, 81.

10. Hugh Kearney, *Scholars and Gentlemen: University and Society in Pre-Industrial Britain, 1500–1700* (Ithaca: Cornell University Press, 1970), p. 33.

11. See Joan Simon, "The Social Origins of Cambridge Students, 1603–1640," *Past and Present*, XXVI (November 1963), 58–67; also Hilde de Ridder-Symoens, "L'aristocratisation des universités au XVIe siècle," *Les Grandes Réformes des universités européennes du XVIe au XXe Siècles*, IIIe Session Scientifique Internationale Cracoviae, 15–17 Mai 1980, pp. 37–47. For a later period in Germany, see Charles McClelland, "The Aristocracy and University Reform in 18th-Century Germany," in *Schooling and Society: Studies in the History of Education*, ed. Lawrence Stone (Baltimore: Johns Hopkins University Press, 1976), pp. 146–173.

12. Philippe Ariés, *Centuries of Childhood: A Social History of Family Life*, trans. Robert Baldick (New York: Vintage Books, 1965), pp. 142–143, 152, 171. See also Astrik L. Gabriel, "The College System in the Fourteenth Century Universities," in *The Forward Movement of the Fourteenth Century*, ed. Francis Lee Utley (Columbus: Ohio State University Press, 1961), pp. 79–124, and "Preparatory Teaching in the Parisian

Colleges during the 14th Century," *Garlandia: Studies in the History of the Medieval University* (Frankfurt/Main: Josef Knecht, 1969), pp. 97–124.

13. See August Tholuck, *Vorgeschichte des Rationalismus: Das akademische Leben des 17. Jahrhunderts*, section 2, *Die akademische Geschichte* (Halle: E. Anton, 1854), pp. 147–148.

14. See Gerald Strauss, *Luther's House of Learning: Indoctrination of the Young in the German Reformation* (Baltimore: Johns Hopkins University Press, 1978), pp. 154–155, and "The Social Function of Schools in the Lutheran Reformation in Germany," *History of Education Quarterly*, XXVIII (Summer 1988), 205–206; see also Friedrich Paulsen, *Geschichte des Gelehrten Unterrichts*, 2nd ed., vol. I (Leipzig: Veit, 1896), pp. 318–322.

15. Gerhard Meyer, *Die Entwicklung der Straßburger Universität aus dem Gymnasium und der Akademie des Johann Sturm* (Heidelberg: C. Winter, 1926); and Charles Borgeaud, *Histoire de l'Université de Genève: L'Académie de Calvin* (Genève: Georg, 1900). On Leyden and Franeker, see Samuel Eliot Morison, *The Founding of Harvard College* (Cambridge: Harvard University Press, 1935), pp. 145–146.

16. On the English schools see their respective histories and the general works of Joan Simon, *Education and Society in Tudor England* (Cambridge: Cambridge University Press, 1966); Howard Staunton, *The Great Schools of England* (London: Strahan, 1869); and Lawrence A. Cremin's summary in *American Education: The Colonial Experience, 1607–1783* (New York: Harper & Row, 1970), pp. 167–176.

17. On the scientific societies and the academies, see Martha Ornstein, *The Role of the Scientific Societies in the Seventeenth Century* (Hamden, CT: Archon Books, 1913); Herbert McLachlan, *English Education under the Test Acts: Being the History of the Non-Conformist Academies, 1662–1820* (Manchester: University Press, 1931); Francis R. Johnson, "Gresham College: Precursor of the Royal Society," *Journal of the History of Ideas*, I (October 1940), 413–438; and R. J. W. Evans, "Learned Societies in Germany in the Seventeenth Century," *European Studies Review*, VII (1977), 129–151.

18. On the conservatism of schooling in Catholic areas, see Grete Klingenstein, "Despotismus und Wissenschaft: Zur Kritik norddeutscher Aufklärer an der österreichischen Universität, 1750–1790," in *Formen der europäischen Aufklärung*, ed. Friedrich Engel-Janosi et al. (Wien: Verlag für Geschichte und Politik, 1976), pp. 126–157, and Notker Hammerstein, *Aufklärung und katholisches Reich: Untersuchungen zur Universitätsreform und Politik katholischer Territorien des Heiligen Römischen Reiches deutscher Nation im 18. Jahrhundert* (Berlin: Duncker &

Humblot, 1977). For Lutheran and reformed countries see A. Tholuck, *Vorgeschichte des Rationalismus: Das akademische Leben des 17. Jahrhunderts: Die akademischen Zustände* (Halle; E. Anton, 1853). A good summary description of teaching at Oxford and its "academic ethos" as a defense of tradition is given in Peter Slee, "The Oxford Idea of a Liberal Education 1800–1860: The Invention of Tradition and the Manufacture of Practice," *History of Universities*, VII (1988), 66–67.

19. See Heinz-Elmar Tenorth's summary statement in Detlef K. Müller, Fritz Ringer, and Brian Simon, eds., *The Rise of the Modern Educational System: Structural Change and Social Reproduction, 1870–1920* (Cambridge: Cambridge University Press, 1987), p. 220.

20. For Prussia, see Hans-Georg Herrlitz, *Studium als Standesprivileg: Die Entstehung des Maturitätsproblems im 18. Jahrhundert* (Frankfurt am Main: S. Fischer Verlag, 1973).

21 For Germany, see Karl-Ernst Jeismann, "Das höhere Knabenschulwesen," in *Handbuch der deutschen Bildungsgeschichte*, ed. Karl-Ernst Jeismann and Peter Lundgreen, vol. III, *1800–1870* (München: Verlag C. H. Beck, 1987), pp. 152–172; and Brian Simon, "Systematisation and Segmentation in Education: The Case of England," in Müller et al., *The Rise of the Modern Educational System*, pp. 88–108.

22. On this, see Fritz Ringer's introduction to Müller et al., *Rise of the Modern Educational System*, pp. 1–12.

Chapter 2: Grammar Schools, Colleges, and Academies in Early America

1. From "New England's First Fruits," reprinted in Samuel Eliot Morison, *The Founding of Harvard College* (Cambridge: Harvard University Press, 1935), p. 432.

2. "Law of 1647," reprinted in *Record of the Governor and Company of the Massachusetts Bay in New England*, ed. Nathaniel B. Shurtleff, vol. 2, *1642–1649* (Boston: William White, 1853), p. 203.

3. James Axtell, *The School upon the Hill: Education and Society in Colonial New England* (New Haven: Yale University Press, 1974), p. 179.

4. Kenneth B. Murdock, "The Teaching of Latin and Greek at the Boston Latin School in 1712," *Publications of the Colonial Society of Massachusetts*, XXVII, (March 1927), 27, 28.

5. Robert Middlekauff, *Ancients and Axioms: Secondary Education in Eighteenth Century New England* (New Haven: Yale University Press, 1963), pp. 88–91.

6. See Murdock, "Teaching of Latin and Greek," p. 24, and Robert Middlekauff, "A Persistent Tradition: The Classical Curriculum in Eighteenth-Century New England," *William and Mary Quarterly*, 3rd series, XVIII (January 1961), 54–56.

7. Samuel Eliot Morison, *Harvard College in the Seventeenth Century*, vol. I (Cambridge: Harvard University Press, 1936), p. 165.

8. Frederick Rudolph, *Curriculum: A History of the American Undergraduate Course of Study Since 1636* (San Francisco: Jossey-Bass, 1977), pp. 32–33.

9. See James J. Walsh, *Education of the Founding Fathers of the Republic: Scholasticism in the Colonial Colleges* (New York: Fordham University Press, 1935), p. 101; and Middlekauff, *Ancients and Axioms*, pp. 54–56.

10. Morison, *Harvard College in the Seventeenth Century*, I, 200.

11. Ibid., p. 186.

12. Ibid., p. 184, 185.

13. Ibid., p. 252–253.

14. Ibid., p. 254.

15. Ibid., p. 259.

16. Ibid., p. 262.

17. See Walsh, *Education of the Founding Fathers*, p. 127: for a description of a disputation, see pp. 308–309.

18. Ibid., p. 103.

19. See David Potter, *Debating in the Colonial Chartered Colleges: An Historical Survey, 1642 to 1900* (New York: Teachers College, Columbia University, 1944), pp. 37–38. See also Rudolph, *Curriculum*, pp. 45–46.

20. Morison, *Founding of Harvard College*, p. 252.

21. Axtell, *School Upon the Hill*, pp. 201–244.

22. See my *From Crisis to Crisis: American College Government, 1636–1819* (Cambridge: Harvard University Press, 1982), pp. 112, 128–141.

23. Samuel Eliot Morison, *The Intellectual Life of Colonial New England*, 2nd ed. (New York: New York University Press, 1956), p. 90.

24. Axtell, *School Upon the Hill*, p. 177.

25. Clifford K. Shipton, "Secondary Education in the Puritan Colonies," *New England Quarterly*, VII (December 1934), 655; and Pauline Holmes, *A Tercentenary History of the Boston Public Latin School, 1635–1935* (Cambridge: Harvard University Press, 1935), p. 252.

26. Jon Teaford, "The Transformation of Massachusetts Education, 1670–1780," reprinted in *The Social History of American Education*, ed. B. Edward McClellan and William J. Reese (Urbana: University of Illinois Press, 1988),pp. 29, 30, 34.

27. Middlekauff, *Ancients and Axioms*, pp. 105–106.

28. Shipton, "Secondary Education," pp. 660–661.

29. Morison, *Intellectual Life*, pp. 76–78; and Shipton, "Secondary Education," 659, 660–661.
30. Reprinted in Teaford, "Transformation," p. 35.
31. Ibid., pp. 29, 30, 35.
32. Ibid., p. 31.
33. See Leonard W. Labaree et al., eds., *The Autobiography of Benjamin Franklin* (New Haven: Yale University Press, 1980), pp. 196–197, and p. 196 n. 7., and *The Papers of Benjamin Franklin*, vol. III (New Haven: Yale University Press, 1982), pp. 397–421.
34. Laurence M. Crosbie, *The Phillips Exeter Academy: A History* (Norwood, MA: Plimpton Press, 1924), pp. 311, 289.
35. Ibid., p. 304.
36. Ibid., pp. 290–293.
37. Ibid., p. 293.
38. Ibid., p. 33.
39. On the history of the New York Board of Regents, see Frank C. Abbott, *Government Policy and Higher Education: A Study of the Regents of the University of the State of New York, 1784–1949* (Ithaca: Cornell University Press, 1958). For a more detailed discussion of the New York academies, see my "The Regents of the University of the State of New York, 1784–1920," in *The Colonial Experience in Education*, ed. António Nóvoa, Marc Depaepe, and Erwin V. Johanningmeier, *Paedagogica Historica*, supp. ser., 1 (1995), 317–333.
40. Abbott, *Government Policy*, p. 24.
41. Committee on Colleges, Academies, and Common Schools, Regent Minutes, *Assembly Journal*, March 25, 1822.
42. George Frederick Miller, *The Academy System of the State of New York* (Albany: J. B. Lyon, 1922), pp. 102–103.
43. Regent Minutes, *Assembly Journal*, March 25, 1822.
44. Regent Minutes, *Assembly Journal*, April 12, 1826, and April 6, 1830.
45. Regent Minutes, *Assembly Journal*, January 12, 1826.
46. Regent Minutes, *Assembly Journal*, January 12 and April 12, 1826.
47. Regent Minutes, *Assembly Journal*, March 17, 1829.
48. Regent Minutes, *Assembly Journal*, February 28, 1832.
49. Abbott, *Government Policy*, pp. 37, 39.
50. *Annual Report of the Superintendent of Common Schools, 1831–1832*, Assembly Document No. 17, January 7, 1833, p. 21.
51. Abbott, *Government Policy*, p. 51.
52. *Annual Report of the Superintendent of Common Schools, 1840–1841*, Assembly Document No. 100, January 30, 1841, p. 110.
53. *Annual Report of the Superintendent of Common Schools, 1839–1840*, Assembly Document No. 120, February 11, 1840, p. 16.

54. Report of the Executive Committee of the State Normal School, January 13, 1848, in *Annual Reports of the Secretary of State* (New York).
55. See Abbott, *Government Policy,* p. 51.

Chapter 3: The Nineteenth-Century Liberal Arts College

1. Robert Middlekauff, *Ancients and Axioms: Secondary Education in Eighteenth Century New England* (New Haven: Yale University Press, 1963), pp. 92–102.
2. See "Original Papers in relation to a course of Liberal Education," *American Journal of Science and Arts,* XV (January 1829), 338.
3. See William D. Carrell, "American College Professors: 1750–1800," *History of Education Quarterly,* VIII (Fall 1968), 289–305, and "Biographical List of American College Professors to 1800," 358–374. Also Theodore Hornberger, *Scientific Thought in the American Colleges, 1638–1800* (Austin: University of Texas Press, 1946), pp. 26–27.
4. See Joe W. Kraus, "The Development of a Curriculum in the Early American Colleges," *History of Education Quarterly,* I (June 1961), 64–76.
5. John W. Vethake, quoted in *Social Theories of Jacksonian Democracy,* ed. Joseph L. Blau (Indianapolis: Bobbs-Merrill, 1954), p. 212.
6. For the concept of the "booster college," see Daniel Boorstin, *The Americans: The National Experience* (New York: Random House, 1965), pp. 152–161; and for "the Great Retrogression," see Richard Hofstadter's "The Old-Time College," in *The Development of Academic Freedom in the United States,* by Hofstadter and Walter Metzger (New York: Columbia University Press, 1955).
7. See my *From Crisis to Crisis: American College Government, 1636–1819* (Cambridge: Harvard University Press, 1982), chap. 12, and "The American Revolution and the American University," *Perspectives in American History,* X (1976), 279–354.
8. As David Potts recently pointed out, the so-called Yale Report actually consists of three separate papers, two from the college faculty and one from a committee of the corporation; see Potts, "Celebrating Roots: Sesquicentennials and the Distinctiveness of the Liberal Arts College," *History of Higher Education Annual,* XI (1991), p. 18 n. 5; and Brooks Mather Kelley, *Yale: A History* (New Haven: Yale University Press, 1974), p. 162.
9. "Original Papers," pp. 328–330.
10. Ibid., p. 337.
11. Ibid., p. 344.

12. Henri I. Marrou, *A History of Education in Antiquity* (New York: Sheed & Ward, 1956), p. 303.
13. "Original Papers," pp. 350, 351.
14. Ibid., p. 345.
15. Ibid., pp. 300–301.
16. Sheldon Rothblatt, *Tradition and Change in English Liberal Education: An Essay in History and Culture* (London: Faber & Faber, 1976), p. 130.
17. For the Yale Report as a forward-looking document, see J. C. Lane, "The Yale Report of 1828 and Liberal Education: A Neorepublican Manifesto," *History of Education Quarterly*, XXVII (Fall 1987), 325–338.
18. "Original Papers," p. 301.
19. Ibid., p. 303.
20. Edward Copleston, *Reply to the Calumnies of the Edinburgh Review Against Oxford, Containing an Account of Studies Pursued in that University*, 2nd ed. (Oxford: Cooke, Parker, & Mackinley, 1810), p. 146.
21. Ibid., p. 149.
22. Ibid., pp. 132–133.
23. Ibid., pp. 151, 154–155.
24. Ibid., 151, 177.
25. Peter Slee, "The Oxford Idea of a Liberal Education, 1800–1860: The Invention of Tradition and the Manufacture of Practice," *History of Universities*, VII (1988), 66.
26. "Original Papers," p. 323.
27. Ibid., p. 323.
28. John F. Fulton, *Benjamin Silliman, 1779–1864: Pathfinder in American Science* (New York: Henry Schuman, 1947), pp. 160–161.
29. Chandos Michael Brown, *Benjamin Silliman: A Life in the Young Republic* (Princeton: Princeton University Press, 1989), pp. 137–138, and Kelley, *Yale*, p. 161.
30. George William Pierson, *Yale: An Educational History, 1871–1921* (New Haven: Yale University Press, 1952), p. 37.
31. For the description of Yale's curriculum, I have relied heavily on Kelley, *Yale*, pp. 156–160, and, to a lesser degree, on John C. Schwab, "The Yale College Curriculum, 1701–1901," *Educational Review*, XXII (June 1901), 1–17.
32. "Original Papers," p. 299.
33. Kelley, *Yale*, pp. 134, 135.
34. Brown, *Silliman*, p. 129.
35. Ibid., p. 135.
36. Rachel Laudan, *From Mineralogy to Geology: The Foundations of a Science, 1650–1830* (Chicago: University of Chicago Press, 1987), p. 21.
37. Cf. Brown, *Silliman*, p. 204.

38. See Herbst, *From Crisis to Crisis,* pp. 139–140.
39. Frederick Rudolph, *Curriculum: A History of the American Undergraduate Course of Study Since 1636* (San Francisco: Jossey-Bass, 1977), pp. 76–79, 81–83.
40. "Original Papers," p. 315.
41. Ibid., p. 316.
42. Ibid., p. 313.
43. Pierre Bourdieu, "Systems of Education and Systems of Thought," *International Social Science Journal,* XIX (1967), quoted from reprint in *Readings in the Theory of Educational Systems,* ed. Earl Hopper (London: Hutchinson University Library, 1971), p. 170.
44. "Original Papers," p. 300.
45. Ibid., p. 319.
46. Ibid., pp. 321–322.
47. See Lane, "Yale Report," for the argument that the report was not a "reactionary plea" but "a conservative effort" to preserve tradition while at the same time adapting to "the needs of an expanding entrepreneurial society."

Chapter 4: The People's College

1. The term *people's college* was used in the nineteenth century to describe schools that provided educational alternatives to the liberal arts college. In this and subsequent chapters I use the term to refer to an urban high school whose primary purpose was to prepare its students for entry into the world of work.
2. Edward Krug, *The Shaping of the American High School* (New York: Harper & Row, 1964), p. 445.
3. See Elmer Ellsworth Brown, *The Making of Our Middle Schools: An Account of the Development of Secondary Education in the United States* (New York: Longmans, Green, 1902), pp. 297–322, and Emit Duncan Grizzell, *Origin and Development of the High School in New England Before 1865* (New York: Macmillan, 1923), pp. 94, 132.
4. See Brown's account in *Making of Our Middle Schools,* pp. 307–308.
5. Quoted, ibid., pp. 299–300.
6. On this issue, see Michael B. Katz's classic, *The Irony of Early School Reform: Educational Innovation in Mid-Nineteenth Century Massachusetts* (Cambridge: Harvard University Press, 1968).
7. Josiah Quincy, in *Report of a Sub-Committee of the School Committee* (Boston, 1828), quoted in *The Educating of Americans: A Documentary History,* ed. Daniel Calhoun (Boston: Houghton Mifflin, 1969), p. 136.

8. See also the account given in David Tyack and Elisabeth Hansot, *Learning Together: A History of Coeducation in American Public Schools* (New Haven: Yale University Press, 1990), pp. 124–128.

9. See my *And Sadly Teach: Teacher Education and Professionalization in American Culture* (Madison: University of Wisconsin Press, 1989), pp. 92–94.

10. "Report of Dr. Larkin Dunton on the Boston Normal School," *15th Annual Report of the Superintendent of Public Schools of the City of Boston, March 15, 1895* (Boston: Rockwell & Churchill, 1895), p. 297.

11. Brown, *Making of Our Middle Schools*, p. 311.

12. David L. Labaree, *The Making of an American High School: The Credentials Market and the Central High School of Philadelphia, 1838–1939* (New Haven: Yale University Press, 1988), pp. 14–15.

13. Ibid., pp. 15, 16, 109–110.

14. Ibid., p. 22.

15. Quoted, ibid., p. 20.

16. See ibid., pp. 4–5, 22–23, 34.

17. See Brown, *Making of Our Middle Schools*, p. 307.

18. Carl F. Kaestle, *The Evolution of an Urban School System: New York City, 1750–1850* (Cambridge: Harvard University Press, 1973), p. 173.

19. Quotation is from *Report of the Select Committee Appointed to Inquire into the Application of the Literature Fund which is Apportioned by the Regents of the University to the City and County of New York* (New York, 1847), pp. 20–24, quoted in *The College of the City of New York: A History, 1847–1947*, by S. Willis Rudy (New York: City College Press, 1949), p. 13.

20. Kaestle, *Evolution of an Urban School System*, pp. 106–107.

21. Rudy, *College of the City of New York*, pp. 33, 34, 39.

22. Ibid., p. 41.

23. Cf. the discussion of this issue in chapter 5 of Tyack and Hansot, *Learning Together*, pp. 114–145.

24. See Reed Ueda, *Avenues to Adulthood: The Origins of the High School and Social Mobility in an American Suburb* (Cambridge: Cambridge University Press, 1987), p. 57.

25. See ibid., chap. 3, pp. 40–58 passim.

26. Ibid, pp. 41–42.

27. The quotations are from the Somerville Annual School Committee Report of 1857, p. 13, and 1846, pp. 22, 23, quoted, ibid., p. 41.

28. See ibid., p. 46, table.

29. See ibid., p. 52.

30. Quoted in Theodore R. Sizer, *Secondary Schools at the Turn of the Century* (New Haven: Yale University Press, 1964), p. 261.

31. Labaree, *Making of an American High School*, p. 34.
32. I am using the concept of "defining institution" as discussed by Hilary Steedman in "Defining Institutions: The Endowed Grammar Schools and the Systematisation of English Secondary Education," in *The Rise of the Modern Educational System: Structural Change and Social Reproduction, 1870–1920*), ed. Detlef K. Müller, Fritz Ringer, and Brian Simon (Cambridge: Cambridge University Press, 1987), pp. 111–134. The quotation is from p. 112.

Chapter 5: State Systems of Secondary Education

1. See O. Burton Adams, "Yale Influence on the Formation of the University of Georgia," *Georgia Historical Quarterly*, LI (June 1967), 175–185.
2. On the University of the State of New York, see chapter 2, above, and on the University of Georgia, see my *From Crisis to Crisis: American College Government, 1636–1819* (Cambridge: Harvard University Press, 1982), pp. 169–170, 209. The Senatus Academicus is described in Robert Preston Brooks, *The University of Georgia under Sixteen Administrations* (Athens: University of Georgia Press, 1956), p. 7.
3. In the Minutes of the Board of Trustees, ms., November 12, 1803, p. 70, typescript, p. 63. Deposited in the General Library, University of Georgia, Athens.
4. Elbert W. G. Boogher, *Secondary Education in Georgia, 1732–1858* (Philadelphia: Boogher, 1933), p. 60.
5. Minutes of the Board of Trustees, ms., p. 104, typescript, p. 90. General Library, University of Georgia, Athens.
6. Minutes of the Senatus Academicus, November 13, 1827, typescript, pp. 179–180, University of Georgia Libraries, Department of Records Management and University Archives, November 4, 1976.
7. Cf. E. Merton Coulter, "The Ante-Bellum Academy Movement in Georgia," *Georgia Historical Quarterly*, V (December 1921), 11–42.
8. See Richard Malcolm Johnston, "Early Educational Life in Middle Georgia," *Report of the Commissioner of Education for the Year 1895–1896*, vol. I (Washington, DC: Government Printing Office, 1897), pp. 839–886.
9. William H. Kilpatrick, "The Beginnings of the Public School System in Georgia," *Georgia Historical Quarterly*, V (September 1921), 3–19.
10. See the discussion of the term *union school* in *The Making of Our Middle Schools*, by Elmer Ellsworth Brown, (New York: Longmans, Green, 1902), p. 302.

11. In *Annual Report of the Regents*, University of the State of New York, 1884, p. 13.
12. Regents' Minutes of January 12, 1866, pp. 203–204, in *Annual Report of the Regents*.
13. Regents' Minutes of January 13, 1870, pp. 23–24, in *Annual Report of the Regents*.
14. Regents' Minutes of March 29, 1870, pp. 26–27, in *Annual Report of the Regents*.
15. Regents' Minutes of March 20, 1878, p. xii, in *Annual Report of the Regents*.
16. Minutes of the 24th Convocation, July 6–8, 1886, p. 89, in *Annual Report of the Regents, 1887*.
17. *Annual Report of the Regents, 1882*, p. xxiii.
18. *Annual Report of the Regents, 1882*, p. xiv.
19. See Howard H. Peckham, *The Making of the University of Michigan, 1817–1967* (Ann Arbor: University of Michigan Press, 1967), pp. 5–9.
20. Quoted in Floyd R. Dain, *Education in the Wilderness*, vol. 1 of *A History of Education in Michigan* (Lansing: Michigan Historical Commission, 1968), p. 105.
21. Willis Frederick Dunbar, *The Michigan Record in Higher Education* (Detroit: Wayne State University Press, 1963), p. 61; *Report of the Superintendent of Public Instruction of the State of Michigan, January 5, 1837* (such reports hereafter cited as *MICHREP*) (Detroit, 1837), p. 33, and *MICHREP, 1839* (Detroit, 1839), pp. 231, 258.
22. *MICHREP, 1842*, vol. II (Detroit, 1842), pp. 287–288.
23. *MICHREP, 1843* (Detroit, 1843), p. 376.
24. *MICHREP, 1847* (Detroit, 1848), pp. 102, 103–106. The italics in the quotation are mine.
25. Visitors' Report in *MICHREP, 1848* (Detroit, 1848), pp. 13–21; and *MICHREP, 1850* (Lansing, 1850), p. 3.
26. Regents' Report in *MICHREP, 1853* (Lansing, 1853), p. 18; Detroit Board of Education Report, ibid., p. 146; Report from Battle Creek, ibid., p. 169.
27. *MICHREP, 1855, 1856, 1857* (Lansing, 1858), p. 47.
28. *MICHREP, 1855 and 1856* (Lansing, 1857), p. 17.
29. *MICHREP, 1855, 1856, 1857*, p. 63; and *MICHREP, 1858* (Lansing, 1858), p. 27.
30. *MICHREP, 1855, 1856, 1857*, p. 49.
31. *MICHREP, 1866* (Lansing, 1866), p. 17.
32. Adapted from table in Calvin Olin Davis, *Public Secondary Education* (Chicago: Rand McNally, 1917), p. 192.
33. See the brief account of the arguments, ibid., p. 194.

34. See "Charles E. Stuart *et al., versus* School District No. 1 of Kalamazoo, *et al.,"* reprinted in *The Michigan Search for Educational Standards,* ed. Charles R. Starring and James O. Knauss (Lansing: Michigan Historical Commission, 1969), pp. 180–181.

35. *MICHREP, 1872* (Lansing, 1872), p. 16.

36. See the text of the decision in Starring and Knauss, *Michigan Search,* pp. 175–188; and Archie P. Nevins, "The Kalamazoo Case," *Michigan History,* XLIV (March 1960), 91–100.

37. *MICHREP 1873* (Lansing, 1874), p. 16.

38. See the syllabus as printed in *MICHREP, 1876* (Lansing, 1877), p. xlix.

39. See Starring and Knauss, *Michigan Search,* p. 102.

40. *MICHREP, 1877* (Lansing, 1878), p.xii.

41. See *MICHREP 1884* (Lansing, 1885), p. x, table. The statement is based on the assumption that only those among the graduates who were listed as having become lawyers, doctors, and ministers were likely to have considered college attendance.

42. Starring and Knauss, *Michigan Search,* p. 102.

Chapter 6: Midwestern Democracy

1. See the statistical tables I assembled in my "Professionalization in Public Education, 1890–1920: The American High School Teacher," in *Bildungsbürgertum im 19. Jahrhundert:* Part I, *Bildungssystem und Professionalisierung in internationalen Vergleichen,* ed. Werner Conze and Jürgen Kocka, (Stuttgart: Klett-Cotta, 1985), pp. 521–528.

2. Theodore R. Sizer, *Secondary Schools at the Turn of the Century* (New Haven: Yale University Press, 1964), pp. 39–40.

3. Paul E. Belting, *The Development of the Free Public High School in Illinois to 1860* (Springfield: Illinois State Historical Society Journal, 1919), p. 170.

4. For a discussion of the conflict between an emerging professional bureaucracy and democratic district control in the U.S. rural heartland, see Wayne E. Fuller, *The Old Country School: The Story of Rural Education in the Middle West* (Chicago: University of Chicago Press, 1982). The quotation about the "educators in overalls" occurs on p. 108.

5. The first quotation is from *The Memorial of a Committee of the State School Convention, December 7, 1844* (Springfield, IL: Walters & Weber, 1845), p. 30; the second, from the *Tenth Biennial Report of the Superintendent of Instruction of the State of Illinois, 1873–1874* (Springfield, 1875), p. 82. Taking the 10th Report as example, hereafter the reports of the Illinois superintendent will be cited as follows: *10th ILLREP, 1873–74* (1875), p. 82.

6. Adapted from Belting, *Development of the Free Public High School*, pp. 164, 185, 186.

7. See Richard vs. Raymond, *Supreme Court Reporter*, v. 92, Ill., p. 612, and Rulison vs. Post, v. 79, Ill., p. 567.

8. *The Memorial*, p. 29.

9. *ILLREP, 1857 and 58* (1859), pp. 41, 42.

10. See Daniel J. Boorstin, *The Americans: The National Experience* (New York: Random House, 1965), pp. 152–161.

11. Belting, *Development of the Free Public High School*, p. 15.

12. Ibid., p. 28.

13. *ILLREP, 1849* (1849), p. 19.

14. *6th ILLREP, 1865–66* (1867), pp. 156, 175.

15. See George H. Genzmer, "Newton Bateman," in *Dictionary of American Biography*, ed. Allen Johnson, vol. 2 (New York: Charles Scribner's Sons, 1929), pp. 44–45.

16. *6th ILLREP, 1865–66*, p. 178.

17. See Helen E. Marshall, *Grandest of Enterprises: Illinois State Normal University, 1857–1957* (Normal: Illinois State Normal University, 1956), pp. 3–16, and my "The Development of Public Universities in the Old Northwest," in *The Northwest Ordinance: Essays on Its Formulation, Provisions, and Legacy*, ed. Frederick D. Williams (East Lansing: Michigan State University Press, 1988), pp. 109–110.

18. See the table in *7th ILLREP, 1867–68* (1869), pp. 524–525, and the convenient but by now outdated lists in Donald G. Tewksbury, *The Founding of American Colleges and Universities Before the Civil War* (New York: Teachers College, Columbia University, 1932), pp. 211–220; and Colin B. Burke, *American Collegiate Populations: A Test of the Traditional View* (New York: New York University Press, 1982), pp. 15–17.

19. *ILLREP, 1851–52* (1853), p. 77.

20. *ILLREP, 1855–56* (1857), p. 13.

21. *ILLREP, 1857 and 58*, p. 42.

22. The numbers are taken from the "Statistical Abstract of Universities, Colleges, etc.," *7th ILLREP, 1867–68*, pp. 524–525. It is interesting to note in this context that as late as 1882 seventy students attended the Illinois Industrial University's preparatory department. They accounted for one-fifth of the undergraduate student body.

23. *6th ILLREP, 1865–66*, pp. 156–157.

24. *8th ILLREP, 1869–70* (1871), pp. 160, 181, 197.

25. *ILLREP, 1857 and 58*, pp. 373, 375.

26. J. B. Roberts, "The American High School: Its Claims and Its Work," *Illinois Teacher*, XVII (December 1871), 437, 449.

27. *9th ILLREP, 1871–72* (1873), p. 105.

28. See note 10, above.
29. *10th ILLREP, 1873–74*, p. 82.
30. Principal Boltwood's report in *11th ILLREP, 1875–76* (1877), pp. 144–145.
31. Ibid., pp. 162–164.
32. Ibid., pp. 147, 148.
33. Ibid., pp. 154, 159.
34. See ibid., p. 162.
35. In ibid., pp. 441, 442.
36. *13th ILLREP, 1878–80* (1881), p. 97.
37. *14th ILLREP, 1880–82* (1883), pp. cvii–cxvi.
38. *13th ILLREP, 1878–80*, pp. 98–99.
39. *16th ILLREP, 1884–86* (1886), p. lxxxiii.
40. Numbers compiled from the *16th ILLREP, 1884–86*, pp. lxxxiv–xcii.
41. George Santayana, "The Genteel Tradition in American Philosophy," *Winds of Doctrine* (New York: Charles Scribner's Sons, 1912).

Chapter 7: Between Town and Gown

1. See the discussion in Joseph Schafer, "Genesis of Wisconsin's Free High School System," *Wisconsin Magazine of History*, X (December 1926), 134–135.
2. See Alice E. Smith, *The History of Wisconsin*, vol. I (Madison: State Historical Society of Wisconsin, 1973), pp. 588–590, Edgar G. Doudna, "The Making of Our Wisconsin Schools," *Wisconsin Journal of Education* (hereafter cited as *WJE*), LXXX (January 1948), 238; and the Introduction to J. W. Stearns, ed., *The Columbian History of Education in Wisconsin* (Milwaukee: State Committee on Educational Exhibit for Wisconsin, 1893), p. 8.
3. *Annual Report of the Superintendent of Public Instruction of the State of Wisconsin* (Madison, 1850), Appendix, 914–915. Hereafter the Wisconsin Superintendent's Reports, whether annual or biennial, are cited as *WISREP*.
4. Thomas C. Reeves, "Education and Culture," in *Racine: Growth and Change in a Wisconsin County*, ed. Nicholas C. Burckel (Racine: County Board of Supervisors, 1977), p. 425; and Anon., *The History of Racine and Kenosha Counties, Wisconsin* (Chicago: Western Historical Company, 1879), p. 420. See also the sketch of McMynn in Stearns, *Columbian History*, p. 502.
5. Siefert's quotations are taken from the *Fiftieth Annual Report of The German English Academy* (Milwaukee, 1901), pp. 12–13; also see Bettina

Goldberg, "The German-English Academy, the National German-American Teachers' Seminary, and the Public School System in Milwaukee, Wisconsin, 1851–1919," in *German Influences on Education in the United States to 1917*, ed. Henry Geitz, Jürgen Heideking, and Jurgen Herbst (Cambridge: Cambridge University Press, 1995), pp. 177–192.

6. Carl Quickert, *The Story of Washington County* (West Bend, WI: Quickert, 1923), pp. 183–184.

7. On this, see Conrad E. Patzer, *Public Education in Wisconsin* (Madison: John Callahan, State Superintendent, 1924), pp. 30–36.

8. See Schafer, "Genesis," pp. 140–143 passim.

9. William English Brown, "Racine County," in *Southeastern Wisconsin: A History of Old Milwaukee County*, ed. John G. Gregory vol. I (Chicago: S. J. Clarke, 1932), pp. 459–460.

10. See *WJE*, n. s., IX (1879), 137.

11. Oliver E. Wells, *WISREP, 1892*, pp. 48–51.

12. See Robert C. Nesbit, *The History of Wisconsin*, vol. III, *Urbanization and Industrialization, 1873–1893* (Madison: State Historical Society, 1985), pp. 336–338.

13. Merle Curti and Vernon Carstensen, *The University of Wisconsin: A History, 1848–1925*, vol. I (Madison: University of Wisconsin Press, 1949), p. 495.

14. Ibid., p. 483.

15. Ibid., p. 484.

16. Ibid., p. 79 n. 9.

17. Ibid., p. 185, 364.

18. Ibid., p. 484–485.

19. Albert O. Barton. "Dane County," in *Southwestern Wisconsin: A History of Old Crawford County*, ed. John G. Gregory vol. II (Chicago: S. J. Clarke, 1932), pp. 836–837, and Schafer, "Genesis," p. 141.

20. Anon., *History of Dane County, Wisconsin* (Chicago: Western Historical Company, 1880), pp. 773–774.

21. Curti and Carstensen, *University of Wisconsin*, I, pp. 492–493.

22. Ibid., pp. 485–486.

23. John Bascom, "The University and the High Schools," *WJE*, XI (April 1881), 155–159; and C. W. Roby, "An Educational Problem," *WJE*, IX (December 1879), 503–510.

24. See Curti and Carstensen, *University of Wisconsin*, I, 395–401.

25. Editorial, *WJE*, XX (November 1890), 468.

26. On this see Nesbit, *History of Wisconsin*, III, 359–362.

27. In *WISREP, 1862*, pp. 62–72.

28. *WISREP, 1867*, p. 50.

29. Statistics of high school graduates are available only as a total of graduates for the years before 1880. They show that of the 1,351 graduates, 850, or 63 percent, were girls.
30. Searing, *WISREP, 1874*, p. xxi.
31. Searing, *WISREP, 1874*, pp. 218–220.
32. See Nesbit, *History of Wisconsin*, III, 362–363.
33. Searing, *WISREP, 1875*, pp. 43–48.
34. Whitford, *WISREP, 1878*, p. 44.
35. Whitford, *WISREP, 1879*, p. 20.
36. In *WJE*, X (January 1880), 7.
37. Robert Graham, *WISREP, 1886*, p. 27.
38. See W. H. Beach, "The Position of the High School in Our System of Education," *WJE*, VIII (March 1878), 132–133; and C. A. Hutchins, "Course of Study in High Schools," ibid., 133–137.
39. R. W. Burton, "Should the High School Be Organized as Supplementary to the Common School, or as Preparatory to the University or College?" *WJE*, X (May 1880), 188.
40. Graham, *WISREP, 1882*, p. 23.
41. Jesse B. Thayer, *WISREP, 1890*, p. 16.

Chapter 8: Growing Pains

1. In Detlef Müller, Fritz Ringer, and Brian Simon, eds., *The Rise of the Modern Educational System: Structural Change and Social Reproduction, 1870–1920* (Cambridge: Cambridge University Press, 1987), p. 220.
2. Ibid., pp. 95–96.
3. See John L. Rury, *Education and Women's Work: Female Schooling and the Division of Labor in Urban America, 1870–1930* (Albany: SUNY Press, 1991), pp. 11ff.
4. See David F. Labaree, *The Making of an American High School: The Credentials Market and the Central High School of Philadelphia, 1838–1939* (New Haven: Yale University Press, 1988), pp. 33–34.
5. U.S. Bureau of the Census, *Historical Statistics of the United States: Colonial Times to 1957* (Washington, DC: Government Printing Office, 1960), p. 207.
6. See Reed Ueda, *Avenues to Adulthood: The Origins of the High School and Social Mobility in an American Suburb* (Cambridge: Cambridge University Press, 1987), pp. 89–90.
7. Ibid., pp. 94, 99–100.
8. In this and the following paragraphs I have relied heavily on Labaree, *Making of an American High School*.

9. Ibid., pp. 150–153.

10. Ibid., p. 150.

11. Ibid., pp. 47–48.

12. Ibid., p. 7.

13. Ibid., p. 155.

14. Ueda, *Avenues to Adulthood*, pp. 90–92.

15. Ibid., pp. 92–93.

16. See *Report of the Superintendent of Public Instruction of the State of Michigan 1876* (Lansing, 1877), p. xlix; and *Report, 1877* (Lansing, 1878), p. xii. (Hereafter such reports are cited as *MICHREP.*)

17. H. H. Belfield, "Manual Training," *57th MICHREP, 1893*, pp. 51–56.

18. Henry Raab, "What Can the Public School Do to Prepare Our Youth for the Work of Practical Life?" *Sixteenth Biennial Report of the Superintendent of Public Instruction . . . 1886* (Springfield, IL, 1886), pp. ccxxxix–cclv. (Hereafter such reports are cited as *ILLREP.*)

19. S. G. Love, "Industrial Education," *New York Regents Report, 1887*, (Albany, 1888), pp. 106, 112. (Hereafter such reports are citied as *NYRE-GREP.*)

20. Alfred G. Compton, "Work-Shop Instruction in the College of the City of New York," ibid., pp. 114–115.

21. See "Manual Training," *64th MICHREP, 1900* (Lansing, 1901), pp. 16–56.

22. A. S. Whitney, "Flexibility of High School Courses," *62th MICHREP, 898* (Lansing, 1899), pp. 180–187.

23. In *17th ILLREP, 1888* (Springfield, 1889), pp. ccvii–ccviii.

24. Oliver E. Wells, "The Free High Schools," *Biennial Report of the State Superintendent . . . 1894* (Madison, WI, 1894), p. 51; and H. W. Rood, R. H. Halsey, and George H. Reed, "Course of Study for High Schools," *Wisconsin Journal of Education* XXIII (August 1893,) p. 187. (Hereafter the superintendent's reports are cited as *WISREP.*)

25. J. Q. Emery, "Manual Training Departments," *WISREP, 1898* (Madison, 1898), pp. 27–30. And see L. D. Harvey, "Manual Training," *WISREP, 1902* (Madison, 1902), p. 77.

26. L. D. Harvey, "Free High Schools," *WISREP, 1900* (Madison, 1901), p. 112.

27. On this see Marvin Lazerson, *Origins of the Urban School: Public Education in Massachusetts, 1870–1915* (Cambridge: Harvard University Press, 1971), pp. 74–80.

28. Ibid., pp. 85–96. See on this also the discussion in *Report of the Commissioner of Education . . . 1887* (Washington, DC, 1888), pp.787–791. (Hereafter such reports are cited as *USREP*).

29. Quoted from the *Princeton Review* (March 1883), in the *USREP, 1885* (Washington, DC, 1886), p. ccvi.

30. See Bernard Mehl, "The High School at the Turn of the Century: A Study of the Changes in the Aims and Programs of Public Secondary Education in the United States 1890–1900," (Ph.D. diss. University of Illinois, 1954), p. 99.

31. Quoted in Charles H. Ham, *Manual Training: The Solution of Social and Industrial Problems* (New York: Harper & Brothers, 1886), p. 332.

32. Much of what I write in this paragraph is based on Berenice M. Fisher's illuminating analysis in her *Industrial Education: American Ideals and Institutions* (Madison: University of Wisconsin Press, 1967), pp. 72–83.

33. Calvin M. Woodward, *Manual Training in Education* (New York: Scribner & Welford, 1890), pp. 41–46, as quoted in Selwyn K. Troen, *The Public and the Schools: Shaping the St. Louis System, 1838–1920* (Columbia: University of Missouri Press, 1975), p. 170.

34. In *20th ILLREP, 1894* (Springfield, 1894), p. 68.

35. Joseph H. Freeman, *22nd ILLREP, 1898* (Springfield, 1898), pp. 51–55.

36, Richard Davis Lakes, "From Manual Training to Trade Instruction: The Evolution of Industrial Education in Cincinnati, 1886–1920" (Ph.D. diss., Ohio State University, 1988), pp. 72, 81.

37. Quoted in Leigh Joseph Altadonna, "The School, Curriculum, and Community: A Case Study of the Institutionalizing of Industrial Education in the Public Schools of Philadelphia, 1876–1918" (Ed.D. diss., Columbia University Teachers College, 1982), pp. 99, 102–105, 142. See also James MacAlister, *Manual Training in the Public Schools of Philadelphia* (New York: New York College for the Training of Teachers, March 1890), and "Manual Training," *Education: A Monthly Magazine Devoted to the Science, Art, Philosophy, and Literature of Education*, XI (September 1890–June 1891), 429–436.

38. On this, see Rury, *Education and Women's Work*, pp. 136–137.

39. Lakes, "From Manual Training to Trade Instruction," pp. 70–72. See also *USREP, 1885*, p. ccx.

40. See *USREP, 1885*, pp. ccix–ccii passim.

41. Freeman, *22nd ILLREP, 1898*, pp. cvi–cxiv.

42. For a discussion of the place of drawing and art in manual education see the addresses in *USREP, 1896*, vol. II, pp. 1321–1329.

43. Wellford Addis, "Manual and Industrial Training," in *USREP, 1887–88* (Washington, DC, 1889), pp. 825ff.

44. Wellford Addis, "Manual and Industrial Training," *USREP, 1888–89*, vol. I (Washington, DC 1891), p. 411.

Chapter 9: The Committee of Ten

1. See the preface to Theodore R. Sizer, *Secondary Schools at the Turn of the Century* (New Haven: Yale University Press, 1964), pp. xi–xiv, and the excellent discussion of Eliot's role in Edward A. Krug, ed., *Charles W. Eliot and Popular Education,* Classics in Education # 8 (New York: Teachers College, Columbia University, 1961.)
2. These and other quotations from the committee report are taken from the text as reprinted in Sizer, *Secondary Schools*, pp. 209–271. The passages quoted here are from pp. 260–262.
3. Ibid., pp. 264–265.
4. Francis W. Parker, "The Report of the Committee of Ten: Its Use for the Improvement of Teachers Now at Work in the Schools," *Addresses and Proceedings of the National Educational Association* (Washington, DC, 1894), p. 449.
5. Edward A. Krug, *The Shaping of the American High School* (New York: Harper & Row, 1964), pp. 39–92 passim. The quoted passage occurs on p. 45 and is taken from Charles W. Eliot's "Undesirable and Desirable Uniformity in Schools," *Addresses and Proceedings of the National Educational Association, 1892,* p. 85.
6. Sizer, *Secondary Schools*, p. 262; italics are mine.
7. See Baker's minority report, ibid., pp. 268–271.
8. See Krug, *Shaping of the American High School,* pp. 71ff.
9. G. Stanley Hall, *Adolescence,* vol. II (New York: Appleton-Crofts, 1904), pp. 510–515.
10. Charles W. Eliot, "The Fundamental Assumptions in the Report of the Committee of Ten," *Educational Review* (November 1905), pp. 330–332 passim.
11. Joseph Lindsey Henderson, *Admission to College by Certificate,* Teachers College Contributions to Education, No. 50 (New York: Teachers College, 1912), pp. 23–29.
12. Harold S. Wechsler, *The Qualified Student: A History of Selective College Admission in America* (New York: Wiley, 1977), pp. 28, 33–34.
13. *Bulletin of the University of Georgia* (hereafter cited as *GAUBULL*), IV (Extra, 1904), 83–84.
14. *GAUBULL,* V (January 1905), 6–9.
15. Joseph Spencer Stewart, "The High-School," *GAUBULL,* VI (January 1906), 10.
16. Joseph Spencer Stewart, "The Accredited High School," *GAUBULL,* V (January 1905), 2.
17. Stewart, *GAUBULL,* VI (January, 1906), 5; Sizer, *Secondary Schools,* p. 259.

18. Charles M. Holloway, "College Entrance Examination Board," *The International Encyclopedia of Higher Education,* ed. Asa S. Knowles, vol. 3 (San Francisco: Jossey-Bass, 1977), pp. 930–934.

19. Charles W. Eliot, "The Fundamental Assumptions," *Educational Review,* XXX (November 1905), 330.

Chapter 10: From Manual to Vocational Education

1. "American Industrial Education: What Shall It Be?" *Report of the United States Commissioner of Education . . . 1901* (Washington, DC: Government Printing Office, 1902), vol. I, pp. 217, 220, 221–226.

2. Quoted in Lawrence A. Cremin, *The Transformation of the School: Progressivism in American Education, 1876–1957* (New York: Knopf, 1961), pp. 38–41. See also Berenice M. Fisher *Industrial Education: American Ideals and Institutions* (Madison: University of Wisconsin Press, 1967), pp. 114–128.

3. For the dual system–unit system controversy, see Lloyd E. Blauch, *Federal Cooperation in Agricultural Extension Work, Vocational Education, and Vocational Rehabilitation* (Washington, DC: Government Printing Office, 1935), pp.28–33. See also the articles by David Snedden and John Dewey, conveniently reprinted in *John Dewey: The Middle Works, 1899–1924,* ed. Jo Ann Boydston, vol. VIII (Carbondale, IL, 1962), pp. 117–127, 411–413, 460–465.

4. See the excerpts from the commission report as given in Marvin Lazerson and W. Norton Grubb, *American Education and Vocationalism: A Documentary History, 1870–1970* (New York: Teachers College Press, 1974), pp. 69–75.

5. See Layton S. Hawkins, Charles A. Prosser, and John C. Wright, *Development of Vocational Education* (Chicago: American Technical Society, 1951), pp. 32–37.

6. C. P. Cary, "Free High Schools," in *Eleventh Biennial Report of the Department of Public Instruction . . . 1904* (Madison, WI, 1904), pp. 80–83. (Such reports hereafter cited as *WISREP.*)

7. Cary, "Commercial and Manual Training Courses," *13th WISREP, 1908,* part I, p. 27.

8. See Ann M. Keppel and James I. Clark, "James H. Stout and the Menomonie Schools," *Wisconsin Magazine of History,* XLII (Spring 1959), 200–210.

9. Charles McCarthy, "German Trade Success Explained by Industrial Education System," in *Vocational Education in Wisconsin,* ed. Arthur M. Evans (Chicago: Commercial Club, 1913), pp. 2–8.

10. W. E. Hicks, *Annual Report of the Public Continuation Schools of Wisconsin, No. 7, July 1, 1912–June 30, 1913* (Madison: Wisconsin State Board of Industrial Education, 1913), p. 22.

11. Anon., "The Educational System of Wisconsin," *Wisconsin Blue Book* (Madison: State of Wisconsin, 1958), p. 170.

12. Kathleen A. Paris, *A Political History of Vocational, Technical, and Adult Education* (Madison: Wisconsin Board of Vocational, Technical, and Adult Education, 1985), pp. 20, 86, 102.

13. Ibid., p. 39.

14. Ibid., pp. 38–41.

15. Joseph H. Freeman, "Industrial Training," *Twenty-Second Biennial Report of the Superintendent of Public Instruction . . . 1898* (Springfield, IL, 1898), pp. cvi–cvii. (Such reports hereafter cited as *ILLREP*.)

16. Alfred Bayliss, "The High Schools," *25th ILLREP, 1904*, pp. 26, 27.

17. *29th ILLREP, July 1, 1910–June 30, 1912*, p. 315.

18. David John Hogan, *Class and Reform: School and Society in Chicago, 1880–1930* (Philadelphia: University of Pennsylvania Press, 1985), p. 170.

19. For these and subsequent statistics on Illinois high school enrollments see various biennial reports of the state superintendent of public instruction.

20. Edwin G. Cooley, "The Need of Vocational Schools in the United States: A Statement" (Chicago: Commercial Club, 1912), 10 pp; see especially the summary, p. 10.

21. Paul H. Hanus, "The Industrial Continuation Schools of Munich," in *Beginnings in Industrial Education and Other Educational Discussions* (Boston: Houghton Mifflin, 1908), p. 92.

22. For a good summary of Kerschensteiner's views see Michael Knoll, "Dewey versus Kerschensteiner: Der Streit um die Einführung der Fortbildungsschule in den USA, 1910–1917," *Pädagogische Rundschau*, XLVII (1993), 131–145.

23. I have relied heavily on chapter 3 of Julia Wrigley, *Class Politics and Public Schools: Chicago, 1900–1950* (New Brunswick: Rutgers University Press, 1982), pp. 48–90.

24. John Dewey, "Education vs. Trade-Training: Reply to David Snedden," *New Republic*, May 8, 1915, pp. 42–43.

25. John Dewey, "Splitting Up the School System," *New Republic*, April 17, 1915, p. 283.

26. David Snedden, "Vocational Education," *New Republic*, May 8, 1915, pp. 40–42.

27. Dewey, "Education vs. Trade Training," p. 42.

28. Harvey A. Kantor, *Learning to Earn: School, Work, and Vocational Reform in California, 1880–1930* (Madison: University of Wisconsin Press, 1988), pp. 42–43.

29. Melville Dewey, "Secretary's Report," *Regents' Report 1893*, pp. r268–r270.

30. John Kennedy, "Report of the Committee of Ten," *Regents' Report 1894*, p. 275.

31. See reports and discussion on "Business Education," *Regents' Report 1898*, pp. 366–417.

32. *Secondary Education*, Bulletin 27 of the New York State Department of Education (November 1905), p. 9.

33. See *Journal of Regents' Meeting*, October 28, 1909, pp. 169–171.

34. In *Eleventh Annual Report of the City Superintendent of Schools for the Year Ending July 31, 1909* (New York: Department of Education, 1909), pp. 117–118.

35. In *Fourth Annual Report for the School Year Ending July 31, 1907* (New York: State Department of Education, 1907), p. 602.

36. In *Tenth Annual Report of the City Superintendent of Schools for the Year Ending July 31, 1908* (New York: Department of Education, 1908), p. 118.

37. In *Proceedings of the Eleventh Annual Convention of the National Association of Manufacturers Held at New York City, May 14–16, 1906* (New York: The Association, 1906), p. 55.

38. In *Proceedings of the Twenty-Eighth Annual Convention of the American Federation of Labor, Held at Denver, Colorado, 1908* (Washington, DC: The Federation, 1908), p. 234.

39. For information on developments in New York City, I have relied on Moses C. Stambler, "The Democratic Revolution in the Public High Schools of New York City, 1898–1917" (Ph.D. diss. New York University, 1964).

Chapter 11: The Legacy of Vocational Education

1. For developments in Cincinnati see Richard Davis Lakes, "From Manual Training to Trade Instruction: The Evolution of Industrial Education in Cincinnati, 1886–1920" (Ph.D. diss., Ohio State University, 1988).

2. See Ibid., pp. 93–135 passim.

3. In the preceding two paragraphs I have drawn heavily on Edward Meredith Fee, "The Origin and Growth of Vocational and Industrial

Education in Philadelphia to 1917" (Ph.D. diss., University of Pennsylvania, 1938), pp.175–209 passim. Also see Leigh Joseph Altadonna, "The School, Curriculum, and Community: A Case Study of the Institutionalizing of Industrial Education in the Public Schools of Philadelphia, 1876–1918" (Ed.D. diss., Columbia University Teachers College, 1982).

4. See David F. Labaree, *The Making of an American High School: The Credentials Market and the Central High School of Philadelphia, 1838–1939* (New Haven: Yale University Press, 1988), p. 163.

5. In Detlef K. Müller, Fritz Ringer, and Brian Simon, eds. *The Rise of the Modern Educational System: Structural Change and Social Reproduction, 1870–1920* (Cambridge: Cambridge University Press, 1987), p. 7.

6. Harvey A. Kantor, *Learning to Earn: School, Work, and Vocational Reform in California, 1880–1930* (Madison: University of Wisconsin Press, 1988), p. 64.

7. See ibid., pp. 134–135.

8. In *Biennial Report of the Superintendent of Public Instruction of the State of Illinois, 1916–1918* (Springfield, 1918), pp. 157–158.

9. These and other Illinois figures are taken from various issues of the biennial reports of the state superintendent of public education.

10. See John L. Rury, *Education and Women's Work: Female Schooling and the Division of Labor in Urban America, 1870–1930* (Albany: SUNY Press, 1991), pp. 139–147.

11. Daniel T. Rodgers and David B. Tyack, "Work, Youth, and Schooling: Mapping Critical Research Areas," in *Work, Youth, and Schooling: Historical Perspectives on Vocationalism in American Education*, ed. Harvey Kantor and David B. Tyack (Stanford, CA: Stanford University Press, 1982), p. 278.

12. Lawrence A. Cremin, "The Revolution in American Secondary Education, 1893–1918," *Teachers College Record*, LVI (March 1955), 295–308.

13. Martin Trow, "The Second Transformation of American Secondary Education," *International Journal of Comparative Sociology*, II (September 1961), 144–166.

Chapter 12: Toward the Comprehensive High School

1. From the Committee of Ten report, as quoted in Theodore Sizer, *Secondary Schools at the Turn of the Century* (New Haven: Yale University Press, 1964), p. 261.

2. For more details see Noah Gayle Simmons, "The Emerging Design for the Comprehensive American High School, 1913–1922—A Study

of the Commission on the Reorganization of Secondary Education"
CEd.D. diss., Washington University, 1960), pp. 146–153.

3. On this, see Edward A. Krug, *The Shaping of the American High School* (New York: Harper & Row, 1964), pp. 295–303.

4. In Clarence D. Kingsley, "Third Report of the Committee on the Articulation of High School and College," *Proceedings and Addresses, National Education Association* (1913), p. 490.

5. *Cardinal Principles of Secondary Education,* Department of the Interior, Bureau of Education, Bulletin No. 35, 1918, (Washington, DC: Government Printing Office, 1918), pp. 5, 9.

6. John Dewey, *Democracy and Education* (New York: Macmillan, 1916), p. 101.

7. On the differences between Dewey's and Kingsley's concepts of "growth," see Lawrence A. Cremin, *The Transformation of the School: Progressivism in American Education 1876–1957* (New York: Knopf, 1961), pp. 122–123.

8. Cf. Lawrence A. Cremin, *American Education: The Metropolitan Experience, 1876–1980* (New York: Harper & Row, 1988), pp. 338–345.

9. *Cardinal Principles,* p. 9.

10. Herbert M. Kliebard, *The Struggle for the American Curriculum, 1893–1958* (New York: Routledge & Kegan Paul, 1987), p. 90.

11. *Cardinal Principles,* p. 9.

12. Ibid., p. 9.

13. Ibid., pp. 10, 11.

14. Ibid., pp. 10, 12.

15. Ibid., pp. 10, 12–13.

16. Ibid., p. 12.

17. Ibid., p. 13.

18. Ibid., p. 16.

19. Ibid., pp. 13–15.

20. Ibid., p. 15.

21. Ibid.

22. Cf. William G. Wraga, *Democracy's High School: The Comprehensive High School and Educational Reform in the United States* (Lanham, MD: University Press of America, 1994), pp. 31, 57–58, and U.S. Bureau of Education, *Biennial Survey of Education, 1920–1922,* Bulletin No. 13, 1924 (Washington, DC: Government Printing Office, 1924), vol. I, p. 313.

23. George S. Counts, *The Senior High School Curriculum* (Chicago: University of Chicago, 1926), pp. 26–29.

24. Leonard V. Koos and staff, *Summary,* Bulletin No. 17, 1932, National Survey of Secondary Education, Monograph No. 1 (Washington, DC: U.S. Department of the Interior, 1934), pp. 1–6.

25. Ibid., p. 31; and Grayson Kefauver, Victor H. Knoll, and C. Elwood Drake, *The Horizontal Organization of Secondary Education,* Bulletin, No. 17, 1932, National Survey of Secondary Education, Monograph No. 2 (Washington, DC: U.S. Department of the Interior, 1934), p. 18.

26. Koos, *Summary,* pp. 36–37.

27. Ibid., p. 32.

28. Counts, S*enior High School Curriculum,* pp. 2, 11, 25, 130, 131.

29. In *The Development of the High School Curriculum,* Sixth Yearbook, Department of Superintendence, National Education Association (1928), pp. 130–138, quoted in Simmons, "Emerging Design," pp. 317–323.

30. *Cardinal Principles,* p. 22.

31. Ibid., pp. 25–26.

32. Ibid., pp. 23–24.

33. Ibid., pp. 24–25.

34. Ibid., 15.

35. Counts, *Senior High School Curriculum,* p. 120.

36. Robert S. Lynd and Helen Merrell Lynd, *Middletown: A Study in Contemporary American Culture* (New York: Harcourt, Brace, 1929), pp. 211, 219–220.

37. *Cardinal Principles,* pp. 18–19.

38. Ibid., 19–20.

39. Ibid., pp. 30–31.

Chapter 13: The High School Under Siege

1. Leonard V. Koos and staff, *Summary,* Bulletin No. 17, 1932, National Survey of Secondary Education, Monograph No. 1 (Washington, DC: U.S. Department of the Interior, 1934), pp. 1–6.

2. See George S. Counts, *The Senior High School Curriculum* (Chicago: University of Chicago, 1926), pp. 26–29.

3. Quotations are from Calvin O. Davis. "The Curriculum and the Seven Objectives," *Ninth Yearbook,* National Association of Secondary School Principals (1925), as cited in Noah Gayle Simmons, "The Emerging Design for the Comprehensive American High School, 1913–1923: A Study of the Commission of the Reorganization of Secondary Education" (Ed.D. diss., Washington University, 1960), pp. 309–312; Leonard V. Koos, *Trends in American Secondary Education* (Cambridge: Harvard University Press, 1927), pp. 8–10, as quoted in Simmons, "Emerging Design," p. 313; and Carter V. Good, "The Objective of Secondary Schools in 1926–28," *Education,* XLVII (June

1927), 585–592; and *The Development of the High School Curriculum,* Sixth Yearbook, Department of Superintendence, National Education Association (1928), as quoted in Simmons, "Emerging Design," pp. 313–316.

4. In *Development of the High School Curriculum,* pp. 159–187, as quoted in Simmons, "Emerging Design," pp. 323–333.

5. See Edward Krug, *The Shaping of the American High School, 1920–1941* (Madison: University of Wisconsin Press, 1972), pp. 209, 214.

6. Julia Wrigley, *Class Politics and Public Schools: Chicago, 1900–1950* (New Brunswick: Rutgers University Press, 1982), pp. 218–219.

7. David Tyack, Robert Lowe, and Elisabeth Hansot, *Public Schools in Hard Times: The Great Depression and Recent Years* (Cambridge: Harvard University Press, 1984), p. 40.

8. Avis D. Carlson, "Deflating the Schools," reprinted in *The Great Depression,* ed. David A. Shannon (Englewood Cliffs, NJ: Prentice Hall, 1960).

9. Quoted in Tyack et al., *Public Schools* pp. 45–47.

10. Quoted from George S. Counts, *Dare the School Build a New Social Order?* (New York: John Day, 1932), as reprinted in *American Education in the Twentieth Century: A Documentary History,* ed. Marvin Lazerson (New York: Teachers College Press, 1987), pp. 97–99.

11. This paragraph borrows heavily from Krug, *Shaping,* pp. 234–240. The quotation is from pp. 239–240.

12. See the excerpts from Wilford M. Aiken, *Thirty Schools Tell Their Story* (New York: McGraw-Hill, 1943) in Lazerson, *American Education in the Twentieth Century,* pp. 109–113.

13. See Robert S. Lynd and Helen Merrell Lynd, *Middletown in Transition: A Study in Cultural Conflicts* (New York: Harcourt, Brace, 1937), pp. 218–220.

14. Lynd and Lynd, *Middletown,* p. 221.

15. Ibid., p. 222.

16. Ibid., p. 223.

17. Ibid., p. 452.

18. Ibid., p. 463.

19. Ibid., p. 175.

20. Ibid., pp. 171, 306.

21. See Ibid., pp. 224, 208, 225, 568.

22. See Ibid., pp. 225, 239–240.

23. Francis T. Spaulding, *High School and Life: The Regents' Inquiry, 1938* (New York: McGraw-Hill, 1939), pp. 123–124. Italics throughout are in the original.

24. Spaulding, *High School and Life,* pp. 125–133 passim.

25. Ibid., pp. 17, 31–32.
26. Ibid., pp. 33, 34.
27. Ibid., pp. 93, 94–115 passim.
28. Ibid., pp. 55, 72.
29. Ibid., pp. 134–144 passim.
30. Ibid., p. 150.
31. Ibid., pp. 54–62 passim.
32. For more on this, see Ibid., pp. 147, 148.
33. Ibid., p. 149.
34. See V. T. Thayer, Caroline B. Zachry, and Ruth Kotinsky, *Reorganizing Secondary Education* (New York: D. Appleton-Century, 1938), pp. 25–50.
35. Educational Policies Commission, *The Purposes of Education in American Democracy* (Washington, DC: National Education Association of the United States, 1938), pp. 24, 25, 146.
36. Educational Policies Commission, *Purposes of Education*, p. 147.
37. For an account of the introduction of educational work in the CCC camps, see Frank Ernest Hill, *The Schools in the Camps: The Educational Program of the Civilian Conservation Corps* (New York: American Association for Adult Education, 1935), pp. 8–13.
38. Clarence M. Dannelly, "Finances and Philosophies," *School Executive*, LXI (October 1941), 25–26.
39. A. C. Payne, reported in news note, *Clearing House*, XV (November 1940), 178, quoted in Krug, *Shaping of the American High School*, p. 323. The entire paragraph is based largely on Krug, *Shaping of the American High School*, pp. 319–327.
40. See Tyack et al., *Public Schools*, pp. 103–112; and Charles H. Judd, "The Real Youth Problem," *School and Society*, LV (January 10, 1942), 32.
41. American Youth Commission, *Youth and the Future* (Washington, DC: American Council on Education, 1942), pp. 30, 36–37.
42. Tyack et al., *Public Schools*, pp. 119, 121; and American Youth Commission, *Youth and the Future*, p. 57.
43. American Youth Commission, *Youth and the Future*, pp. 60–70.
44. Ibid., p. 60.

Chapter 14: The High School in Search of Itself

1. See excerpts from the report of the Special Committee on the Secondary School Curriculum for the American Youth Commission, *What the High Schools Ought to Teach* (Washington, DC: American

Council on Education, 1940), pp. 10–16, 19–29, reprinted in *The American Curriculum: A Documentary History,* ed. George Willis et al. (Westport, CT: Greenwood Press, 1991), pp. 273–283, quotation from p. 281.

2. David Tyack, Robert Lowe, and Elisabeth Hansot, *Public Schools in Hard Times: The Great Depression and Recent Years* (Cambridge: Harvard University Press, 1984), pp. 177–179 passim.

3. Educational Policies Commission, *Education for All American Youth* (Washington, DC: National Education Association of the United States, 1944), pp. v, 1.

4. Ibid., pp. 35, 39.

5. Ibid., pp. 192, 211, 296, 359.

6. *General Education in a Free Society: Report of the Harvard Committee* (Cambridge: Harvard University Press, 1945), p. 11.

7. Norwood Brigence, "General Education in a Free Society," *Vital Speeches,* XIII (February 1, 1947), 249.

8. See Charles A. Prosser, *Secondary Education and Life* (Cambridge: Harvard University Press, 1939).

9. U.S. Office of Education, *Life Adjustment Education for Every Youth,* Bulletin No. 22, 1951, (Washington, DC: Government Printing Office, 1953), p. 46.

10. "Life Adjustment Education for Every Youth" (Washington, DC: Federal Security Agency, Office of Education, n.d.), p. 4. Mimeographed, was issued in 1947.

11. Harl R. Douglass, *Secondary Education for Life Adjustment of American Youth* (New York: Ronald Press, 1952), pp. 171–172.

12. See Mortimer Smith, *And Madly Teach: A Layman Looks at Public School Education* (Chicago: H. Regnery, 1949), and Arthur Bestor, *Educational Wastelands: The Retreat from Learning in Our Public Schools,* 2nd ed. (Urbana: University of Illinois Press, 1985), pp. 82–83.

13. Jerome S. Bruner, *The Process of Education* (Cambridge: Harvard University Press, 1960), pp. 2, 4, 31.

14. Ibid., pp. 12–13, 33, 52.

15. Ibid., pp. 77, 80.

16. James Bryant Conant, *The American High School Today: A First Report to Interested Citizens* (New York: McGraw-Hill, 1959), pp. 12, 15, 40.

17. Ibid., pp. 40, 53, 85.

18. Ibid., pp. 74–75.

19. Ibid., pp. 40, 77–96, 133, 37.

20. Ibid., pp. 85–95 passim.

21. James Bryant Conant, *Slums and Suburbs* (New York: McGraw-Hill, 1961), pp. 145–147.

22. Ibid., pp. 2, 30, 37.
23. Ibid., pp. 39, 147, 6.
24. Educational statistics are notoriously unreliable, and Conant's are no less so. In *Slums and Suburbs* he assigned one-third each of the country's high school students to large metropolitan schools, to the comprehensive schools he approved of, and to schools that were too small. The last group, he wrote, accounted for 80 percent of the country's public high schools.
25. Conant, *American High School Today*, pp. 51–52, 74–76.
26. In Conant, *Slums and Suburbs*, p. 40, and in James Bryant Conant, *The Child, the Parent, and the State* (Cambridge: Harvard University Press, 1959), p. 47.
27. Conant, *American High School Today*, pp. 62–63, 20, 39, 60.
28. Ibid., pp. 55, 67, 58.

Chapter 15: End of an Era

1. James Bryant Conant, *The Comprehensive High School: A Second Report to Interested Citizens* (New York: McGraw-Hill, 1967), pp. 2, 20.
2. Ibid., pp. 19–21; James Bryant Conant, *Slums and Suburbs* (New York: McGraw-Hill, 1961), pp. 2, 41.
3. Diane Ravitch, *The Troubled Crusade: American Education, 1945–1980* (New York: Basic Books, 1983), p. 233.
4. John Holt, *How Children Fail* (New York: Pitman, 1964); Paul Goodman, *Compulsory Mis-Education* (New York: Horizon Press, 1964), p. 21; Edgar Friedenberg, *Coming of Age in America* (New York: Random House, 1965), p. 4; and Charles E. Silberman, *Crisis in the Classroom: The Remaking of American Education* (New York: Random House, 1970), p. 10.
5. James S. Coleman et al., *Equality of Educational Opportunity*, U.S. Department of Health, Education, and Welfare, Office of Education (Washington, DC: Government Printing Office, 1966), pp. 9, 12, 21–22, 28.
6. U.S. Commission on Civil Rights, *Racial Isolation in the Public Schools* (Washington, DC: Government Printing Office, 1967).
7. Christopher Jencks et al., *Inequality: A Reassessment of the Effect of Family and Schooling in America* (New York: Basic Books, 1972).
8. James S. Coleman, Sara D. Kelley, and John H. Moore, *Trends in School Segregation, 1968–1973* (Washington, DC: Urban Institute, 1975).
9. David K. Cohen and Janet A. Weiss, "Social Science and Social Policy: Schools and Race," *Educational Forum*, May 1977, p. 410.

10. Educational Policies Commission, *The Central Purpose of American Education* (Washington, DC: National Education Association, 1961), pp. 12, 19–20.

11. Ralph W. Tyler, "National Committee on Secondary Education: A Report," *Bulletin* (National Association of Secondary School Principals), LI (1967), 94; Harold Howe II, "The Neglected Majority," ibid., 43, 45.

12. Harl R. Douglass, *Secondary Education for Youth in Modern America* (Washington, DC: American Council on Education, 1937), pp. 29–30; *Trends and Issues in Secondary Education* (Washington, DC: Center for Applied Research in Education, 1962), pp. 24–26.

13. B. Frank Brown, *New Directions for the Comprehensive High School* (West Nyack, NY: Parker, 1972), pp. 21, 184, 189.

14. Task Force on Secondary Schools in a Changing Society, *This We Believe* (Reston, VA: National Association of Secondary School Principals, 1975), pp. 10, 36.

15. Ibid., pp. 33, 35.

16. Educational Policies Commission, *Education and the Disadvantaged American* (Washington, DC: National Education Association, 1962), p. 18.

17. See Mayor D. Mobley and Melvin L. Barlow, "Impact of Federal Legislation and Policies upon Vocational Education," in *Vocational Education*, (64th Yearbook of the National Society for the Study of Education) (Chicago: University of Chicago Press, 1965) pp. 200–201.

18. See W. Norton Grubb and Marvin Lazerson, "Rally 'Round the Workplace: Continuities and Fallacies in Career Education," *Harvard Educational Review*, XLV (November 1975), 459.

19. Melvin Barlow, "The Challenge to Vocational Education," in *Vocational Education*, pp. 12–14.

20. Interview with Sidney P. Marland, Jr., in *American Education*, VII (November 1971), 25–26, reprinted in Marvin Lazerson and W. Norton Grubb, *American Education and Vocationalism: A Documentary History, 1870–1970* (New York: Teachers College Press, 1974), pp. 174–176.

21. Michael Timpane, Susan Abramowitz, Sue Berryman Bobrow, and Anthony Pascal, *Youth Policy in Transition* (Santa Monica, CA: Rand, 1976), p. 80.

22. Christopher Jencks, "Cultivating Greater Diversity," *The New Republic* (November 7, 1964), pp. 33–40.

23. The National Commission on the Reform of Secondary Education, *The Reform of Secondary Education* (New York: McGraw-Hill, 1973), See also note 13, above.

24. Panel on Youth of the President's Science Advisory Committee, *Youth: Transition to Adulthood* (Washington, DC: Executive Office of the President, 1973), pp. 80, 84–86.
25. Ibid., pp. 153–155, 156, 157, 160.
26. National Panel on High School and Adolescent Education, *The Education of Adolescents* (Washington, DC: U.S. Office of Education, 1976), pp. 1–10, passim.
27. Timpane et al., *Youth Policy in Transition*, pp. viii–ix, xi, 63, 62.
28. Ibid., pp. 133–134, xii.
29. Ibid., pp. 82, 83.
30. Ibid., pp. 87–91 passim.
31. Mortimer Adler, *The Paideia Proposal: An Educational Manifesto* (New York: Macmillan, 1982), p. 5; National Commission on Excellence in Education, *A Nation at Risk: The Imperative for Educational Reform* (Washington, DC: U.S. Department of Education, 1983), pp. 5, 18; Task Force on Education for Economic Growth, *Action for Excellence* (Denver: Education Commission of the States, 1983).
32. Ernest L. Boyer, *High School: A Report on Secondary Education in America* (New York: Harper & Row, 1983); Philip A. Cusick, *The Egalitarian Ideal and the American High School: Studies of Three Schools* (New York: Longman, 1983); John I. Goodlad, *A Place Called School: Prospects for the Future* (New York: McGraw-Hill, 1984); Theodore R. Sizer, *Horace's Compromise: The Dilemma of the American High School* (Boston: Houghton Mifflin, 1984); and Arthur G. Powell, Eleanor Farrar, and David K. Cohen, *The Shopping Mall High School: Winners and Losers in the Educational Marketplace* (Boston: Houghton Mifflin, 1985).
33. Boyer, *High School*, pp. 56, 67.
34. Cusick, *Egalitarian Ideal*, esp. chap. 5, and Powell et al., *Shopping Mall High School*, p. 68.
35. Cusick, *Egalitarian Ideal*, p. 105.
36. Powell et al., *Shopping Mall High School*, p. 305.

Chapter 16: From the Twentieth to the Twenty-First Century

1. Paul E. Peterson, "The New Politics of Choice," in *Learning from the Past: What History Teaches Us About School Reform*, ed. Diane Ravitch and Maris A. Vinovskis (Baltimore: Johns Hopkins University Press, 1995), p. 237.
2. See John F. Witte, Andrea B. Bailey, and Christopher A. Thorn, *Second Year Report: Milwaukee Parental Choice Program* (Madison: University of Wisconsin Department of Political Science and the Robert La Follette Institute of Public Affairs, 1992).

3. Philip A. Cusick, *The Egalitarian Ideal and the American High School* (New York: Longman, 1983). p. 111.

4. Ibid., p. 119.

5. The reference is to David K. Cohen's chapter "Origins," in *The Shopping Mall High School: Winners and Losers in the Educational Marketplace*, by Arthur G. Powell, Eleanor Farrar, and David K. Cohen (Boston: Houghton, Mifflin, 1985), pp. 233–308. Cohen relied for his figures on V. Grant and L. Eiden (of the National Center for Education Statistics), *Digest of Education Statistics: 1981* (Washington, DC: U.S. Government Printing Office, 1981).

6. David Angus and Jeffrey Mirel, "Rhetoric and Reality: The High School Curriculum," in Ravitch and Vinovskis, *Learning from the Past*, pp. 316, 321.

7. Powell, Farrar, Cohen, *Shopping Mall High School*, p. 68.

8. Torsten Husén, *Education and the Global Concern* (Oxford: Pergamon Press, 1990), p. 9.

9. Angus and Mirel, "Rhetoric and Reality," p. 311.

10. Quotations in this paragraph are from Harvey Kantor and David Tyack, "Historical Perspectives on Vocationalism in American Education," in *Work, Youth, and Schooling*, ed. Kantor and Tyack (Stanford: Stanford University Press, 1982), pp. 1, 2.

11. Herbert M. Kliebard, "Vocational Education as Symbolic Action: Connecting Schooling with the Workplace," *American Educational Research Journal*, XXVII (Spring 1990), 26.

12. Robert Maynard Hutchins, *The University of Utopia* (Chicago: University of Chicago Press, 1953), p. 47.

13. See Husén, *Education and the Global Concern*, pp. 9, 41–43 passim.

14. Torsten Husén, "Problems of Educational Reforms in a Changing Society," *International Perspectives on Education and Society*, IV (1994), 14.

15. See chap. 15, note 25.

16. John I. Goodlad, *A Place Called School: Prospects for the Future* (New York: McGraw-Hill, 1984), pp. 323–326 passim.

17. For those who doubt that it is possible to imbue all students in elementary and junior high schools with a love and habit of learning, I suggest they read Deborah Meier, *The Power of Their Ideas: Lessons for America from a Small School in Harlem* (Boston: Beacon Press, 1995), and sample the contributions to *American Education: Still Separate, Still Unequal*, the fall 1995 issue of *Daedalus: Journal of the American Academy of Arts and Sciences*.

18. See Panel on Youth of the U.S. President's Science Advisory Committee, *Youth: Transition to Adulthood* (Washington, DC: Executive Office of the President, 1973). pp. 91ff; National Panel on High School and

Adolescent Education, *The Education of Adolescents* (Washington, DC: U.S. Department of Health, Education, and Welfare, 1976), p. 5; Carnegie Council on Policy Studies in Higher Education, *Giving Youth a Better Chance: Options for Education, Work, and Experience* (San Francisco: Jossey-Bass, 1979), pp. 94ff.

19. For an interesting discussion about these and other issues involved in the debate over the duration of compulsory education, see Myron Lieberman, *Public Education: An Autopsy* (Cambridge: Harvard University Press, 1993), pp. 54–55.

20. For further examples, see Carnegie Council on Policy Studies in Higher Education, *Giving Youth a Better Chance*, pp. 22ff.

21. W. Norton Grubb, "School Reform and the 'New Vocationalism': What It Is, What It Could Be," draft manuscript, March 1994; to be published in *Phi Delta Kappan* (1996).

22. For more on this, see Panel on Youth of the President's Science Advisory Committee, *Youth*, pp. 169–171.

23. See various works by Torsten Husén: *The School in Question: A Comparative Study of the School and Its Future in Western Society* (Oxford: Oxford University Press, 1979), *Education and the Global Concern*, and others.

Index

Abbott, Frank C., 23-24, 220nn. 39, 40, 49, 51, 221n. 55
ability grouping, 162, 185
Abramowitz, Susan, 245n. 21
academic departments. *See* high schools, academic departments of
"academic rearmament", 178-181, 188, 208
academies: as sources of teachers, 24-25, 44, 58, 69, 80; condemned as "aristocratic", 67-68; discussed, 17-25, 53-60, 79-81; mentioned, 1, 7, 8, 9, 28, 29, 30, 38, 42, 43, 47, 65, 70, 87, 88, 98, 108, 112, 211; replaced by public high school, 50. *See also* scientific academies; female academies
accounting: as high school subject, 95; as Latin school subject, 18
accreditation. *See* high schools, accreditation of
Adams, O. Burton, 225n. 1
Addis, Wellford, 233nn. 43, 44
Adler, Felix, 100
Adler, Mortimer, 198, 246n. 31
adult education, 167-169
advanced placement programs, 179, 184.
advanced secondary education. *See* secondary education, advanced
Aesop, as textbook author, 12
African-Americans, 47, 119, 168, 173, 183, 189-190. *See also* minority students
age of school attendance, 209-210
agricultural experiment stations, 5
agriculture: as high school subject, 23, 47, 59, 113, 114, 118, 120, 125, 135-136, 174, 184, 193; as university subject, 23, 28
Aiken, Wilford M., 241n. 12
Albany, New York, State Normal School. *See* New York, State Normal School
algebra: as academy subject, 21, 23; as high

school subject, 42, 73, 74, 95, 135-136; as university preparatory department subject, 84
Altadonna, Leigh Joseph, 233n. 37, 238n. 3
Altdorf, Germany, Teacher Seminary, 81
alternatives in education. *See* alternative schools
alternative institutions. *See* alternative schools; choice schools
alternative schools, xiii, xv, 190, 191, 195, 196.
American Association of School Administrators, 166
American Education: Still Separate, Still Unequal, 247n. 17
American Federation of Labor, 119, 129-130, 237n. 38
American High School Today, 181-183, 185, 243nn. 16-20, 244nn. 25, 27, 28
American Journal of Science and Arts, 34
American Red Cross, 144
American Youth Commission, 168-169, 171-173, 175, 177, 181, 242nn. 41-44; Committee on the Secondary School Curriculum of the, 172, 175, 242n. 1
ancient history: as academy subject, 21; as high school subject, 158
ancient languages. *See* classics
And Madly Teach, 179
Angell, James Burrill, 108
Angus, David, 203, 204, 247nn. 6, 9
apprenticeship, 1, 8,97, 117, 122, 129, 131, 132, 164, 207, 211
Aramaic, as university subject, 14
architecture: as high school subject, 47, 164; schools of, 5
Ariés, Philippe, 5, 7, 216n. 12
Aristotle, 15, 33
arithmetic: as academy subject, 20, 21, 58; as college or university subject, 14, 27; as high

Index

President's Science Advisory Committee, Panel on Youth, 195-196, 213, 246nn. 24, 25, 247n. 18, 248n. 22
Princeton University. *See* College of New Jersey
printing trades, as high school subject, 174, 184
Process of Education, 179
professional faculties. *See* faculties, higher
professional schools, 1, 5, 28, 37, 38, 51, 74
professorships: in divinity, 28, 35; in law, 28; in mathematics, 27, 28; in medicine, 28; in natural philosophy, 27, 28
progressive education, xiii, 3, 139-140, 179, 207
Progressive Education Association, 159, 160, 161, 179; Commission on Secondary School Curriculum of the, 166
proprietary schools. *See* professional schools
Prosser, Charles A., 130, 176-177, 192, 206, 235n. 5, 243n. 8
psychology, as high school subject, 135-136
Purposes of Education in American Democracy, 166, 240nn. 35-36

quadrivium. See liberal arts
Queen's College, New Jersey. *See* College of New Jersey.
Quickert, Carl, 230n. 6
Quincy, Josiah, 44, 223n. 7

Raab, Henry, 98, 99, 232n. 18
Racial Isolation in the Public Schools, 189, 244n. 6
Racine, Wisconsin, Academy, 80
Ramus, Peter, 15
Rand Corporation, 194, 196-198. *See also Youth Policy in Transition*
Rashdall, Hastings, 216n. 3
Ravitch, Diane, 188, 215n. 2, 244n. 3
reading: as high school subject, 74, 172; as Latin school subject, 18; as university preparatory department subject, 84; as writing school subject, 18
reading schools, 18
Reber, Louis, 123
recitations, as college or university teaching device, 16
reconstructionism, educational, 159-160
Red Book. *See General Education in a Free Society*
Reed, George H., 232n. 24
Reeves, Thomas C., 229n. 4
Regenfuss, Frederick, 81
Reinhold, Meyer, xvi
religion, as writing school subject, 18
Rensselaer, Stephen Van, 23
Reply to the Calumnies of the Edinburgh Review Against Oxford, 32-34
Report of the Committee on Secondary School Studies. See Committee of Ten
Report of the Committee of Ten. See Committee of Ten
rhetoric: as academy subject, 20, 21, 58; as college or university subject, 1, 4, 13-16, 35; as high school

subject, 73, 74, 89; as Latin school subject, 5, 13; as subject of the liberal arts, 1
Richard vs. Raymond, 67, 228n. 7
Ridder-Symoens, Hilde de, 216n. 11
Ringer, Fritz, xi, 93, 133, 218nn. 19, 22, 225n. 32, 231nn. 1-2, 238n. 5
Rise of the Modern Educational System, xi, 93. *See also* Müller, Detlef.
Roberts, J. B., 228n. 26
Robinson, Oscar D., 108
Roby, C.W., 230n. 23
Rodgers, Daniel T., 139, 238n. 11
Rood, H. W., 232n. 24
Roosevelt, Franklin Delano, 167-169
Root, Eleazer, 80, 82
Rothblatt, Sheldon, 31, 222n. 16
Royal Society, London, 27
Rudolph, Frederick, 14, 219nn. 8, 19, 223n. 39
Rudy, S. Willis, 224nn. 19, 21-22
Rulison vs. Post, 67, 228n. 7
Runkle, John, 100, 101, 102
Rury, John, 231n. 3, 233n. 38, 238n. 10

sailing, as Latin school subject, 18
St. Paul's School, London, 6
Salerno, University of. *See* University of Salerno
salesmanship, as high school subject, 134
Sallust, as textbook author, 57
Santayana, George, 77, 229n. 41
Schafer, Joseph, 85, 229n. 1, 230nn. 8, 19
Schneider, Herman, 130, 132
school choice movement. *See* choice schools; student choice
school establishment. *See* schoolmen
School to Work Act of 1994, 212, 215n. 1
schoolmen: accused of bungling, 179, 203; ambivalence concerning manual education, 100, 101, 103, 104, 106; and career education, 193; and education for citizenship, 164; and specialized schools, 165; and the New Deal, 167-169, 188; and vocational education, 117-119; capacity for self-deception and manipulative ingenuity, 177-178; close relationship of public and private, 81; defined, xiv; distrusted for their theoretical viewpoint, 122, 123; fear competition of private commercial schools, 97, 101, 134; oppose district school, 67, 73; professional self-interest of, 66, 79, 94, 98, 191-192, 197, 200, 201-202, 210; referred to, 53, 86, 108, 114, 115, 122, 125, 127, 160, 171, 173, 175, 176, 180, 183, 187, 190, 200, 201, 202, 210; relationship with university faculty, 85; resent private academies, 68-70; see mental training as purpose of high school, 42; support comprehensive high school, 141-156, 208; support high school as connecting link, 65; view high school as democratic institution, 76, 115; want state normal school, 69
school-work relationships or transition, xii, 118, 119, 130, 131-132, 135, 150, 164, 174, 183, 191, 196, 197, 211, 212, 214

260

373.73 H538o 1996

Herbst, Jurgen.

The once and future
school: three hundred